THE
BLACK MAN'S
BURDEN

Other Books on Africa by Basil Davidson

Report on Southern Africa (1952)
The New West Africa: Problems of Independence (1953)
(edited with Adenekan Ademola)
The African Awakening (1955)
The Lost Cities of Africa (1959)
Black Mother: The African Slave Trade (1961)
Which Way Africa? The Search for a New Society (1964)
A History of West Africa, 1000–1800 (1965)
(with F.K. Buah)
African Kingdoms (1966)
(with the Editors of Time-Life Books)
*A History of East and Central Africa to the
Late 19th Century* (1967)
(with J.E.F. Mhina)
Africa in History: Themes and Outlines (1968)
The Liberation of Guiné (1969)
*The African Genius: An Introduction to African Social
and Cultural History* (1969)
In the Eye of the Storm: Angola's People (1972)
*Black Star: A View of the Life and Times of
Kwame Nkrumah* (1973)
*Can Africa Survive? Arguments Against Growth Without
Development* (1974)
Let Freedom Come: Africa in Modern History (1978)
No Fist Is Big Enough to Hide the Sky (1981)
The People's Cause: A History of Guerrillas in Africa (1981)
The Story of Africa (1984)
The Long Struggle of Eritrea (1988)
(edited with Lionel Cliffe)
The Fortunate Isles (1989)
Modern Africa (1990)
African Civilization Revisited (1991)

Basil Davidson

The Black Man's Burden

Africa & the Curse of the Nation-State

'Basil Davidson is the most effective popularizer of African history and archaeology outside Africa and certainly the best trusted in Africa itself.' – Roland Oliver in *The New York Review of Books*'

'It is a great read. His attacking power springs from lucidity, humanity and dramatic artistry... Of the recent general books on nationalism this is the most useful one to recommend to undergraduate historians.' – John Lonsdale in *The Journal of African History*

'Africa and indeed the entire international community owe Basil Davidson, the doyen of Africa's pre-colonial history, a gratitude for reopening discussion on this fundamental issue.' – Adebayo Adedeji

'In this sustained attack upon nation-statism and its oppressive tendencies, Davidson brings to bear his vast knowledge of both Africa and the Balkans. This is a knowledge born not only of study, but of tramping the bush with the guerrillas of Vojvodina and Angola. Davidson's admiration for the democratizing effects of grass-roots mobilization goes right back to his youthful years with Tito's partisans; and his attack upon rampant nationalism in Africa is equally relevant, as he demonstrates, to the bloody disintegration of Tito's federation....' – Gerald Moore in *Le Monde Diplomatique*

'Basil Davidson is thoroughly familiar with the classical sources, and he is also in close touch with the current work and thinking of specialists in contemporary historical and archeological research in Africa... Not the least of his gifts is his capacity for compelling narrative and clear exposition.' – John Fage

'... a poet who writes in prose about the deep emotions that move mankind.' – Christopher Fyfe

'Basil Davidson may know as much about modern Black Africa and Black Africans as anyone in the West. As a scholar-journalist, moreover, he has had closer and more intimate contact with people and events in Africa since 1950 than any academic historian. Throughout, he has been the friend of Africans and, in the early days, a hammer of the imperial powers which still dominated them.' – D.K. Fieldhouse, *The Times Literary Supplement*

'This is a book of major importance. The Black Man's Burden *is not only about Africa, but about ethnicity, nations, and the problem of living together in society everywhere.' –* Eric Hobsbawm

RECENTLY PUBLISHED

Basil Davidson
The Search for Africa
A History in the Making

Basil Davidson says '*The arrangement here is partly by theme and partly by time-when-written; there is also, here and there, an underlying "autobiographical" projection, unfolding firstly the development of an African historiography since its academic establishment some forty years ago and, secondly in that context, my own development.*'

'*He addresses the fundamental issues, not the merely topical. He explores the racism inherent in colonial dispossession and the attempted imposition of "categories of systematic inferiority on colonised peoples". He examines the all-too-familiar paradox – the many critics of independent Africa who find the single-party state intolerable and insist on a multi-party state, and are then astonished that the underlying problems remain. He derides the notion of democracy being contained "in some kind of magic bottle from which it can be poured at will".*' – Michael Wolfers in *The Guardian*

'*This collection of his essays and articles, written between 1953 and 1993 as he watched Africa break free from the colonial yoke, gathers together the answers – and questions – that have come out of Mr Davidson's lifelong fascination with Africa. His favourite culprit for Africa's troubling post-colonial history is "the curse of the nation state." Although his thesis is by now familiar to many, the bloody feuds newly tearing apart states from Rwanda to South Africa make it all the more pertinent.*' – *The Economist*

'*Despite its terrible difficulties, Davidson's Africa is a continent of hope. In both the customary and the more fashioable sense, his work is affirmative.*' – Jeremy Harding in *The London Review of Books*

Contents: Introduction CLAIMS The Search for Africa's Past – Africa & the Invention of Racism – Rescuing Africa's History – Africanism & its Meanings ANTIPATHIES Trigger-Happy Transvaal – Resistance in South Africa – The Roots of Anti-Apartheid – South Africa: A System of Legalized Servitude – Congo Saga – 'A Little Corner of Paradise' – Pluralism in Colonial African Societies SYMPATHIES African Peasants & Revolution – Ideas & Circumstances – The Legacy of Amilcar Cabral DEBATES Nationalism & its Ambiguities – Nationalism & Africa's Self-Transformation – The Politics of Restitution – Southern Africa: Progress or Disaster? ARGUMENTS The Ancient World & Africa: Whose Roots? – The Curse of Columbus – Index

1994   384pp   234 x 156
Paper 0-85255-714-0
Cloth 0-85255-719-1

THE
BLACK MAN'S
BURDEN

Africa and the
Curse of
the Nation-State

BASIL DAVIDSON

James Currey
OXFORD

Baobab Books
HARARE

E.A.E.P
NAIROBI

Fountain Publishers
KAMPALA

James Currey Ltd.
73 Botley Road
Oxford OX2 0BS, England

Baobab Books
PO Box 1559
Harare, Zimbabwe

E.A.E.P.
Kijabe Street, PO Box 45314
Nairobi, Kenya

Fountain Publishers
PO Box 488
Kampala, Uganda

First published 1992
5 6 7 8 9 00 99 98 97 96

British Library Cataloguing in Publication Data
Davidson, Basil
Black Man's Burden: Africa and the Curse
of the Nation-state
I. Title
960
ISBN 0-85255-700-0 (James Currey Paper)

Printed by Villiers Publications Ltd London N3

Oloun paapaa ko gbon to . . .
Not even God is wise enough . . .
—Yoruba proverb

Acknowledgments

I want to record my thanks to many persons in many lands for discussions and advice on the themes of this book, for patience and hospitality, for tolerance and affection, and sometimes for acutely productive disagreement. All that pertains to many years, but on this occasion I want especially to acknowledge the help of the Center of African Studies and the Africana Library of Northwestern University for critically useful assistance in finding books and papers, and in affording me the opportunity to read them.

To Steve Wasserman, editorial director of Times Books, I owe my heartfelt thanks for creative inspiration and editorial skill, as well as for the title I could not find.

Contents

xi

THE
BLACK MAN'S
BURDEN

Introduction

How AND why does one get oneself into a long and difficult work, even a life's work: trying to understand and tell truths, in my case, about a huge and hugely complex continent? It must be hard to say, because it can happen, I suppose, for countless reasons of chance and change; and yet as I look back through the years, I can see that my involvement with Africa had its start, its strange beginning, somewhat in the manner of the young man Marlow in Joseph Conrad's novella, an unforgettable story, called "Youth": of the ever-hopeful Marlow saving himself from shipwreck in the seas of the East, in the ocean lapping Indonesia, and his sighting the East for the first time from a small boat "like faint mist at noon: a jagged wall of purple at sunset"—with a puff of wind that brought the odors of strange blossoms and aromatic wood, "impalpable and enslaving, like a charm, like a whispered promise of mysterious delight."

I don't mean to claim that my seeing Africa for the first time was quite that much of an epiphany. But I think the effect was

3

much the same and that, in essence, so was the experience. Later years and long acquaintance have drowned out Marlow's echoes of romance, even if a certain mystery and sense of them remain; but my first experience has stayed with me, and the course of my life seems repeatedly to have insisted that it should. Let me tell you how it came about. It came about in the terrible year of 1941. That was a year, for us, when everything we loved and cared for seemed likely to be lost.

I was then a captain in the British army, and I was twenty-six. I arrived at my epiphany, if that is what it was, not after shipwreck as Conrad's Marlow did, but after a catastrophe which seemed, at the time, rather much as bad. Months earlier I had been on military duty in southeastern Europe, in Yugoslavia when that Balkan land was overwhelmed by Nazi-Fascist invasion, the Germans and Italians being seconded by the Bulgars and Hungarians. With a few others in the same service I fell into Italian military imprisonment and was confined in Italy; and the chances of getting out of that confinement were certainly no better, in May 1941, than Marlow's of getting to dry land. But the blessed ancestors who were preparing my epiphany, as I am ready to believe, chose this moment to intervene. They arranged that British forces then clearing Mussolini's Fascist Italian armies out of eastern Africa—out of Somalia and Eritrea and Ethiopia—should capture the Italian commander-in-chief, who was the duke of Aosta.

Now this duke of Aosta was cousin to the king of Italy, and the king of Italy got hold of a suitable intermediary and asked the British government to send his cousin back to him. "Nothing doing," said the British government, "you don't have any important prisoners of ours to give us in return." But the British government relented, kings being kings, and agreed to give back the duke of Aosta in exchange for one hundred men of ours whom they held, including several very junior officers; and the ancestors (bless them) decided that I should be among the latter. Being reckoned in value as no more than one percent of a duke might not be flattering, but I was in no position to object.

Returned to England by one route or another, I was granted ten days' leave to see my mother, who found the whole thing very puzzling, for the story of the duke of Aosta came out only later, but also very pleasing; and then I was sent back to my unit in the Middle East, in Egypt, and more exactly near the legendary city of Cairo. But at once it became apparent that the ancestors still had their eye on me. By enormous privilege I was spared the long sea journey around the Cape of Good Hope and flown from embattled England in a grand new Boeing flying boat. This was a wonderful machine, almost magical in those days, that performed with superb confidence as a military ferry up and down the east Atlantic seaboard. It carried me and some others to Portugal without the slightest hesitation, and then far south to Bathurst (Banjul today) in the Gambia, a mere curtain of rain as I remember it, of pelting rain like they had in the movies those days, and then eastward to the port of Lagos on the coast of Nigeria. From there a transport plane was to carry me far across the Sahara Desert and its confines to Khartoum on the Upper Nile, and thence I would get to Cairo. And all this duly came about, if you can believe it, with practically no delay.

The first refueling stop on that improbable journey from the Niger to the Nile was to be "somewhere in the north of Nigeria," an unknown point on an atlas map, as far as I could find out. But the port of Lagos already seemed to me, as it still does,

5

a perfectly horrible place to be, and anywhere else would be better. In Lagos there was nothing but damp and squalor; and if Lagos was in Africa, there was nothing to prove it. Happily, the ancestors were still around to speed me on my way, and were able to persuade the army authorities even down to the local transport department. Within a day or perhaps two I was being flown northward to that "somewhere in the north of Nigeria." And that is where I saw Africa for the first time.

Of type and name I have long forgotten, the plane from Lagos yawed and buzzed and shook for a couple of hours and more, and then slid down into a landscape of sand as flat and featureless as the eye could ever see, and utterly empty of anyone or anything. Thus arrived nowhere, we got out of the plane and a wall of sodden heat rushed against me like a fearsome animal. But after a while, gulping for breath, I saw that I was wrong about this place being empty: sitting in the middle distance were two huts of tin and timber, and these were the airport terminal.

But they were not all, even if they seemed so. I walked across the intervening sand with our navigator sergeant, a brisk lad from my mother's county, which is Lancashire; and as we walked, he raised a pointing arm to the horizon and confided, "There's a city over there, a big African city nobody's ever heard of." I had to believe him, for he'd flown this trans-African ferry route before. But there was nothing I could see.

We paused and stared. And as I stared, there came to me— I am not inventing, this is how it came to me—the intimation of a glance into the past that was also, to me, a foretelling of the future. Who knows? Such moments happen, and are not to be explained. There came to me through that distance the out-line of a presence, of a wall both tall and long, a city wall. Very big was this wall, said our navigator-sergeant. It was built of mud and timber, and it went right round a city lost in this African nowhere. One day, he said, he was going to get himself inside that city. All he could tell about it, meanwhile, was its name. "Kano, K-a-n-o. Ever heard of it? Of course you haven't. It's there, though."

He spat into the sand but with a certain respect. "It's old, they say. Five hundred years old, they claim. Don't see how it can be, though."

I found out later. Kano was seven hundred years old, if not a lot more. But even five hundred years meant history, and there wasn't any history in Africa, as far as I'd ever been taught. Perhaps one should find out. Perhaps, but now there was the war.

That day was long ago, and the tides of life have flowed between. All the same, this moment of glimpsing the walls of Kano, half-guessed through midday haze and heat, has stayed with me. The odors that came on the puff of wind, although I doubt if there was any wind, were not of strange blossoms and aromatic wood. They were of bone-dry sand and the oven-scorched air of the savannah. Yet they brought with them, infallibly as it seemed to me, a challenge to learn: a challenge to know what was so much unknown that it could appear to me, as it did that day, as though nobody anywhere had ever seen those walls before me.

The war went on with millions for company, and me among them. Years of army service followed, passed in my case mostly with anti-Nazi irregular forces in Yugoslavia and Italy until, blessedly in 1945, another plane took me home again. When that lovely survival arrived, I went back to my prewar trade of journalism and, more testing still, a youthful ambition to write history. This would be, as I thought, the history of Eastern Europe, where I had wandered in student times and soldiered during the war, and any thought of Africa and the challenge of the walls of Kano retired to the back of my mind or was forgotten. At about then, however, Eastern Europe also vanished behind the barricades of the Cold War, and seemed in all probability bound to stay there. What I had thought could be my life's working plan vanished with it. But the vision of Africa in 1941 was still with me, and in 1951 I would embark on African studies that would hold me for the rest of my life. I traveled and listened and learned; and gradually I began to ask of history those questions that had first come drifting over the horizon of my consciousness ten years earlier.

Since then I have continued to learn about Africa: enough, at least, to have reached the point of understanding that there must always be areas of knowledge that I have not entered and may never enter. Yet you can only do so much in a lifetime and must be grateful for that. Here in this book I present in summary and perspective whatever wisdom I have gathered in these forty-odd years of African study; and in this sense, a vital one to me, these pages offer the conclusions of a lifetime.

What follows, essentially, is a meditation on the nature of the African experience but, centrally, since Africans began to emerge from foreign rule, from colonial rule, in the 1950s. This has been an experience which inspired high hopes and promised liberating freedoms, and these were justified and real in their results. They gave new life to a continent of peoples long reduced to silence and subjection. That this should be so cannot surprise the historian, for the history of Africa's self-development, before foreign rule began, has shown that these peoples achieved much in the past, and will in all likelihood achieve much again.

But the actual and present condition of Africa is one of deep trouble, sometimes a deeper trouble than the worst imposed during the colonial years. For some time now, deserts have widened year by year. Broad savannahs and their communities have lost all means of existence, or else are sorely threatened. Tropical forests such as the world will never see again have fed the export maw. Cities that barely deserve the name have spawned plagues of poverty on a scale never known in earlier times, or even dreamed of. Harsh governments or dictatorships rule over peoples who distrust them to the point of hatred, and usually for good and sufficient reason; and all too often one dismal tyranny gives way to a worse one. Despair rots civil society, the state becomes an enemy, bandits flourish. Meanwhile the "developed" world, the industrialized world, has continued to take its cut of Africa's dwindling wealth. Transfers of this wealth to the "developed" countries of Europe and America have annually expanded in value: in 1988, for example, to what was then a record figure, an immense figure, paid out to "developed" creditors.[1] And multitudes starved.

And so the historian, emerging from the study of past centuries when Africa generally knew no such misery and crisis but, generally, a slow expansion of wealth and self-development, meets questions not to be avoided. What explains this degradation from the hopes and freedoms of newly regained independence? How has this come about? Where did the liberators go astray?

9

No doubt human blunders and corruption can supply some easy answers, and have their abrasive part in the story. Yet human failures are always with us. They can seldom reveal the root of the matter. Africa's crisis of society derives from many upsets and conflicts, but the root of the problem is different from these: different and more difficult to analyze. The more one ponders this matter the more clearly is it seen to arise from the social and political institutions within which decolonized Africans have lived and tried to survive. Primarily, this is a crisis of institutions.

Which institutions? To this the answer is easier. We have to be concerned here with the nationalism which produced the nation-states of newly independent Africa after the colonial period: with the nationalism that became nation-statism. This nation-statism looked like a liberation, and really began as one. But it did not continue as a liberation. In practice, it was not a restoration of Africa to Africa's own history, but the onset of a new period of indirect subjection to the history of Europe. The fifty or so states of the colonial partition, each formed and governed as though their peoples possessed no history of their own, became fifty or so nation-states formed and governed on European models, chiefly the models of Britain and France. Liberation thus produced its own denial. Liberation led to alienation.

The questions multiply. This result in alienation was certainly not intended. Did it come about because Africa really had no past experience of its own self-governing institutions? How true is it that old Africa, precolonial Africa, never developed a nationalism that could evolve and maintain a civil society within accepted frontiers? Europeans of the nineteenth century believed that Africans had never built nations but, at best, only tribes. Europeans have often continued to affirm that "tribalism" has been, and is now, Africa's bane. But what was this tribalism? What is it today?

A meditation of this kind provokes knotty questions, and tribalism is one of them. A terrain full of pitfalls opens out beyond it. In a large historical sense tribalism has been used to express the solidarity and common loyalties of people who share among themselves a country and a culture. In this important sense, tribalism in Africa or anywhere else has "always" existed and has often been a force for good, a force creating a civil society dependent on laws and the rule of law. This meaning of "tribalism" is hard to distinguish in practice from the meaning of "nationalism." Before the period of modern imperialism Europeans visiting and reporting on Africa seldom drew any such distinction.

But the "tribalism" that we see today is evidently quite another thing. This modern tribalism flourishes on disorder, is utterly destructive of civil society, makes hay of morality, flouts the rule of law. It is the reverse of the civil society revealed by the records of history increasingly and intensively inspected, since the 1950s, by historians from many cultures and countries. This was the civil society undermined and finally brought down by the decades of alien rule after Africa's imperialist partition in the 1880s, leaving as it seemed no valid structures for the future. And this of course was why British colonial policy claimed that its task in Africa was "nation building," it being supposed in London that the task had been beyond the capacity of Africans themselves. At first, the British set themselves to the work of inventing tribes for Africans to belong to; later, with possible independence looming ahead, they turned to building nation-states. Because, according to the British, there were no African models, these states would have to be built on European models. So these, being alien models, failed to achieve legitimacy in the eyes of a majority of African citizens, and soon proved unable to protect and promote the interests of those citizens, save for a privileged few.

Left with the shells of a fragile and fallible civil society, the majority have sought ways of defending themselves. The principal way they have found of doing this is through "tribalism," perhaps more accurately, clientelism: a kind of Tammany Hall–style patronage, dependent on personal, family, and similar networks of local interest. Insofar as it is a "system," clientelism has become the way politics in Africa largely operates. Its rivalries naturally sow chaos. Like the economic misery now afflicting much of Africa, this tribalism—the term is always slippery—"reflects, in significant part, pathological characteristics of the contemporary [African] state": of the postcolonial or, as some prefer to call it, the "neocolonial" nation-state which came from decolonization.[2]

These quoted words are Crawford Young's, and here he was thinking especially of the neocolonial nation-state of Zaire, once the Belgian Congo. But his words apply widely, as we shall discover. Next door to Zaire, in the republic of Chad (although the description of Chad as a republic had become absurd), another observer found in 1989 that "the vexatious feuds of the warlords have troubled the whole continent, embarrassed the Organization of African Unity, burnt the fingers of all but the most resilient peace-makers, and provided endless opportunities for international mischief-makers to dabble to their hearts' content." Chad was now "a shell of a country"; yet this same Chad, "with its petty and violent political conflicts, its drought and its under-development, and its systematic self-handicapping, sometimes seems a paradigm of Africa's dilemma."[3]

Other African voices speak the same warning. Africa may have "space, people, natural resources," says one of them, "but Africa is nothing, does nothing, nor can do anything"; and this was not the voice of some crude chauvinist but that of Edem Kodjo, a secretary-general of the Organization of African Unity.[4] As to the supposedly sacred frontiers of this nation-statism, added Kodjo, "the people trample them underfoot." And this was even welcomed, as overwhelming evidence could also show. For by this time "there may be few African frontiers today, certainly in West Africa, across which, day by day or night by night, people do not take themselves and their goods in more or less complete defiance of the constitutional law."[5] Alienation of people from the state could not go much further.

So an analysis of Africa's troubles has also to be an inquiry into the process—the process, largely, of nationalism—that has crystallized the division of Africa's many hundreds of peoples and cultures into a few dozen nation-states, each claiming sovereignty against the others, and all of them sorely in trouble.

Then what may happen in Africa save even worse disaster? This great question of the early 1990s prompted others no less awkward. Other new nation-states were also on the rocks, but this time in Europe itself, the Europe which had vanished behind the barricades of the Cold War but was now quite suddenly freed from those barricades.

These were the product of imperial systems internal to Europe, initially those of Ottoman Turkey, Habsburg Austria, and tsarist Russia; and their shipwreck in the democratic storms of 1989, when their Stalinist overlord in Moscow lost power to protests and huge overturns, was impressively complete. They too were countries that were not or no longer colonies, but nonetheless had been obliged to accept foreign control in all major policy matters. They too, Romania and Hungary and neighbors such as Czechoslovakia and Poland, had ceased to live within their own history. They too suffered an acute alienation.

Basic parallels between these two great zones of imperial and postimperial involvement, African and European, might be obvious enough. But were there parallels beyond the obvious? What could be learned from the difficult and delicate attempt at historical comparison?

A buzz of questions: perhaps best handled, to begin with, by stripping customary verbiage from the rhetoric of nationalism, and taking a look at the spiny contradictions that evidently lie beneath. For if nationalism has been and can be a liberating force, why then has it so often become the reverse?

For reasons that also have their personal angle, I shall begin with the Hungarians. They are a people long and sometimes brilliantly concerned with national history and identity, with what has been often called national spirit. So I propose to start with scenes in a modest urban square, in shape a truncated triangle rather than a square, that opens along the broad Danube promenade of Budapest, Hungary's national capital, just before you reach the Margaret Bridge across that famous river.

This square in Budapest can barely hold five hundred persons when tightly packed, as it sometimes is for reasons that will emerge. Although not much to look at, the square makes a fine place to look out from. I lived in an apartment alongside it many years ago, and every day looked out across the mud-brown flow of the Danube to city heights which climbed then, and perhaps still do, into noble streets of palaces and mansions above the wide Hungarian plain.

More to the point, this square beside the mighty river has been a place of history. Witness to that is a monumental plinth in the middle of the square and, raised on this plinth, the statue of Sándor Petöfi, poet of Hungary's national freedom. Here it was, in 1956, that dissident Hungarian writers bravely met to launch their rebellion against the Stalinist dictatorship of Mátyás Rákosi and his infamous acolytes; this was where they made their challenge that would explode into an outraged people's insurrection.

They met in Petöfi Square and declaimed their verses and spoke their protest because it had been Petöfi who long before had found the well-remembered words they needed. For October 1956 was a time, though by no means past the worst of it, when the freedom of the Hungarians was forfeit to the tyranny of a foreign power, locally manned but not locally commanded: the power, that is, of the empire ruled from Moscow. Hungary was not a colony but its regime, in the language of African nationalism, was certainly neocolonial. The effect was much the same. So the poets of 1956 met and recited Petöfi's promise of a century earlier:

> *Eszkesünk, eszkesünk,*
> *Rovák tovább nem leszünk!*

15

This we swear, this we swear,
Slaves we will no longer be!

Their insurrection was put down in blood by the Soviet armed forces. Another thirty-three years had to pass before history was able to reward those rebels of 1956, or the few of them still living, with a clear proof that they had been in the right and that their rising, however stifled, had been a prelude to liberation. Hungarians in 1990 were at last on their way to recovering the power to make their own history, and to trying once more to govern themselves in civic freedom.

But here, too, nationalism has shown itself a contradictory creature. Its brutalities have outmatched its mercies, its losses have effaced its gains, and several times over. Petöfi's poetic spirit, hovering above his effigy in stone upon its plinth beside the Danube, can recall occasions of another kind from that of the dissidents' brave gathering of 1956. I recall one of them myself, because I happen to have known Petöfi Square on one of those occasions. This was during the grim wartime year of 1941, facing a different tyranny (and, since I have already mentioned 1941, a little earlier than my misfortunes in invaded Yugoslavia).

The Danube's deep winter ice had mostly cleared, as I recall it, leaving the river for once almost as blue as the old romantic song says it is; and spring was on the threshold. But there was no glimmer of springtime in the air that day. Instead, peering across the river from Petöfi Square on that chill March morning of 1941, I saw marching troops and army transports heading south along the quayside; and I knew that Hungary's fragile bid for neutrality between the Democratic powers and the Nazi-Fascist "Axis" (as they liked to call it, even if the wheels squeaked badly) was at an end. They were troops and trucks of Hitler's Wehrmacht on their way to invade a Yugoslavia which, from being neutral, had suddenly become recalcitrant to Hitler's will. And with those German units there were Hungarian troops and trucks bound on the same mission of destruction.

These Hungarian regiments in Germany's service would crash into Yugoslavia a few days later. They would assist the Nazi forces in the reduction of that country to a reeking shambles; and in due course they would seize and kill all the Jewish people they could lay their hands on as well as slaughtering countless other people too. Petöfi that March morning watched them on their way; and so did I, but briefly. A young man caught in the maul of catastrophe, I as yet understood little of its implications. But I understood the implications of those troops and trucks. I bid farewell to Petöfi; and I ran for my life.

Now this Hungarian assault upon a then peaceful neighbor was made for various reasons. The chief of these reasons was that the Hungarians who were then in government would not reject Hitler's demand for their submission and assistance. This was not because they were much in favor of obeying Hitler, simply that they foresaw that disobeying him must have painful consequences. This was political calculation. But the reasons that were given out, then and later, were quite different; they were the reasons of high-flown nationalism. Hungary should recover lands lost to Yugoslavia at the end of the First World War; Hungarians should arise and awaken to their national duty. So Hungarian troops marched southward to the thrum of national anthems and the flourish of national flags; and any hapless person who stood in their way was thrust into jail as a traitor to a holy cause, or else, of course, taken aside and shot.

They went south and assisted in the dismemberment of Yugoslavia, their next-door neighbor, into satellite zones of German or Italian or other military subjection. At the same time, they helped themselves to a handsome slice of Yugoslavia for the greater glory of the Hungarian nation-state, declaring meanwhile that they were acting in the sacred name of national fame and self-respect. Petöfi continued to stand in icy calm upon his plinth beside the Danube, while the emancipated "slaves" of his unforgotten song thrust other peoples into slavery.

The war continued; and before the war was over the Hungarian people would have to pay a terrible price for their nationalism. All this became part of the endless tragedy of those years, affecting millions, countless millions. Meanwhile, for me this was an unforgettable introduction to the perversities of nationalism, to the Janus-like nature of the "national spirit" that demands freedom with one face and denies it with the other. But whatever may be found to explain this resolute two-facedness, it remains that the nation-state in Eastern Europe—but just as in Africa—has failed to meet the high claims of its promoters and the promises of its propagandists.

There must be reasons for this general and continental failure, and at this point in time, with fresh and hopeful solutions so urgently needed, these are reasons that we have to know about. It may be fairly easy to understand that new nation-states, emerging from imperial or colonial oppression, have to modernize their institutions, their modes of government, their political and economic structures. Very well. But why then adopt models from those very countries or systems that have oppressed and despised you? Why not modernize from the models of your own history, or invent new models?

In Africa, just as in Central and Eastern Europe, the search for answers has to begin nearly a century and a half ago: that is, around the 1850s. This takes us back to times both terrible and dramatic: in the African case, to the Atlantic slave trade during years when that great persecution was at last being chased and harried to its end. It takes us, however unexpectedly, to the decks of a British warship named the *Bonetta* in the year 1848, and to men and women, more dead than alive, who were rowed ashore from the *Bonetta* and somehow managed to stay alive.

Africa Without History

THEY CAME ashore in nakedness and hunger, but were lucky to be alive. The months before had been a living nightmare; for many now the deliverance from that nightmare would be a brief prelude to death itself. The slave trade had begun to kill them; disease would finish the job. And whatever the survivors would then remember could be only a series of jagged and traumatic sufferings. Seized in their villages along the West African coastland, these once able-bodied men and women had been dragged to slave prisons on the coast itself, infamous barracoons where, well guarded by their captors, they had lingered for weeks, even months, until a slaving ship bound for the Americas at last came by, and anchored for just long enough to buy them from their captors.

Once they were aboard the ship for the Americas, their misery became worse. Privations had been bad in the "old days" of the Atlantic slave trade, before the trade began to be made illegal early in the nineteenth century: according to such statistics as may be found, about one in seven of all the captives shipped for the Americas were dead before the voyage was over. But now, in the middle years of the nineteenth century, the mortality was higher still, for the old "close packing" of the legal slave trade, horrible enough as that had been, had given way to the dense packing of the smuggling trade. There had once been "regulations" for the treatment of captives; even these flimsy protections had now vanished.

"The form of stowage," wrote an eyewitness who was a British naval officer in 1849, one among many such who carried out his government's orders to stop and suppress this smuggling slave trade along the African seaboard, "is, that the poor wretch shall be seated on his hams, and the head thrust between the knees, and so close that when one moves the mass must." Because of this "stowage," reported this Lieutenant Patrick Forbes, captain of HMS *Bonetta*, in an account characteristic of such reports, the body of the victim "becomes contracted into the deformity of the position, and some that die during the night, stiffen in a sitting posture; others, who outlive the voyage, are crippled for life. . . ." By the 1840s, in this smuggling trade, a three-foot head clearance was considered to be normal. The head clearance on the slave decks "sometimes measure four feet six inches; while, on the other hand, that of the *Tragas Millas* [a slave smuggler overhauled and captured by the *Bonetta*] was fourteen [inches], and of the *Pharafoel* [another smuggler stopped and taken by the *Bonetta*] eighteen inches, intended for children only. One of these hellish nurseries," adds Lieutenant Forbes, who had seen them, "was taken in 1842 by HMS *Fantome*. She measured eighteen tons and had, beside a crew of five Spaniards, one hundred and five slaves (with one exception, a girl of fourteen) under nine and over four years of age.''[1]

Forbes's eyewitness account of slave ship conditions is only one among many made by officers of the British naval blockade instituted after 1807, when Britain had banned the further conduct in British ships of the slave trade that an earlier Britain had done so much to extend and profit from. The blockade continued into the 1860s, when smuggling at last petered out; and while the fate of the victims of the trade was unbelievably harsh, it was often sad for the naval crews as well. But naval employment was hard to find in the years after the defeat of Napoleon and France, and Forbes no doubt counted himself fortunate to be given command of the *Bonetta*. She was a ninety-foot brig converted to a brigantine—that is, to a two-masted sailing ship rigged square on the forward mast and fore-and-aft on the main mast, so as to give greater maneuverability; and she had three guns, with a crew of fifty to sixty men. Not a great command, and a service under conditions perilous to health, but evidently better than half pay or no pay ashore.

So the captives taken out of slave ships by the British naval patrols had reason to be grateful. Instead of being hijacked to the Americas under terrible conditions for the many weeks of the ocean crossing, they had only a few days of sailing to the port of Freetown in the colony of Sierra Leone, and there they were set free. But the naval patrols were few and far between; many slave ships evaded them. Lieutenant Forbes had no illusions about this. He thought that the blockade was a mercy for those who were saved, but after six months' service on the patrol he knew that most victims were not being saved. The smuggling slave trade being "a vast speculation," capable of yielding "vast gains" to the slave merchant ashore, "the profitable result is pretty well calculated by the merchant, and although it is a lottery to the people employed, he is safe enough. He fits out four, and expects to lose three vessels; if he should lose only two, he would consider himself lucky."

Forbes's calculations were of little comfort to the anti-slave-trade campaigners at home. Using such official statistics as there were, he estimated that the blockade, however admirable when it succeeded, could never be of much use in the suppression of the trade. "During 26 years," he found from the figures that he had (and we know now that they gave a broadly true picture), "103,000 slaves have been emancipated" by the warships of the naval blockade, "while in the same period, 1,795,000 slaves were actually landed in the Americas." The task was simply too big for the scale of measures used. In the 1840s each slow-moving warship had to patrol some forty miles of coastline. The chances of escaping capture were many for the slavers, no matter what their victims might have to suffer in consequence.

Even so, it is certain that many more than 50,000 captives were taken out of slave ships by men-of-war like the *Bonetta* and put ashore at Freetown, capital of the little West African colony formed years earlier for free blacks from Britain.[2] Most of these captives had been seized, as prospective slaves in the Americas, not far from the coastland of the countries that are now Ghana, the Ivory Coast, Togo, and Nigeria. But many came from much more distant lands, and a few even from the coasts of East Africa as far north as the Kenya of today. Once taken out of slave ships by their naval rescuers, they were known as "recaptives" in the curious language of those times: captives, that is, taken into slavery for shipment to the Americas, but "recaptured" and set free by the crews of the naval blockade. In the same decades a few thousand other recaptives were likewise set ashore at Monrovia, capital of America's colony for free blacks, Liberia.

A large though unknown number of these recaptives died within months or a few years of being set ashore; but a substantial core of survivors stubbornly remained. Coming from distant homelands along the coast, at first speaking a multitude of mutually incomprehensible languages, this unique community of rescued people rose gradually from great wretchedness in their new land to become a people with a notable history ahead of it. Save in Liberia and two or three free black communities in the New World, there was no other people like them. They had been liberated from the destiny of enslavement across the seas. At the same time, they were now cut sharply adrift from their own homeland cultures, and in the circumstances could not rejoin those cultures. They had to build a new life for themselves, and necessarily within a culture which they must forge for themselves. Ashore in Sierra Leone, settled in villages around Freetown or in Freetown itself, they little by little created a common language, a modified English known as Krio (Creole in English), invented forms of self-administration or adapted those they remembered from home, and at the same time embraced an ardent Christianity in place of their native religions.

The recaptives were all absolutely African in their origins; and yet they were divided from Africa by an acute experience of alienation. Africa had sent them into slavery. Europe, but especially Britain, had rescued and set them free. Converted to

Christianity by the campaigning missionaries of the nineteenth century, the liberated victims naturally looked to Britain as the shrine of salvation. Banding together, the recaptive villages around Freetown saw that freedom was a mercy to be used. They went into local business, local politics, local administration. They took jobs in government, and in time "a small, prosperous bourgeoisie emerged among people who had arrived in Freetown naked and penniless from the slave ships."[3]

Of the peoples of the vast interior lands behind the coast, they knew and could know little or nothing. They saw themselves in any case as the agents of Christian civilization in an Africa sorely in need, as they thought they knew from their own experience, of every form of salvation. Hardworking and self-improving, the recaptive community in due course produced theologians, political thinkers, men of capable action and, increasingly, men of relative wealth. And for a while, before the racist constrictions of a new age of imperialism struck at them in the 1890s, these men and women felt the winds of a liberating history in their sails; and they prospered. By the 1860s the list of their distinguished citizens, as medical doctors and teachers and writers and administrators, was already a long one. Whatever Europeans could do, these adopted Europeans would prove that they could do as well or, if necessary, better.

So it was, however unforeseeably, that rural Africans put ashore from warships like the *Bonetta* became, in an important and even decisive sense, the literate intellectuals of early colonial Africa. It was through them, and their educated colleagues in towns like Cape Coast who had not been captured and "recaptured," that the political ideas of nineteenth-century Britain took root on African soil. Nationalism, and its manifest destiny

26

in the sovereign nation-state, was foremost among these ideas. Alienation, one may say, thus became naturalized.

It would be easy and popular, long afterward, for patriotic Africans to think harshly of the recaptives and their influence upon the shape of things to come. With Christianity and Constitution as their watchwords, the recaptive thinkers held that Africa needed to be saved, and salvation must come from outside the continent. So their influence during the early colonial period was procolonial, and during the late colonial period would help to frame the structures of political sovereignty within which most colonies were to achieve their independence. This was an influence which took it for granted that a more or less total alienation from Africa's own past was entirely desirable since, as it was argued, no progress could otherwise become possible.

The principal agents of Christianity and Constitution lived in various towns and ports along the West Coast. Freetown in Sierra Leone was the earliest colony of modernizing literacy, and perhaps in the long run the most influential; but others soon emerged, the work not of recaptives but of men (as yet, of very few women) who were never victims of the slave trade: at Cape Coast in the Gold Coast (modern Ghana), on Lagos Island and Abeokuta, Nigeria, at Bathurst (Banjul) in the Gambia, and one or two other points of burgeoning urbanism as well, of course, as Monrovia in America's "Black Star" colony of Liberia.

As their influence widened, its principal missionaries became those whose homelands, or whose parents' homelands, had been in what was to become Nigeria, and whose original cultures were Yoruba and Igbo. Known as Saro or Aku, they had the enterprise and courage to return to their homelands, where, as they thought, their duty must be to introduce the light of civilization to an unregenerate paganism, and the advantages of British democracy to a savage despotism. Not surprisingly, they were received with no joy. But they persevered. Interlopers with a self-appointed mission to preach abrasively in these southern towns of what was not yet Nigeria, they were allowed the rights of residence, but with no enthusiasm.

"In all the towns where they were admitted," Professor E. A. Ayandele, a leading historian of Nigeria, would remind a modern audience some eighty years later, "the Saro were treated like a separate class, an aberration, that should not be integrated into [local] society." They should be tolerated, for after all they were fellow Yoruba, "but the essence of the matter is that they were culturally and, in their disposition, fifth columnists who would mentally and ideologically team up with the British invaders [then pushing in, *manu militari*, from Lagos Island, annexed in 1861] rather than sympathise with the unlettered masses."[4]

They would thus be seen, and rightly, as willing and conscious agents of the great colonial enclosure of the last years of the nineteenth century. Vividly eloquent spokesmen for the colonial Pax Britannica, "they were essentially co-operationists," in a judgment of Ayodele Langley's—and Langley is another West African historian whose voice commands respect—"with exceedingly limited political objectives." As it transpired, "a sub-elite whose interests generally coincided with, and were in fact protected by, the foreign rulers they were agitating against."[5] In short, the descendants of the recaptives and their nonrecaptive colleagues constituted the core of that "nationalist petty bourgeoisie" whose unhappy destiny in postcolonial Africa was to play out the role of an otherwise nonexistent bourgeoisie on British or French lines. In the tragic melodrama of postcolonial Africa, they were to portray the missing prince of Denmark.

Yet their ranks included talented and admirable men; and what else should they have done? Back in the mid-nineteenth century, all conceivable present and future power seemed to reside in Europe, but more particularly in imperial Britain; and without this power they or their fathers or mothers would have died in the infamous and stinking decks of slave ships, or else would have joined nameless legions in plantation slavery across the seas. They were enthusiastic about that imperial Britain and its navy; and they saw it as their dual task to assimilate the culture and intentions of their liberators and to transmit these to their fellow Africans.

They thought about the future of the countries that were now their own, of what that future might be in terms of progress and self-development; and, at least in the early years of their activity, the conclusions to which they came chimed closely and naturally with the trend of British official thought on the same subject, and could seem likely to be realized. Were they not a pioneering leadership in these lands so sorely in need of redemption? The Saro and their colleagues thought they knew what the British had in mind; and they approved of it.

What did the British have in mind? In the 1860s, however unexpectedly in the light of what was actually going to happen, the men in charge in London had come around to the belief that Britain should abandon her colonial enterprise on the West Coast of Africa, and withdraw from the little "settlements" she had formed there. The furious rivalries of late-nineteenth-century imperialism had yet to rise and dominate the scene. Meanwhile, to hold unprofitable territories abroad was an offense to Britain's doctrines of "free trade" and "the open door." Besides, the West African "settlements" were giving more trouble than they were worth. Now that there was no more need for shore stations such as Freetown to support the naval blockade against slaving—shore stations, in any case, where British officials died of fevers almost as soon as they got there—the "settlements" should be handed over to the locals. The Saro and their like were accordingly led to believe that some kind of African self-government, even political independence, was on the way.

Could anything be more sensible? The "settlements" were small and of small value. The British had the mouth of the Gambia River, Freetown farther east, some forts on the Gold Coast and, east again, a handful of footholds on the coast of the Bight of Benin; the French had fewer still, the Portuguese one or two paltry possessions, and that was about all. But small though they were, these places gave trouble, and they even cost money. Why bother to keep them?

In 1856, with such sentiments gaining ground, some of the British "settlements" threw up a flurry of tax disputes, always a fertile source of colonial trouble; and the imperial government in London sent out a Major Orde to report and advise the Colonial Office. He was followed by a former governor, Sir Benjamin Pine. Much was said, and very much was written in pen and ink laboriously transcribed. But decisions proved difficult. What seemed simple at a distance became, as invariably in colonial experience, complex and tiresome at first hand.

In 1865, baffled by conflicting detail, the men in London gathered from their cabs and carriages and arrived at the usual imperial solution of insoluble problems. They decided to appoint a Select Committee of the House of Commons which, in due course, would report, and then the report could be noted and filed, and life would continue as before. But on this occasion the Select Committee decided to put the cat among the pigeons. It concluded, to surprise and even uproar in fashionable circles, that the acknowledged African chiefs, in this case of the Gold Coast "settlements," should best be "left to their own jurisdiction, with only an appeal, when necessary, to the British magistracy."[6]

This was going to raise another difficulty, as we shall see, and a big one at that. To the Saro and their recaptive colleagues, meanwhile, it appeared to promise self-government in the foreseeable future. For it said that "the object of our policy should be to encourage the natives in the exercise of those qualities which may render it possible"—the prose was nothing if not prudent, and yet sufficiently clear—"for us more and more to transfer to them the administration" of all political and bureaucratic power, "with a view to our ultimate withdrawal from all [settlements] except, probably, Sierra Leone." Just how ultimate was "ultimate" seemed secondary: here was a blueprint for the years immediately ahead. In the committee chairman's own words, the British had got themselves into "a scrape" in undertaking to govern West African countries, and should now get themselves out of it "as speedily as we honourably can, leaving the tribes in a fair way of being able to hold their own and govern themselves."

Of course, it was not going to happen that way. Precisely the reverse was going to happen. Fewer than ten years would pass before the policy of armed invasion and permanent colonial dominion overhauled and sank, for long years ahead, any policy of peaceful withdrawal. The "scrape" would now become Britannia's mighty enterprise of empire building in Africa. Not for another century would withdrawal come to seem, for patriotic Englishmen or persons claiming to be such, anything less than dastardly betrayal of the national mission, no doubt promoted and paid for by the French or, after 1917, by the Russians.

Yet the Select Committee had its brief moment of patriotic fame. It advanced the conviction that free-born Englishmen could never stand by and consent to or applaud the subjection of foreign peoples. It reflected the liberal enthusiasm which, only five years earlier, had encouraged and enabled a British government to help Italians to liberate Italy from the odious tyranny of non-British empires. It was another victory, however rapidly denied by events, for the radical campaigns against slavery and the slave trade. Short-winded, this liberal enthusiasm fell away as times changed and imperialism followed. Yet the Select Committee's recommendations were to remain important for African politics. They wrote into British imperial doctrine that the ultimate future in West Africa must always lie in a restored African sovereignty. This was a thought that took root and remained alive through all the colonial years that came after. At the time, this briefly surviving policy of withdrawal proved strong enough to raise, and insist upon, a crucial question for West Africans, who were becoming aware that a new history was being made around them. As and when the British packed their official bags, and went, who were to be Britain's residuary legatees in Africa? Who could and should then take power, and within what structures of government?

This was going to be a great dispute. It signaled to the future, moreover, an enormous dissidence. Its outcome even today is still unresolved.

The Select Committee had said that power should be returned to acknowledged African chiefs and kings; and these, notably in the Gold Coast, were by no means the fevered apparitions of colonial invention or promotion. On the contrary, they were often persons of genuine authority and expertise who drew their status and prestige from a long precolonial history, in itself one of successive changes and developments. To reject their claims to take over from the British when Britain withdrew must be tantamount to rejecting the claims of Africa's self-development through countless centuries. In that case the institutions of renewed African independence would have to evolve out of a void, or rather out of the utterly different history of England.

To the recaptives and their colleagues—the latter, mostly, in Cape Coast and on Lagos Island—this "defence of the traditional rulers" as the proper legatees of the British could be nothing but an argument in favor of the unrepentant savagery which, as they rather understandably saw it, had delivered their parents to the slaving ships and enslavement in the Americas. By this time, around the 1860s, the literate groups along the seaboard from Lagos Island to the Gambia were sending sons and sometimes daughters to graze in the learned pastures of London's law schools and courts, fount and teacher of all sophisticated wisdom. These alumni came home with a reinforced conviction that the job to be done, after British withdrawal, could not possibly be entrusted to "tradition."

Postcolonial independence would have to be in the hands of literate and civilized men who understood constitutional law and practice, and could move around at ease in the world of

33

nation-statist sovereignties. However few in number they might be, they were self-selected as an elite as much by their capacity for hard work as by their educational advantages. While the new nations took shape from British withdrawal, the Western-educated elites would substitute themselves for the eventually elective people, and steer the right course until the people, at some time or other, would have learned to do it for themselves. Nation-states had to be formed. They were the men who knew how to form them.

The "acknowledged African chiefs" found this deeply offensive and obviously perverse. Their forms of government might need to be modernized, their institutions reformed, their powers redefined. They could admit as much, and they had plenty of experience, like their forebears, in finding new solutions to new problems. Besides, the more eloquent among them could not easily be written off as old-style "reactionaries" or quaint survivors of a past better forgotten. Far from that, some of them had been or remained pioneering members of associations devoted to the cause of self-improvement as for example of the Aborigines Rights Protection Society, which was also, in its way, a forerunner of the nationalism of later times.

At the old and important "settlement" town of Cape Coast, eastward from Freetown along the seaboard of the Gold Coast, where some of the old tin-roofed houses can still be seen clustering beneath the walls of the grim castle of slaving times, and the ancient guns still point out to sea, the offense to tradition seemed especially great. Here was where the venerable partnership in trade between African chiefs and European mariners had long given rise to mutual acceptance and respect. In the 1860s the chiefs' principal spokesman was a certain King Aggrey.

And when the great dispute came up, this local but well-seated monarch went so far in defense of the rights that he conceived as being inherent to his kingship as to cause the British to send him into exile. He thought, as did his friends, that justice and good sense alike pointed to the "acknowledged chiefs" as those who should inherit British power, because it had been British power which had disinherited the chiefs and kings of past days.

So who was going to win, the "traditionalists" or the "modernizers"? The question lies at the heart of the whole matter of Africa's emergence in the modern world, even though, however ardently disputed along the West Coast or elsewhere in colonial Africa, it was a question little noticed in London or in other capitals where the modern world was run. As to the final answer, we scarcely have it even today. During the colonial period that followed after the 1880s, it was to be the acknowledged chiefs and kings who might have seemed to be winning the argument. But when independence at last came again, it was they who were the losers: but losers who could and did argue that the "modernizers" were bound to make a mess of it.

It was not really a battle between tradition and modernization. Enterprising chiefs and kings were as eager as anyone else to assimilate the fruits of modernization, so long as these could be made digestible to accustomed ritual and historical custom; while the best of the modernizers well understood that there must be some accommodation with tradition. The ideological war as it developed—and a war it soon became—stood on different and more principled issues. No matter how much they spoke in defense of the virtues of Africa's cultures, the "modernizers" were necessarily standing on the ground of European culture. When it came right down to it, the Inns of Court or the Palace of Westminster or their "foreign" simulacra would always know better; and to the "modernizers" this seemed as obvious as it did to the British. The notable case of James Africanus Horton makes the point.

Horton's father had been take captive by slavers in eastern Nigeria. Sold at the coast some time during the 1820s, and then "recaptured," he was put ashore at Freetown in the usual rags and misery of a new recaptive. Joining other Igbo recaptives who lived in a village on Freetown's outskirts, Horton's father became a skilled joiner and a self-respecting Christian citizen of the Sierra Leone colony. He adopted the name of a British missionary and was married with Christian rites. His son James was born in 1835 and was sent to school. James proved to be a brilliant pupil, and would add the name Africanus to his own in proud assertion of his African origins.

The mid-nineteenth century was an age of vigorous self-improvement and therefore of strong belief in the values of literate education. Urged on by his carpenter father, James got himself by diligence and talent into the missionary Fourah Bay Institution (later, College and, eventually, University) and was soon able to make his mark. "After a year there," his biographer Christopher Fyfe records, "he was chosen, with two others, to go to Britain to study medicine: the War Office, alarmed at the high mortality rate among white army medical officers, had decided as an experiment to try training Africans."[7] So the carpenter's son was admitted to King's College, London, where he took a medical degree, and then went to Edinburgh University, where he took another. His medical career brought him back to West Africa and raised him before retirement to the rank of lieutenant colonel in the British army's medical service.

So far, so good. His case was exceptional but not so rare. In the mid-nineteenth century there was little racism in the British colonial service: in the 1840s "almost every senior official post including governor and chief justice [was] held by a man of part-African [most of them Caribbean] descent." That began to change in the 1860s, and Horton, in his turn, would then become the victim of the racism that imperialism brought in its train. Meanwhile, as it seemed, the case for Africa could and should be argued. Horton set himself to arguing that case in books and articles as well as in the circle of his friends. He had triumphed over every obstacle in his personal path and won admiration even from those in London whose prejudices were strong. Now he devoted himself to the political modernization of the Africa he knew.

His line of thought, admirably developed in his book of 1868, *West African Countries and Peoples*, was that Africans must be free to develop themselves.[8] Given this freedom, they would show themselves as capable as any people anywhere. For this, however, they would need Christianity and British example, since the necessary tools of progress, literacy, and the discipline of learning would otherwise lie beyond them. To this extent, and it was a large one, Horton rejected "tradition." The "acknowledged chiefs" to whom the great Select Committee of 1865 had awarded responsibility for the future must have their place, but within entirely new and non-African structures. Horton examined the territories where Britain claimed supremacy in West Africa, traveled in them, studied their condition, and prescribed for each of them in turn.

There should be independence for each of these territories, but within constitutions framed on British lines and administered with paternalist authority. On the whole, Horton preferred the structures of monarchy, and wherever local kings had genuine claims in local history, for example among the Fanti of the Gold Coast, he thought that an authoritative monarchy should be installed. Elsewhere, if conditions fitted, there could be republics, as for example among the Ga to the east of the Fanti. But salvation had to come from outside. Otherwise there would be disaster. Whatever Africa might have achieved in the past could not avail: left to govern themselves as they were, he wrote, "the base being rotten, the whole fabric will, within a very short time, tumble to the ground. Confusion, massacre, and bloodshed would be the inevitable result."

From this it followed that "before the people be given up to govern themselves a new order of things must be established . . . under the auspices of the British Government," and protected, whenever necessary, by Britannia's guardian hand. Never less than thorough, Horton went into detail. Enlightened administrations under British guidance would be legitimized by manhood suffrage and equipped with modern services in health and education; in due course these new kingdoms and republics of British creation would grow into the prosperous and fruitful products of a new civilization. Africa would be free: except, of course, that in terms of political and literate culture, Africa would cease to be Africa.

And this is largely what was going to happen in all those British colonies where there were no large white settler minorities to make distracting uproar. "Nation building," as Horton and his colleagues were to conceive it, would move from one stage of cultural alienation to another, and would eventually reap a harvest in political futility, a fate that could not be foreseen at the time. What was foreseen by Horton and his colleagues, during his lifetime and later, was that Africa's peoples would be transformed into nation-states on the British or another European model. Thus, they would become civilized at last, because "civilization must come from abroad."

This conviction that "no nation can civilize itself" was to be the governing thought in the anticolonial drama, however contradictory that may seem. The point was made repeatedly. One who made it clearly but was not himself of recaptive descent was the Gold Coast clergyman Attoh Ahuma in a book of 1911, nearly half a century after Horton's principal work was published. Ahuma was among those who argued that Africans must be proud of their continent and its cultures. And he had himself renounced his given name of Solomon for a local African name. But in his *Gold Coast Nation and National Consciousness*, he nonetheless urged that it was the task of enlightened Africans to "help one another to find a way out of Darkest Africa. The impenetrable jungle around us"—and you can see its fringes from Ahuma's hometown of Cape Coast, closing down the northern horizon—"is not darker than the dark primeval forest of the human mind uncultured." Therefore, "we must emerge from the savage backwoods and come into the open where nations are made."[9]

This was paying homage to Africa while preaching "traditional" Africa's incompetence to help itself; and the more perceptive writers, like Ahuma, were spasmodically aware of the problem this raised. They accepted the need for modernization of structures if independence was to be fruitful, and argued,

39

reasonably enough, that a "foreign model" could be made to fit provided that Africans did the fitting. At any rate, after their attention was drawn to Japanese resurgence, with Japan's defeat of Russia in the war of 1904, they pondered a possible comparison. How did a nonwhite people defeat a strong white power?

It is probable that men such as Horton were aware, if distantly, of the innovative reforms of the Japanese Meiji period in and after 1867. What is certain is that reforming moves in the Gold Coast—above all the famous Fanti Confederation of that same year of 1867—were soon being seen as similar to Japan's modernizing reforms. Ahuma even suggested that the Ga people of Accra could be compared with Japanese contemporaries. Another member of the Gold Coast literate group, John Mensah Sarbah, argued with great clarity just where the comparison could be shown to fit.

In forming their self-defensive federation or bond of 1867, wrote Sarbah in 1910, "Fanti patriots, and the Japanese emperor with his statesmen, were both striving to raise up their respective countries by the proper education and efficient training of their people. The same laudable object was before them both. The African's attempt was ruthlessly crushed and his plans frustrated."[10] Colonial usurpation, in short, had taken over. But Japan had not been invaded and subjected to the imposition of a totally external culture. Japan had remained independent. Standing on this independence, Japan had been able to look to the West and gradually take from the West whatever might be useful, rejecting what was not useful. Modernization, in other words, did not have to mean alienation.

But in Africa—and the case became general—modernization had to mean precisely that. In the 1870s the British, and the

French still more, turned sharply to military enclosure. Armies marched and colonies were defined, filling up the "empty map." And with this there came by the end of the century a stifling tide of Eurocentrism, of the racism that held that Europeans are naturally and inherently superior to Africans, with lesser codicils assuring that Englishmen are superior to Frenchmen (or the reverse), and so on down the line. The crude and inchoate prejudices of the slaving centuries were gathered together in a skein of racist ideology, while on the ground, out there in Africa, the old acceptance of innate equality between all human beings was thrown overboard. Africans would do what they were told, and their countries would be "developed" for them.

Such views, we should remember, were sincerely held and strictly applied in practice. As Christopher Fyfe, the authoritative historian of Sierra Leone, writing of this new dispensation throughout this new colonial Africa, has observed: "In the large new protectorates that were tacked on to existing small British colonies in West Africa," as the imperial powers carved up the continent and drew lines across the little-known interior, "there was no place for literate Africans. There, whites ruled and blacks obeyed. Inexorably, the racial rule of the protectorates seeped into the colonies"—the initially enclosed coastal enclaves—"where, as the twentieth century advanced, Africans were squeezed out of the senior official posts they had held in Horton's day, and replaced by Europeans."[11]

So it came about that by 1912 Africans in Sierra Leone, for example, held only one in six of the senior official posts, whereas as recently as 1892 they had still held nearly half of those posts. Such plans as Horton's, for African self-adjustment to the challenges of the West, went by the board: constitutions were to be London's initiative, work, and decision. The contrast with Japan after 1867 could really not be more acute. Japan was able to accept "Westernization" on its own terms, at its own speed, and with its own reservations, ensuring as far as possible that new technology and organization were assimilated by Japanese thinkers and teachers without dishonor to ancestral shrines and gods. Japanese self-confidence could be salvaged. Such an outcome was impossible in dispossessed Africa.

In retrospect, the whole great European project in Africa, stretching over more than a hundred years, can only seem a vast obstacle thrust across every reasonable avenue of African progress out of preliterate and prescientific societies into the "modern world." It achieved the reverse of what occurred in a Japan made aware of the need to "catch up with the West." It taught that nothing useful could develop without denying Africa's past, without a ruthless severing from Africa's roots and a slavish acceptance of models drawn from entirely different histories.

The children of the recaptives reflected the full force of this alienation, for it was Africa, after all, that had consigned their parents to the damnations of slavery. But the same alienation invaded all those West Coast and other Africans who now began to receive the benefits of literate education in mission schools in several colonies. Above the entrance to every school there was an invisible but always insistent directive to those who passed within the magic gate to the "white man's world": ABANDON AFRICA, ALL YE WHO ENTER HERE. There would be a vigorous reply to that, later on, when an African Christianity arose to claim its moral birthright. But this would be a protest in response to what was already an established order.

42

"Those who are instructed in the English language," the Afro-Caribbean diplomat and civil servant Edward Wilmot Blyden wrote to a sympathetic Mary Kingsley in 1900, "are taught by those from whom they have received their training that all native institutions are, in their character, darkness and depravity, and in their effects only evil and evil continually. . . . The Christianised Negro looks away from his Native heath. He is under the curse of an insatiable ambition for imitation of foreign ideas and foreign customs."[12] Whatever messages came from "outside" seemed only to reinforce this ambition as a necessary road to salvation.

Africa's own experience and achievement could teach nothing: it was "only evil and evil continually." And this was a lesson that gathered behind it the full force of whatever the outside world, with all its technical skills and military power, seemed able to teach. It was an alienation displayed in its purest form by transatlantic black people who had come to develop their freedom in Sierra Leone's "sister territory" of Liberia. They were sure, in the words of the famous black American surgeon Dr. Martin Delany, writing in 1859 after a visit to the Niger, that "the claims of no people are respected until they are presented in a national capacity."[13] Since Africans themselves were thought to have produced no such capacity, the liberators must do it for them. Those newly educated Africans along the coast who were not recaptives, notably at Cape Coast, were still close enough to native roots to retain some respect for those roots. But the American Liberians had no such reservations. They meant to build a "national capacity" on entirely non-African lines, convinced that nothing else was possible or, if possible, desirable.

43

Basil Davidson

There is the striking case of Alexander Crummell (1810–98) of Monrovia. His grandfather had been a chief in Sierra Leone, a chief in the "savage backwoods" before the slave trade hijacked him to North America. Grandson Alexander, resettled in Liberia from New York as a free American, considered reasonably enough that the land from which his ancestor had been driven as a slave was, in Alexander's words of 1870, "a seat of ancient despotism and bloody superstition." There could be no question of reforming its own institutions: these must simply be abolished so as to make way for the importation and exercise of "the genius of free government."

And if it were to be objected that "we have no right to command, or press such regulations upon our native population"—upon all those in the "savage backwoods" now governed by American Liberians—then the answer could not be in doubt. "Both our position and our circumstances make us the guardians, the protectors, and the teachers of our heathen tribes."[14] With some differences in language, it was precisely what the white settlers would say, in their more solemn moments, about their duties to the "savage backwoods" in colonies such as Rhodesia, Kenya, Madagascar, or wherever else white settler communities had the whip hand. The results in misgovernment would be much the same.

It could easily seem then, and perhaps it still does, that this enterprise of civilizing Africa by alienating Africa from itself had become necessary to meeting the challenge of self-rule in the modern world. Wasn't Africa's own world, wherever the grim decades and centuries of the slave trade and slavery had done their work, now far advanced in moral and political decay? Hadn't Africa failed signally to "save itself"? Such questions

44

became pressing in those times, and the problem of answering them without confirming their expected reply was repeatedly enlarged by the educated groups' response to the increasing racism of the colonial enclosures. The whole white establishment, in contrast with earlier years, multiplied its sneers and contempt for literate Africans, "useless visionaries, detestable clerks" as one colonial governor called them in speaking the mind of other colonial governors.[15] But the sneers seem only to have encouraged the visionaries and clerks into trying to prove that the sneers were not deserved.

It was bound to be a losing game. While white officials and their wives looked down their noses, the educated men and their wives abounded in the very proofs of "progress" that were certain to stretch the noses further. They formed learned societies. They presided over racecourses. They founded musical circles, debating clubs, charitable exercises. Above all, they started newspapers—several dozen in British West Africa alone—and wrote in them with the fire and fury of a true literary vocation. They promoted more constitutions that stayed on paper. They elaborated federal projects that met the same fate. Nothing abashed, they showed themselves masters of British law and science. They read voraciously. They knew everything.

It did them no good. The more they proved they knew, and the more artfully they argued their case for admission to equality of status, the less they were listened to. Better by far, pestered officials were bound to think, the "uncorrupted child of nature" than these wretchedly "Europeanized Negroes." But the latter still held fast to their belief in liberation by the imperial model, and persistently buttressed their case by polite behavior. As late as 1896, to pick from the records only one choice flower of this behavior, there was the marriage at Freetown, a brilliance well remembered, of City Councillor C. C. Nicholls and Miss Laura Henrietta Thomas. It occurred "with all the pomp and splendour," wrote the *Sierra Leone Times* of December 12 in that year, "which such an occasion fully justified." The bride was "richly attired in a costume of Duchesse Satin, made in the style of Mary Stuart, embroidered with pearls and trimmed with Chiffon and Orange blossom. The train, which measured 5½ yards, hung gracefully from the right shoulder," while "the Bridesmaids had on salmon pink" and "wore large picture hats trimmed with white ostrich plumes."[16]

Who could do better, who could do as well? If money was the test of civilization, there was obviously plenty of that, and as for polite behavior, the whole affair "presented an imposing and brilliant scene that has hardly been excelled before."

But it scarcely helped. Imperial racism proceeded as before. Only a few years after these grand nuptials, African doctors in the tradition of James Africanus Horton were excluded from the newly reorganized West African Medical Service. Twenty of them had qualified from the West Coast by the turn of the new century; and some of them, like Dr. J. F. C. Easmon, had made important contributions to medical science. Easmon's had been in the difficult field of research into blackwater fever. None of that did any good either. Despite solid evidence to the contrary, a departmental committee in London, reporting in 1909 on the condition of the medical service, found itself "strongly of the opinion that it is in general inadvisable to employ natives of West Africa as medical officers in the Government service." There was indeed no effective evidence save racist prejudice that the committee should arrive at this unanimous opinion: but the opinion was not seriously questioned except, of course, by the African medical men.

"In any case," pursued the same report as if admitting a clandestine doubt, "the Committee are certainly of the opinion that if natives either of West Africa or of India are employed, they should be put on a separate roster . . . and European officers should in no circumstances be placed under their orders."[17] This notion that Europeans should never be obliged to serve under Africans, no matter what degrees of competence there might be to advise that they should precisely so serve, became the touchstone of all imperialist culture. It was, in this large and decisive sense, the European response to African acceptance of colonial alienation. Yes, to become civilized Africans they must cease to be Africans, but in order to ensure that this should duly and completely happen, they should never be allowed to become Europeans. They should wander in some no-man's-land of their own until the trumpet of destiny, at some unthinkable time in the future, should swing wide the doors of civilization and let them in.

The British were the most systematic in imposing this sentence to nowhere, but at least they were less hypocritical than others. They held out no empty promise of "assimilation" to the white man's condition, and they gave rather few lectures on the universal rights of man. Indulging in both, the French were just as systematic in their racism while camouflaging its reality behind Jacobin verbiage that promised much and meant, in practice, remarkably little. The Belgians took their line from the French, although with less verbiage, while the Italians, Portuguese, and Spanish (with the Germans out of the picture after

47

1918) generally retired behind a miasmic fog of Christian beatitude which none of them intended to honor, or even thought they should honor.

The consequences that flowed from this were many and profound. For one thing, they seemed to confirm the educated groups' conviction that nothing in Africa's experience could be valid for the future. This racism of imperial government went hand in hand with a growing reliance on the "savage backwoods" for the purposes of colonial rule. Nothing, it seemed, was to change except that the "acknowledged chiefs" were now the agents of foreign domination instead of being, as in the past, the guardians of African tradition and self-respect. There was simply no place, as Christopher Fyfe has observed, for literate Africans except as clerks and policemen. Thinkers, ideologues, debaters of possible alternatives, were no more than a nuisance or, after the Russian Revolution of 1917 and the great panic about Communism of the 1920s (exceeded in dimensions only by the similar great panic of the late 1940s), they were subversives to be watched, followed, pushed around and, when necessary, exiled. As those years went by, the gap between the educated groups and the "savage backwoods" grew ever wider, leaving the educated groups to insist vainly upon their relevance or founder in their futility.

Another consequence was added. All the lessons of imperialism, as the colonial years went by, seemed to agree that Martin Delany, back in the 1850s, had been right: that "the claims of no people are respected until they are presented in a national capacity." That was what the British imperial rulers were also saying, even if they showed no sign of listening to those claims: "nation building" was now the great British slogan. Then the educated men would come into their own. So the aims of nationalism must be right; and this must be the nationalism that could produce the nation-state on the British model. Nothing else would be practicable; no other instrument of liberation was thinkable. None of the abrasions of European racism could obscure this evident certainty.

Nationalism thus acquired an irresistible virtue. Doubts about the desirability of multiplying the number of nation-states might be voiced in the homeland of the nation-state, but the homeland could afford such luxuries, seeing how little the doubts would count for. The stately Lord Acton did indeed observe in Horton's time that nationalism was a bad thing, since "nationality does not aim at liberty or prosperity, both of which it sacrifices to the imperative necessity of making the Nation the mould and measure of the State." He believed that the course of nationalism "will be marked with material as well as moral ruin." But that kind of liberal self-indulgence was all very well for the *beati possidentes*, comfortably installed in their power and wealth while apprehensive of upstart rivals. Outside the portals of the National Liberal Club, it had less appeal. To colonized Africans, told repeatedly that they were not free because they were not nations, it had no appeal at all.

The resultant poverty of speculative thought, in this political context, reached down the years. And speculative thought was made poorer still by the barricades raised against it, as imperial powers saw that looming ghost of the first half of the twentieth century, socialism in one or other of its forms, and tried in every way to exorcise it. There would in effect be no speculative thought on the crucial subject of structural alternatives until well after the Second World War or even, more widely, until

49

the collapse of the postcolonial nation-state in the 1980s. There were some exceptions, notably in the minds of revolutionary thinkers such as Amílcar Cabral (1924–73), but these thinkers were to have small chance of demonstrating what they meant.

One may think, even so, that the largest and most serious consequence of this ideological poverty lay in the general acceptance by literate Africans, at least down to the 1970s and perhaps beyond, of their necessary self-alienation from Africa's roots. What Horton and others had argued in the 1860s, but from a sensitive understanding of what the "savage backwoods" really were, and of the capacities and potentials to be found there, became ever more vulgarized and narrowed to an unthinking truism. This necessary self-alienation was preached from every kind of pulpit, and repeated to the point of arriving at simple nonsense. So we find, in 1963, a solemn essay by an accredited authority, American in this case, who tells us that "in building the newest nations, most of the population [of Africa, in this statement] cannot be taught overnight, or even in a few generations, the skills necessary to participate meaningfully and effectively in politics."[18]

The statement might be absurd, but it said only what was widely seen as obvious. Learned scholarly foundations, great international banking agencies, a host of specialized institutes devoted to "aid for Africa," have all abounded in versions of the same nonsense: a successful nation-statism in Africa must dispense with, or better still ignore, every experience of the past. Tradition in Africa must be seen as synonymous with stagnation. The ballast of past centuries must be jettisoned as containing nothing of value to the present. And yet these convictions were never seriously questioned, at the level of policy, until it would at last be seen, and even could no longer not be seen, that the imported model was a dismal failure.

Is there then anything useful to be said, at this late date, about the nonimported model, the essentially native African model of community self-government? No people can ever return to its past, of course, but there is value in considering what the past can say about its own models, even if only to suggest an experience helpful to the way ahead. In short, were there no nations or nation-states in Africa's precolonial history?

The Road Not Taken

ONE OF the achievements of our bloodstained century, if it may be called an achievement, is so clearly to have revealed the two faces of nationalism: its capacity for enlarging freedom, and its potential for destroying freedom. The rise and havoc of Fascist nationalism in one or other of its forms were a mortal threat to millions of people, and the threat was made good. But for colonized peoples, however much they incidentally suffered in the Second World War, the reality of Fascist nationalism produced the opposed reality of anti-Fascism; and anti-Fascism, unstoppable as it proved, became antiracism; and antiracism led in due course to an end of colonization.

Among the liberating effects of this antiracist nationalism was a denial, in our context here, of the Africa-has-no-history assertion that had helped to justify the colonial mission and its dispossessions. After 1945 this denial was placed on the ground of proven or well-attested fact instead of standing, as it had done, on the ground of imagination and romance. Among the earliest solid results was a book of 1956, *Trade and Politics in the Niger Delta* by the late Onwuka Dike of Nigeria.[1] He had decided, against orthodox advice, to write his thesis from the standpoint not of the "expansion of Europe," a safe one to adopt in those days, but from the standpoint of resistance to that expansion. He saw, as others were beginning to see, that an African self-assertion could never hold its own, intellectually, unless it could stand on Africa's own history. The following thirty years or so saw Africa's own history placed on firm ground.

With much else, this called for a reassessment of whatever had been known, or was thought to be known, about the precolonial past. In Europe quite a bit was then seen to have been known, but generally forgotten; while if memories had survived "in the bush," these had, in the professional view, been downgraded more often than not to the rank of ornamental folklore. There were exceptions, and especially with these exceptions the work of reassessment would produce results.

Once upon a time, around 1690 or so, the great tropical forestland behind the West African seaboard, known to seafaring Europeans as the Gold Coast, was inhabited by various groups or clans of a people called Akan. These groups were usually at peace with one another but suffered from being subject to other clans, who were also Akan, to whom they were obliged to pay tribute. If they could unite their forces, they might throw off this subjection and, should matters then go well, turn the tables on their stronger neighbors. But they had not been able to unite: clan rivalries had prevented them.

There came to them a man called Agyei Frimpon. He was a man they knew by reputation, for in living among their strong

53

neighbors he had acquired spiritual insights and power. They welcomed him and named him *Okomfo* Anokye, *okomfo* meaning, in the Twi language of the Akan, a priest or guardian of ancestral shrines. Priest Anokye let them know that he had come with a mission. This was to make the clans in question, those of Asante (or Ashanti in a more familiar English usage), into a powerful nation. In short, he wanted to enable them to unite against their neighbors.

Word got through to the leading man of these clans, King Osei Tutu, and Tutu, clearly well briefed, called a great gathering of chiefs and elders and queen mothers—for the Akan gave and still give great value to the influence of women—at his forest capital of Kumase, "Under the Kuma Tree." And there, as local memory recalls it (and recalled it for the benefit of a friendly European, Captain R. S. Rattray, about 230 years later), Priest Anokye drew upon his spiritual power "and brought down from the sky, in a black cloud and among rumblings, and in air thick with white dust, a wooden stool with three supports and partly covered with gold." It was, in fact, a stool of the kind upon which leading Akan sat in council, or at other times in everyday circumstance. But this was a special stool brought down from the heaven of the Akan high god Onyame, and with the mission conferred by Onyame upon Priest Anokye.[2]

The multitude that day watched in pent silence as this Golden Stool, Sika Dwa, descended from its black cloud and came to rest not upon the ground but upon the knees of King Osei Tutu. Whereupon Priest Anokye "told Osei Tutu and all the people that this stool contained the *sunsum* (soul or spirit) of the Asante nation, and that their power, their health, their bravery, their welfare were all in this stool." The stool was never to be sat upon by anyone, not even by the king, or ever allowed to be seized by hostile agency, much less destroyed, because in that case "the Asante nation [would] sicken and die."[3]

Myth or reality? Both, of course; but the myth was a function of the reality, not the reverse. This arrival of the Sika Dwa in the midst of a great assembly had no doubt been preceded by appropriate discussions and arrangements, all of them tending to agreement on the need for interclan unity; and King Osei Tutu and Priest Anokye were in any case historical persons. What remained was the need not only for a symbol that could embody the idea of unity where no unity had existed before, but no less for a symbol acceptable to Akan concepts of ritual for change. Akan persons of authority had sat on stools made for them since times beyond memory, and new aspects of authority, introduced to meet this or that contingency of social change, had required the making of new stools for new wielders of authority. Such stools possessed the prestige of custom and clan solidarity, but they did not come down from heaven in a black cloud or any other sort of cloud. They belonged to the person in authority who had the right to sit on them, and were of bureaucratic rather than mystical importance.

The Golden Stool thus produced was different not because it was unique, although unique it was, but because it could belong to no living person. It stood for the spiritual power that commanded all persons and all things, and commanded, in this case, the clans of the Asante and their fortunes and their fate. One may compare its power and meaning with the power and meaning of the English Crown: not the crown the monarch wears, any more than the Sika Dwa was or is the stool on which the king of the Asante sits, but the Crown which no one has ever

seen or ever can see: the initiating symbol of the English nation's unity and welfare, ritually acquired and ineffably empowered by convenience, coercion, and the manifold accretions of
history. The Golden Stool, like the English Crown or comparable symbols, embodied a transcendental power beyond its material existence.

Yet the Golden Stool, however mystically descended, was
above all an artifact of practical statesmanship. Having produced
the symbol and seen it accepted, Anokye was at once ready with
its mandatory charter. This consisted in a unifying constitution
expressed in seventy-seven laws. These laws, in the sociologist
Naomi Chazan's accurate words, "set out the structure of the
government [and] the divisions of labour, and the main elements
of early Asante political culture."[4] The clans thus unified were
to abandon their separate charters of origin and legitimacy or
else consign these to silence. Henceforth, their legitimacy would
be drawn from the charter of the Golden Stool.

These unifying laws were accepted as wise and desirable by
the clans situated nearest to Kumase, where Osei Tutu reigned,
and then by clans more distant, and eventually under initial
coercion by other peoples who fell within the Asante nation's
widening power. Meanwhile, the Sika Dwa remained true to its
origin: it remained an artifact of statesmanship used or abused
according to the ups and downs of Asante history and the wisdom or foolishness of their rulers. All this has much to say
about the manner of formation of ancient communities in Africa, although the Asante case of the Sika Dwa has rare virtues
in its dramatic clarity of demonstration. It may be seen as a
paradigm of the sociopolitical process; and this is the sense in
which Ivor Wilks has described Asante self-assertion as "a

model of early change.''[5] No one aware of this history, or its manifold parallels, is likely to suppose that Africans have lacked the skills necessary ''to participate meaningfully and effectively in politics.''[6]

What had happened to the Asante clans before the coming of the Golden Stool is less well known but can be broadly sketched. Their remote ancestors had lived in the lands north of the Gold Coast seaboard (in modern Ghana) from time immemorial, certainly for many centuries. Gathering forest food and hunting game, they had secured for themselves a steady but slow increase in their numbers. Extended families had grown into clans, and their clans, by the time the earliest Europeans dropped anchor along their seaboard late in the fifteenth century, were developing into small but structured states. Of these, by 1620, the Portuguese who came here thought there might be as many as twenty. At this point these people, the Akan, embarked on major changes in their way of life, the most important of which was a concentration of effort upon the cultivation of food. They began clearing forests for new farms and fields, and gradually achieved a successful tropical agriculture. Scholars are divided about the reasons for this development. Some see it as the climax in a movement to tropical farming. Others put emphasis on the arrival of new crops from tropical America, crops deriving from plants brought across the Atlantic in ships that were now, increasingly, a transoceanic link in Europe's maritime trade. Both explanations are clearly valid. New crops did arrive— manioc (cassava), pineapples, and others—but the skills to cultivate them were already present.

The Akan in any case felt the need for more land to clear and use for farming. Looking for it, they moved steadily northward

into the forest. Clearing more land, they needed more labor. Given their stage of economic development, this had to be wage-less labor as in nearly all neighboring African societies. In practice, this had to mean subjected labor: in one local form or another, slave labor. This was not, of course, the chattel slavery of transatlantic plantations but the coercive means by which a clan or other unit could enlarge its labor force. It was not, as in chattel slavery, an irreversible rejection from the society that employed it: on the contrary, it supposed an organic absorption of subjected persons into the society that used them. Slaves bought or captured for farming work were normally accepted into the family or other unit for which they toiled. They could found families of their own but also inherit within that unit. In a short time, according to Rattray, they "merged and intermarried with the owner's kinsmen"—or rather, given Akan matrilin-
earity, with the owner's kinswomen, but Rattray was writing before gender liberation became an issue—to the point "that only a few would know their origin." They became, in short, citizens of the Golden Stool.

Osei Tutu, the first of the Asante kings to be chartered by the Golden Stool, is thought to have been born around 1645. This was then the threshold of the time when the Asante clans of the Akan had developed to a point of wealth and confidence at which subjection to neighboring states such as Denkyira was becoming an unacceptable burden. After the unity forged by Priest Anokye, Osei Tutu organized an army that was able, notwithstanding some defeats, to throw off the burden and make Asante into a nation-state. But is the term permissible?

Like all such terms, "nation-state" tends in application to be what you think it is. The Europeans who first came in close contact with Asante, increasingly in the nineteenth century, certainly thought and wrote of Asante as a nation-state, even if they only used for it the term "nation," because it had all the attributes that justified the label. It had a given territory, known territorial limits, a central government with police and army, a national language and law, and, beyond these, a constitutional embodiment in the form of a council called the Asanteman, even if, during the nineteenth century, the charter of the Golden Stool remained a secret to outsiders. Moreover, as is now more clearly understood, Asante possessed a history of its own state formation, processual and perfectly understandable once you knew the salient facts.

Besides this, the Asante polity proceeded to behave in the best accredited manner of the European nation-state. Having achieved its own unity and independence, it went to war with neighbors and subdued them, obliged them to pay tribute, and otherwise bullied them as and when its rulers felt best or able. By 1750 this powerful nation-state had secured effective control of the whole of what would become, two centuries later, the republic of modern Ghana. The Asante nation-state had become an empire-state.

All this, in continuing terms of being able to "participate meaningfully and effectively in politics," brought corresponding changes in structure and systems of control. But the principles which had guided the charter of the Golden Stool, it seems, generally held firm. For example, while the concept of a national unity framed upon an overarching rule of law was modified to the extent of allowing non-Akan subject peoples to maintain their own separate charters of identity, the acknowledged spokesmen of these subject peoples were obliged to recognize the supremacy of the Golden Stool and its inherent charter. They had to attend the *odwira*, or annual yam festival, this being a means of insisting on the primacy of national over subnational or regional rights and obligations, and, in Wilks's phrase, performed as an embodiment of the "overriding national purpose."[7]

This enshrinement of unity of purpose as a necessary condition of political health was buttressed, here and elsewhere in precolonial Africa, by other principles of good government. The yam festival was an occasion for music and display, for the luxury of expensive gowns and cloaks, the brilliance of great umbrellas twirled above the heads of those who could claim to deserve them, or the banging away of countless muskets, along with much persiflage and courtly intrigue, diplomatic or merely personal. But its celebration of Asante union was carefully accompanied by a down-to-earth insistence on the power sharing that sustained unity of purpose. The festival coincided with the annual meeting of the Asantemanhyiamu, the representative assembly of the Asanteman or Asante nation. This was "a kind of parliament," wrote a British observer in 1886, at which "all matters of political and judicial administration are discussed by the King and Chiefs in Council, and where the latter answer all questions relating to their respective provinces, and are subject to the consequences of appeals, from their local Judicial Courts, to the Supreme Court of the King in Council."[8]

There must be a unifying force, but this had to depend upon a system of participation that must not only work, but must publicly be seen to work. And to these two principles applied since the initial act of union, one may add a third, again characteristic of precolonial political institutions in every African region where stable societies produced one or other form of central government. This third principle may be called a systemic distrust of power. It took a multitude of different forms. The Asante system, for example, had markedly aristocratic tendencies in that power resided in chiefs by ascription as well as in chiefs by appointment. Asante government could be severely autocratic no matter what the laws laid down by Priest Anokye might command. But the Asante were not a people, at least by present observation, greatly given to any modest shrinking from the public eye. They have not feared to shine. Their laws and customs have registered the fact.

"Tell him," the assembled people will admonish (or, at any rate, used to admonish) a newly enstooled person of authority:

> "Tell him that
> We do not wish for greediness
> We do not wish that his ears should be hard of hearing
> We do not wish that he should act on his own initiative . . ."

but he should consult with representatives of the people, and pay attention to other useful maxims of the like import.[9]

The subject here is a large one, but the drift of the evidence all goes one way. Power was exercised by powerful persons, but with constitutional checks and balances tending to prevent abuse of power. Despots certainly arose; they were dethroned as soon as could be. Between ruler and people—one can say between state and people—there was an acknowledged recognition of ties of mutual obligation and respect. Centralized power, at least within the limits of human frailty, was exercised within structures that were devolutionary in their intention and usually

Basil Davidson

in their effect. Asante had well-policed main roads for foot messengers and a complex network of administrative communications, and was altogether a powerful state. Yet its executive power derived from the degree in which its founding principles were observed: in the rule of law, in the diffusion of executive power, and in the encasing of that power within political and legal checks upon its use, just as Asante's blunders and disasters came from failure to maintain those principles.

I shall not be thought to be asking, I hope, for any belief in a smooth and regular process of stability and compromise. Humanity seems not to work in that way. The detailed history of Asante, available at least from about 1700, shows that the system had to absorb repeated and sometimes abrasive adjustment to ambitions, corruptions, careers, and circumstances that threatened uproar and upset, and not seldom produced disgraceful setbacks to law and order. What is significant, in our context here, is that this polity had found the means and ability to weather such storms. Up until the late nineteenth century and a time of momentous change on the eve of colonial enclosure, the system proved self-adjusting even in moments of catastrophe. Over at least two centuries there had been nothing that in the least resembled the structural crisis that was to follow colonial enclosure.

Was Asante exceptional in these respects? The records and analyses now in hand for many other polities suggest generally that it was not. In many ways, no doubt, Asante was peculiar to itself. Yet it functioned on principles of constitutionalized delegation and devolution of executive power, and of inherent checks and balances, such as may be seen at work under different appearances in the history of a whole range of contemporary

62

polities. Of those, for example, of the Mossi, of the Yoruba, of the Mandinka, and of others in West Africa and of polities in other regions of the continent. If one were to make a comparative listing of political structures in precolonial Africa, the result would confirm that precolonial political cultures undoubtedly displayed a great diversity, but an even greater unity of underlying concept.

So much nonsense has been written over the last hundred years about the arbitrary and unpredictable nature of precolonial African political communities and their modes of existence that their systemic regularities, and the reasons for these realities, have become hugely obscured. Those communities about which we now have copious information, perhaps some sixty or so out of several hundred, can be seen to have operated according to established charters of self-identity that are comparable with each other, and even, in their substantial objectives, identical with each other. They supposed, for their good operation, an accepted manipulation of the symbols of institutional power. The Asante case is particularly interesting concerning this manipulation of power through manipulation of the symbols of power, but this is probably only because we know a lot about it.[10] All these systems had to depend upon intelligent manipulation or, if they were unfortunate, had to suffer from stupid manipulation. Symbols far greater than the Sika Dwa have shown us the same outcome: the Crown of England for one example, the Cross of Christ on a continental scale.

The political sociology of Africa, in brief, has been peculiar to itself but peculiar in no other sense. Its seeming eccentricity or inexplicability or unpredictability has existed only in the eyes of those who have not really looked.

* * *

The Asante polity could apparently adjust, and rather well, to new problems raised within its own culture and circumstances. But why, it may be asked, did that mature Asante of the late nineteenth century seem unable to adjust to problems raised by external challenges—above all, by the challenges of European modernization? Why, for example, was there no strong development of merchant capitalism to meet the thrust of European companies and corporations? Why no innovating initiatives to help defend Asante's interests against this restless world now lapping at Africa's shores of consciousness?

These are reasonable questions even while they imply an unwillingness to innovate that was never really present; and the answers are crucially important to an understanding of today as well as yesterday. This is because the whole weight of argument for "technical aid to Africa" has rested on a false assumption that the societies of Africa, or at any rate of tropical Africa, have survived without possessing an efficient rationale of "marginal advantage": they have not, in other words, operated by asking in a given situation what is better and what is worse. They have simply, on this general assumption, wandered through their history on a purely hit-and-miss trajectory.

Cohorts of "technical aiders" of one sort or another, often with a certain measure of idealism, have sought in Africa to solve indigenous problems, notably in matters concerning the production of food, that Africans have not been thought to have solved or even been able to solve. The same order of assumption has been applied to problems of a political or sociopolitical nature. Incapable of building its own nations or nation-states—the two terms seem often to be used interchangeably—these

64

people must be shown how. Once shown how, naturally on the findings of European experience and example, then all must be well.

Complacent assumptions of this kind have lately taken some hard knocks, but this is not to say that they have vanished from the scene. It is still worth asking why leading polities in West Africa, by 1850 in contact and sometimes close contact with Europe for three or four centuries, should have failed to make adjustments in their modes of production and exchange, adjustments that could have helped them to meet the external challenge of imperialism. One answer is that there was in fact no sufficient chance for adjustment. The long trading contact, opened after about 1450 along the western seaboard, had remained culturally narrow and was successively narrowed again and again by the reductive influence of the slave trade after the British and the French got into it. Then came, very suddenly, the colonial enclosure, and with that enclosure all contact was reduced to a master-and-servant relationship.

The Japanese example is once more instructive. What would have happened in and to Japan if the Western world had made Japan a target for colonial enclosure and dispossession in the second half of the nineteenth century? Precisely at the time, that is, when Japan was entering a period of radical and internally directed reform of structures and commercial habits? Supposing that Western enclosure and dispossession could have succeeded and did succeed, and rule by Western agencies—in the event, undoubtedly rule by racist discrimination—had taken from the Japanese all scope for their own initiative and enterprise? One may reasonably reply that in this case the modernizing revolution of Japan could not have been carried through:

repression and stagnation would have replaced all those self-adjustments comprised in and after the Meiji reforms that brought Japan into the modern world on its own feet. Western judgments would surely then have said of Japan what the late Professor H. E. Egerton was to say in 1922 of colonized Africa: that what had happened there, with the imposition of Western rule, was "the introduction of order into blank, uninteresting, brutal barbarism."[11]

Japan is not Africa, of course, and I will pursue the comparison no further. But there is another answer to the "no-adjustment" argument. Let us take a brief look, in this context, at what was really happening in Asante—even though other examples would be perfectly possible and relevant—when the British policy of enclosure and dispossession was being decided upon.

Asante in the 1880s was undoubtedly strong in its power and structure but was also in the throes of structural change. Its rulers faced a growing threat from British power along the coast, and the more perceptive of them now understood that this threat was in the nature of an imperial ambition which they probably could no longer or not much longer meet in military terms. Earlier in the century they had tried a policy of military self-defense and had managed to prevail or at least to force a stalemate. But British military pressure had continued, and had then been able to show, in Britain's invasion of 1874, that the military balance had shifted to the British side.

After that invasion, and Britain's brief occupation by force of the Asante capital of Kumase, there were those in Asante, or at least in Kumase, who thought that peaceful compromise must now be the right course. The British had withdrawn from Kumase, true enough, but they had inflicted harsh losses. In

W.E.F. Ward's description, "the fall of Kumase had shaken the Asante state to its roots, and many of the great feudatories"— the senior officeholders, or *amanhene*, though few have agreed that their relationship with their king was feudal in its nature— "were thinking of breaking away" from the unity of the Golden Stool.[12] Yet the British had nonetheless withdrawn, glad to extract their forces from what their veteran commander, Sir Garnet Wolseley, called the worst of the many colonial wars in which he had fought; and a new Asantehene could set about restoring royal authority and reducing breakaways.

For some twenty years, after 1874, the politics of the Asante state swung between one internal pressure and another. But those who were for structural change as a means of adjustment to the British threat, and all it implied, gained in strength. Not only in Asante: a sense of necessary internal change, as part of the answer to facing external challenges increasingly perceived if far from clearly understood, had begun to acquire a wide presence some years before the invading European armies marched. Kings and great chiefs saw a new danger. What they now began to fear, as well as outright military invasion, was that European pressure and example would undermine their political power by reducing their economic power: by curtailing royal monopolies, promoting discontented subjects, and fomenting rebellions against tradition.

At least in coastal and near-coastal Africa, much had been changing. With the virtual end of transatlantic demands for slave labor, internal wars and raids induced by the hunt for enslaveable captives had gone out of fashion. In the widening peace before the 1890s, new kinds of trade were possible and, as enterprising merchants rapidly discovered, were increasingly desirable. For those brief years, before European trading companies followed invading flags in order to build their own monopolies, there appeared to be a real chance that African trading companies would continue to prosper and, in prospering, inspire those economic reforms whereby Africa should be enabled to meet the commercial challenges of capitalism.

Thrusting African merchants along the western seaboard, men such as King Ja Ja of Opòbo, who now soared to commercial power on the export of palm oil, began to induce the rise of a capital-owning and -investing group that might have hope, given time, of becoming a middle class of nation builders in the European sense of the term. But they were not given time. They were at once found inconvenient and, being stubbornly competitive with European merchants, they were soon found intolerable. Ja Ja and his kind were all attacked, expropriated, exiled, or otherwise done away with as the European dispossession continued. It remains that the potential they had represented, in terms of structural adjustment, was in substance no different from the potential realized by the Japanese after 1867.

The potential they had represented was not small. In that brief interval before expropriation, perhaps twenty or thirty years, Asante had seen the rise of a "new class," in Ivor Wilks's term, a new group of "wealthy persons," the *asikafo*, or men of commercial enterprise, eager to take advantage of opportunities they saw ahead of them. By the 1880s such persons "should properly be regarded as constituting a small but growing bourgeois middle class with distinct interests and aspirations transcending loyalties and allegiances of a traditional kind."[13] Here again, but now in terms substantially economic, was rivalry between Tradition and Progress. In England's history, that was

a rivalry settled by forty or so years of internal strife and
civil war after 1642, leaving England in 1688 with a Glorious
Revolution to open wide the gates to private enterprise and
capitalist supremacy. Two centuries later something of the same
complex process, working its way slowly to the surface of events,
was clearly going forward in parts of Africa. Asante was one of
those parts.

Until now the Asante polity had relied for its commercial
operation upon state enterprise controlled and monopolized by
the king and his appointed agents. It had relied, that is, on
"mercantilist" policies to which the *asikafo*, the new "private
enterprisers," were understandably hostile. The *asikafo*, in this
comparison, stood for the City of London against the English
king's royal prerogative: they were for the opening up of Asante
by whatever means of private enterprise that might come to
hand. If this should damage the interests of the king and his
court, that was the price of progress; if instead it brought wealth
to the *asikafo*, that would be the reward of enterprise. The
issues would scarcely have presented themselves to the Asantehene and his chiefs on one side, or the *asikafo* on the other, in
quite these terms. But it would not be rewriting history to use
such terms in explaining this rivalry. Consciously or not, the
asikafo were for "moving with the times," while the king and
his court were not.

Wherever European pressures had appeared, this rivalry was
not in fact a new one. As many as four centuries earlier, the
king of the royal state of Benin, afterward part of southern
Nigeria, had created new chieftainships for the benefit of better
relationships with European sea traders while, at the same time,
taking care to prevent these new chiefs from going into business

on their own account.[14] In the Asante case, under the conditions of the 1880s, the king and his administrative stool holders saw their route to self-defense in measures to extend the royal monopoly but this time in partnership with a British royal monopoly. Their bid for self-adjustment took the form of offering the British monarch, Queen Victoria, a huge commercial concession. This was no less than acceptance of British commercial invasion in order to dissuade British military invasion. Britain should be asked to develop Asante in return for golden prizes, but the development should in no way undermine the royal power.

The implications, insofar as these were thought through, were breathtaking. Far away in southern Africa, when this extraordinary offer was made in 1895, a British company chartered by the Crown had acquired extensive mining and commercial rights from another African monarch sorely threatened by British military invasion. This was Cecil Rhodes's British South Africa Company, and the concession was intended by King Lobengula of the Ndebele to dissuade the British from a war of dispossession. It would in fact do nothing of the kind, and the Ndebele were duly and completely dispossessed. Yet the king of Asante's ambassadors then in London offered the British a concession, they explained, which would give a British chartered company "the same extensive rights as at present enjoyed by the British South Africa Company" in the lands that would become Rhodesia.[15]

Now it might be thought that the British government, eager to acquire a monopoly of commercial control over wide West African lands, but far less eager to meet an almost certain high cost of conquest, would have jumped at this offer. But the

British ministers in charge at home now wanted more than monopolist commercial control; they wanted territorial ownership. Partly in order to keep out the French, then pressing down from the interior lands of the Western Sudan, but even more, as most of the evidence seems to show, because a demand for territorial ownership had become an imperial obsession and even a popular cause. Rejecting the offer of commercial domination of Asante without cost or warfare, another British army marched on Kumase. This time the British did not withdraw. Asante was enclosed as a "protectorate" of the Crown in 1901 and, in practice, a region of the Gold Coast Colony. The financial cost of much of this was then quietly shunted onto the invaded people.

But with this, as events have shown, the whole scope for possible development into modernizing structures was stopped dead, and could not be started again so long as colonial dispossession continued. What might have happened if the Asante offer had been accepted by the British government, and a chartered company on Rhodesian lines installed in Asante, is open to anyone's guess. There would at least have been no British or other white farming settlers, or so one may suppose; but the end result, otherwise, is likely to have been much the same. All roads, in those days, led to dispossession, but the *asikafo* had at least demonstrated their capacity for self-adjustment. As it was, they remained alive, but not their chances of enterprise. They, too, were expropriated in one way or another. Everyplace that wealth could be extracted by commercial means fell within the scope of European companies, mostly British, based along the coast.

These took control of the export trade, fixed prices, and milked producers at the rates thus fixed. Government in all matters was reserved for Europeans acting as servants of the British Crown. The grandchildren and great-grandchildren of the recaptives and other Westernizing educated groups, for long so prominent in government and its services, were removed from all positions of authority. Every last shred of their argument of being empowered to lead the "West African settlements" to self-government under African rulers but British institutions—every last bit, that is, of Horton's policy of the 1860s—was torn up and thrown away.

The irony of this was to be very sharp. No more than sixty years or so after preferring to invade Asante with military force rather than accept the Asante offer of a more or less unfettered commercial control of that country and its wealth—a control, moreover, that would cost next to nothing in administrative terms, since Asante would continue to administer itself—British imperial government found that it had little to gain, after all, from territorial possession and reverted to the policy of withdrawal set forth in 1865. They turned back to a policy of "decolonization" within British institutions, just as Horton had recommended. But if Horton's spirit got to hear of this, circling as an adopted ancestor above the roofs of the University of Edinburgh, whose first African graduate he had become a hundred years earlier, he could scarcely have approved. In terms of political and structural development, these had been, for the most part, wasted years.

Wasted years because, in every crucial field of life, the British had frozen the indigenous institutions while at the same time robbed colonized peoples of every scope and freedom for self-development. Horton had foreseen, and rightly, that renewed independence within the African institutions of the 1860s would not be able to meet the challenge of an outside world, a Western world of which Africans knew little or nothing, and that there must be a developmental period of adjustment. His recommendations had been intended to provide for that.

No such period followed colonial invasion. What did follow was an ever-widening conflict of sympathy and purpose between the old nationalists, standing for the resurrection of precolonial powers and prerogatives, and new nationalists for whom the old powers and prerogatives had no more value, but were mere obstructions to modernizing progress. Left to their old privileges and restored to power, the chiefs and kings could only be a drag on liberated Africa. So the new nationalists argued; and what they argued seemed manifestly true. It remained that in jettisoning the heritage of chiefs and kings, the new nationalists were obliged to accept another heritage, that of the nation-statism which came from Europe. They were obliged to accept the alienation they had set themselves to oppose and reject.

When the Gold Coast Colony and Protectorate eventually became independent Ghana in 1957, the celebrations were both vivid and popular. But the king of Asante was not present at them. He refused to attend the great festivities of Independence Day. For him, as for others of his kind, this independence could only be a perverse denial of the old independence, and the new nationalists no more than usurpers of the legacy of Africa's own development. The royal absence was little remarked at the time. But it was to cast ahead a shadow that would be long and dark.

Shadows of Neglected Ancestors

As it was to turn out, the nationalists of most of the colonies were to hustle themselves or be hustled during and after the 1950s into British or French political institutions, and had little time or opportunity to consider what the further implications might then be. Liberation from colonial rule, all too clearly and as it seemed urgently, had to go hand in hand with liberation from whatever was or seemed to be "traditional": from all those "savage backwoods" that the pioneering nationalists, recaptive in origin or not, had condemned as useless or deplorable. For how, after all, were independence campaigns to be conducted, still more independent constitutions to be framed, by men trained neither in literacy nor in law? The answer seemed obvious, so obvious that it was scarcely raised. The whole question of structural and cultural alienation, so pressing an issue even by the 1970s, had to go after 1945 practically by default. What European and American experts and legislators held to be patently true—that precolonial Africa had acquired no experience relevant and valid to any process of self-government—was simply accepted.

One of the consequences of this acceptance became a general debasement of the argument about institutions to the level of what was said to be "democracy versus tribalism" or some comparable dichotomy, rather as though Africa's problem in becoming independent from colonial rule was not to modernize its own institutions—see again Japan—but to suppose there had been none, or none of any relevance. The problem, on this generally accepted view, was for Africans to overcome an atavistic tendency to live in "tribes" and to begin living in "nations." Much was written on the supposed miseries of this incorrigible "tribalism," and most of what was written, as may now be seen, completely missed the point. Not until years later, when a lot of damage had been done, was it understood that precolonial tribalism was no more peculiar to Africa than nineteenth century nationalism was to Europe. The one, like the other, might be useful and progressive; or, according to circumstance, it might be neither.

Then it was seen, among much else, that a host of foreign constitution makers and commentators had been wrong. The history of precolonial tribalism (by no means necessarily the same thing as later forms of tribalism) was in every objective sense a history of nationalism: of sociopolitical categories, that is, corresponding to the origins and development of unifying community formation in one terminology or another. This was a history indigenous to the continent and specific to itself, and Asante was only one case in point, even if a singularly clear one.

75

However "exotic" Asante might appear in its African guise, it was manifestly a national state on its way toward becoming a nation-state with every attribute ascribed to a West European nation-state, even if some of these attributes had still to reach maturity. It possessed known boundaries, a central government with police and army, consequent law and order, an accepted national language; and beyond these it even possessed, by the 1880s, an emergent middle class capable of envisaging the role of capitalist entrepreneur. Thereupon its whole dynamic and potentials were suddenly dispossessed by colonial takeover, and all indigenous development stopped. In the measure that development began again—as with the development of indigenous cocoa farming—this had to occur within the constricting limits of foreign dispossession. Not until independence were there any serious efforts, for example, to provide development capital to this capital-demanding cocoa industry.

What might have happened if indigenous development could have continued, and precolonial structures had remained free to mature into modern structures, can indeed be anyone's guess. Suppose that the sovereignty of Asante had not been hijacked, and the *asikafo* had continued to grow in wealth and numbers to the point of being able to install a liberal-capitalist structure of self-government. Could then the resultant Asante nation-state have answered to the needs of the twentieth century? Would it have acted as a magnet of progress for its neighbors? Or would it have become a curse and a burden?

We shall get further in another direction of thought. Now in the 1990s, with disaster having followed on colonial dispossession, it must be useful to look at what was seldom or never discussed before: at the possibly permanent and surviving value of the experience that came *before* dispossession. Not as colorful folklore, nor as banal assertion of Africa's possessing a history of its own, but as a value that may be relevant to the concerns and crises of today.

A first point in any such discussion has to insist that Asante was not an exception but an example of a general process, an immensely long and complex process, of political self-development across much of the continent.

Africa's history can be said to have begun, as a record or description of that process, with the onset and spread of farming after the seventh millennium before the Christian era: after, say, about 6000 B.C. It then entered a new phase, ancestral to modern times, with the introduction of iron-bladed tools, above all iron-bladed hoes, around 500 B.C. This second major spur to social and productive development, again a long and complex process, was that of metal technology—the mining, smelting, and forging of iron ore, and of some other minerals—and it began first in the grasslands of the Central and Western Sudan as well as in those of the upper Nile Valley. This ushered in a period, many centuries long, of sociopolitical growth and corresponding structural development.

Historians have generally called this long period the African Iron Age. It saw the spread of metal technology right across the continent: by the fourth century of the Christian era, as far as the lands of what are now the southeastern provinces of South Africa. This Iron Age established polities and economies capable of a steady expansion of population and the command of environment. It fathered most of those diversities of African culture that we think of as "traditional." It functioned as the great

77

"central period" of African development. And it came to an end in the nineteenth century of our era by reason partly of its own success, producing demands that Iron Age structures could no longer satisfy, but much more by reason of European dispossession.

It is therefore right to think of the African Iron Age, although the term itself is reductive since much was involved besides the technology of metals, as the period in which Africa's peoples completed the mastery of their continent at a preindustrial level of production. Every habitable region was made to yield a slowly increasing supply of food for a slowly increasing population; and to that end were applied a range of productive techniques from elementary soil analysis through irrigation to forms of fertilization and food storage. Intraregional marketing developed as settlements grew in size and number. Conflicts remained small in scale. Sacred or profane, the acts of life evolved.

What actual sizes of population carried through this "taming of a continent," as I have elsewhere ventured to call it, is impossible to say. In 1977 an impressive seminar of demographers at the University of Edinburgh looked at this particular question, and found that "no overall estimates for the population of Africa at given periods in the past could be more than vaguely approximate." But even the vaguely approximate can be useful in default of anything at all precise, and the experts present also found that they could probably agree with several broad propositions.[1]

One of these was that "from the period of the Early Iron Age the agricultural populations of Africa seem to have grown gradually from very small numbers, though perhaps in fluctuating cycles rather than steadily, up to the onset of the colonial period'' in about 1880.[2] Other guesses have suggested that the total population outside the lower valley of the Nile, some two thousand years ago, was on the order of three or four million. Around 1850, still intelligently guessing, one might put the total population as being between 100 and 150 million, with probability around the lower end of the range.

This increase is interesting in that it seems generally to have been in line with the expansion of productive capacity. Famines there must have been, but as exceptions and not as indicating a surplus of population such as normally could not be fed, and even fed well. On the contrary, the dual increase of people and food seems to have been fully self-sustainable, save in times of cyclical climatic drought, and was perhaps an optimum for preindustrial societies.

All this had equally to allow for the frictions and servitudes that came with the demand for exploitable labor when the Iron Age, no doubt early in its life, duly slammed shut the gates of Eden. The myths and legends that have come down to us from that remote past certainly speak of competitive warfare in this grand adventure of settlement in lands unknown amid the solitude of far horizons. But they speak as much or more of dramas of the spirit that were afterward rehearsed in ritual dance and song, celebrating human survival against every mystery of death; and these are dramas of the psyche, calling up the freedoms and coercions of archetypal consciousness, whether of blessing or of curse, that belong to the realm of the ancestors. Behind those dramas may be glimpsed the challenges of this long development as few persons became many persons, as methods of work diversified, as new problems of community sponsored new kinds of authority, and as all these asked for the creation of new modes of psychological reassurance. The language of legend spoke in the idiom of saints and heroes, while mediators became priests and lineage leaders became kings.

These were societies, in other words, self-governed by a rule of law. This was a fact exceedingly hard for the outside world or at any rate for Europeans and North Americans, becoming aware of Africa in the last decades of the nineteenth century, to recognize and accept. To most overseas travelers and chance observers, Africa seemed to live in a malevolent condition of chaos; and for this almost universal conclusion among Europeans and North Americans, we can now ascribe several reasons. One was that the impression was partly true. After about 1850 travelers and observers in East Africa began to enter lands ravaged by a relatively new slave trade; and they found, from the Swahili coast westward to the great lakes, or from the Southern Sudan southward through Mozambique, appalling evidence of death and devastation because of this slave trade. Travelers elsewhere in Africa, especially West Africa, found no such situation, save here and there as the older West Coast slave trade gradually vanished; but they saw societies which had been ravaged in earlier years by the same slaving curse and were now trying, with difficulty, to regain stability.

A more important reason for misunderstanding, at least in years long after the slave trades were banished, lay in the appearance of this rule of law. It had to take what the modern world, the industrialized world which is also a largely secularized world, has seen as a purely religious guise. Each of these evolving societies, from lineage group to clan to cluster of clans, had to shape its behavior to fit its environment, its possible resources in food and shelter, its scope for political development. Otherwise it would perish; and no doubt many such evolving societies, failing to adjust successfully, did perish. But the successful ones, those whose ancestors we hear of now, had to follow rules that were explanatory as well as mandatory.

The rules had to be explanatory so that people, knowing the reasons for them, would understand why survival depended upon following them. They had to explain from hard experience what was possible, as well as desirable, for a given community in its place and circumstance. Therefore, they had to be the fruit of painstaking observation and analysis of soils and seasons and all the manifest diversities of nature, including human nature. In short, they had to be severely reasonable within their own cultures, the very reverse of the blind dictates of superstition that nineteenth-century Europeans supposed to reign supreme on the "dark continent."

But explanation, given the frailties of human nature, could not be enough. The rules had to be mandatory as well. They had to possess the coercive force of a "system" of rewards and punishments. Obey the rules for social survival, and you will prosper. Break them, and suffering will befall. But why, and through what means? The substantial answer, as in all preindustrial societies, had to come from spiritual agencies: from the reservoirs of belief that feed and preserve social consciousness and cohesion. This rule of law, one may say, had to be the complex product of a process of trial and error in search of survival and expansion. Duly codified and modified and taught from one generation to the next, it had to rely for its effective-

81

ness upon the psychological supports of Good and Evil, of reward and punishment, whereby survival and expansion could alone be possible.

More than twenty years ago, I concluded a long inquiry into the nature of Africa's religions by writing: "Religion appears in all its varied African garb as the projection and affirmation of certain norms which govern the evolution of society. It is the selective codification, for its impact on everyday life, of a 'two-way' network of moral pressure: of the workings of the principle of Good in its positive sense, on behalf of whatever supports or guards a specific social system; and of the workings of the same principle in a negative sense—the sense of Evil which promotes or provokes, chiefly as one form or other of punishment or deterrent, whatever may go against that system."[3] I find no need to amend that conclusion in the light of much of value on this subject written by others later.

Now this rule of law, these codes of acceptable behavior, whether social or personal, had also to allow for the problem of change and initiative. This could be no simple problem, nor, so far as we know, was it ever comfortably solved; and we can easily see why. Once a community had achieved stability within its environment, each of these evolving African societies had to stick closely to its rules for survival. It had to be severely conservative. Yet at the same time it had to allow for its own success: for the changes, that is, which must follow the growth of a community from few to many, from small to large, from old needs to new needs, such as its stability could no longer absorb. In this long process of settlement and migration across these endless lands south of the Equator, the rules had to provide, among much else, for arrivals and departures. So there had to be rules—accepted customs duly empowered by accepted rituals—so that newcomers could be made welcome and absorbed or, in the same process, younger sons and families permitted to leave and seek new land elsewhere and form new units duly sanctioned by appropriate rules. This dichotomy of conservatism and change was in these societies the great provider of emotive tension, just as, under different labels and appearances, it may be in every living society.

What the "white man's world" has so often seen as the mystifications of mumbo jumbo and the gibberings of witchcraft, the "black man's world," knowing its own reality, has recognized as, typically, the codified guarantee of survival and expansion in an immense process of continental growth and settlement. One can, of course, transcribe this guarantee in a variety of ways. Allowing for myriad diversities of appearance in creed and custom, it is for instance possible, as I have suggested earlier in this book, to conceive of this rule of law in terms of a number of guiding principles of social behavior.

One of these concerned a principle of conservation. A successful balance with nature had to be a stable balance: rocked severely by internal rivalries, these little "ships of state" would be all too liable to sink with no hope of being saved. Excessive greed could be one means of sinking the boat, for slender resources must be sensibly shared, as for example in Max Gluckman's story of wild bees' nests in Bembaland. Finding one nest is good fortune because honey is a blessing, finding two is better still, but persisting in your search for bees' nests that are never plentiful and finding three—that is the work of witchcraft: it is the influence of greed, for which the powers of Evil will find a way to punish you. You will then miss your aim in hunting a leopard and narrowly escape a wound as the leopard strikes back. But the miss by your thrown spear will not be accidental: it will be the punishment called up by your greed. Restitution is compensation and therefore conservation, whichever way you have to take it. Homicide is a crime, but the killing of one person may not be best answered by the killing of the killer: it may be better answered by providing the deprived family with a person to take the place of the lost person. Broadly, this principle of "leveling compensation" was a norm of African judicial practice, even while it must have been often breached in everyday life; and this norm was applied to all situations of imbalance caused by infringements of the given community's rule of law.

The old English maxim that "power corrupts" accordingly had its place in these societies. Ruling powers tend by their nature to become oppressive powers: powers which therefore threaten the balance of social stability. Chiefs and kings were consequently bound to offend the rules and lead to trouble, sooner or later, because greed and egotism would attend their power and even the best would fall by the wayside. A regulatory principle must accordingly express a permanent distrust of power. This regulatory principle is well attested in evidence from many African peoples in precolonial times. But in reading of these matters one should bear well in mind, as Gwyn Prins and others have insisted, that descriptive accounts of state structures have been "types of traditions invented for particular purposes at particular times."[4] The essence of history being process, what we have learned about structures can never be a final outcome, rounded and complete, but always only an imprint of changing circumstance and pressure.

So it has come about, or it used to come about, that accounts brought back by external researchers (or, often, internal informants) tended to assert that the state structures they had looked at possessed some immutable quality of permanence. Because People X do this now, we may infer that they did it then: yet circumstances may have meanwhile changed and, with circumstances, so may the rules governing behavior. A cheerful skepticism is needed. But with this warning it may be said that what we now know about African societies in the precolonial past does seem to be sufficient, and sufficiently tested, to allow the generalizations I have been making here.

This inbuilt distrust of executive power is part of that evidence. Again, in Zambia (Northern Rhodesia as he knew it, and as it was before 1964) Max Gluckman found that the Barotse, who lived and still live near the headwaters of the Zambezi River, and have long had a kingship and corresponding chiefly powers, "are apparently terrified of giving away power [meaning executive power of any kind, and] always think of the dual pressures of the ambivalence of power on an individual to whom power comes or in whom power is vested."[5] The concept repeatedly recurs in other societies, and may be said, with due precaution not to write it into rigid doctrine, to have formed a constant element in their chartered systems of social coherence, or, in familiar jargon, in the ideologies (or religions) of these systems. Power from inheritance should be balanced by power from appointment. Power from spiritual authority should be shared: among constituent interest groups, and through the operation of chartered checks and balances.

The outcome, perhaps needless to say, could never be a final and congealed harmony but was always a process of invention and adjustment according to the pressures and accidents of life. Yet it was a process that embodied the essence of principles such as those I have touched upon here: a rule of law derived from experience and experiment in a given ecological and social situation, but turned into myth and thereby given mandatory force by attribution to ancestral and therefore spiritual powers whose authority derived in turn from God. This distrust of the executive capacity as being all too able to upset the acquired balance with nature, or with society, marched together with an insistence on the distribution of executive power. In other words, a well-built polity had to be a participatory polity. No participation had to mean no stability. In "traditional" Africa this concept of an indispensable participation formed the hearthstone of statesmanship. Standing on that, power would prosper; but not otherwise.

This has been obvious in all "segmentary societies" where delegation of powers to chiefly persons was limited or minimal or nonexistent. The community met as equals and decided things accordingly. This was how the numerous Igbo communities of eastern Nigeria are said to have behaved whenever they had refused, as most did, to agree to chiefs and kings. Across the river Niger, among the Yoruba, it was different. There they created chiefs and kings in a big way. Their hierarchical and aristocratic society—or societies, for the Yoruba have had many different communities—has often been described; here I am using Naomi Chazan's recent observations. The Yoruba "myth of origin" has been "essentially, a charter for the rulers, the descendants of Oduduwa," God's agent in forming the Yoruba, indeed all humankind; and this myth "provides legitimacy for the distribution of power on a regional basis" as between one

Yoruba community and other Yoruba communities. Similarly, the myth of origin "regulates the types of relationship between ruler and ruled."[6]

This might suggest a rigid structure with no allowance for the process of change or for checks on executive power. It seems to me that the Yoruba structure really has been rigid; but it is certainly very old and its evolution over many centuries has clearly allowed both for the process of change and for checks on the executive. One such check on the executive power of Yoruba kings lay in controls invested in dependent councils of chiefs, but also in other and nondependent councils. Thus, the *alafin*, or king, of the powerful Yoruba state of Oyo made state policy and took state decisions, but in company with his senior office-holders, the *oyo mesi*, who were drawn from the acknowledged leaders of constituent lineages: "big men" from "big families."

Yet the *oyo mesi*, all too likely as Yoruba aristocrats to throw their weight about, were flanked by an association called the Ogboni that was aimed at tying together "all individuals in the polity regardless of their social, economic, or political standing."[7] This was what allowed for historical process, so that newly emerged interests or groupings, "not specifically accounted for in the myths, did develop," in Chazan's words, "side by side with existing structures." The "ideal model" of Yoruba community, articulated by hierarchies of power and obligation provided by sanction of the myths of origin, was thus made viable over time (over a great deal of time) by "articulators of solidarity"—we can think of them as claimants to equality of rights—provided by associations like the Ogboni.

The point here is a general one. These precolonial societies, or those that endured for centuries and were successful in mastering their historical process, and about which we consequently know a good deal, were centrally concerned in securing and sustaining their legitimacy in the eyes of their peoples. They endured because they were accepted. And they were accepted because their rules of operation were found to be sufficiently reasonable in providing explanation, and sufficiently persuasive in extracting obedience. What this says, in tremendous contrast with times during and after colonialism, is that these communities achieved an accountability of rulers to ruled and, quite persistently, the other way around as well. Dissidence and protest might be frequent. The structures of accountability could well enough absorb them.

Sometimes we can follow all this in fascinating detail, as with Asante during its great epoch of the eighteenth and nineteenth centuries. In other cases we can only note the results. Such was the case with Ufipa, a little-considered and yet notable example.[8]

Ufipa today is a place rather than a state. The place is an upland area of Tanzania, southeast of Lake Tanganyika; and its inhabitants, the Fipa, are or rather were members of a cluster of loosely related communities organized in states or, as some may prefer it, "protostates." Its extent measures some 25,000 square miles, about that of the republic of Ireland or half of the state of Arkansas: not a very big country, but not a very small one either. It may have had about 100,000 inhabitants when its first European visitor, the explorer-missionary David Livingstone, managed to walk there in the middle years of the nineteenth century.

Utterly unknown to the European world (in the event, imperial Germany) that was about to invade and dispossess it, Ufipa had been important to the wider life of East Central Africa. Like some of their neighbors, the Fipa were inventive and productive. One of their admired skills was the smelting and forging of iron, mostly for hoe blades. They produced these in forced-draught kilns built of hard-packed earth. About ten feet in height, each being normally packed with about seventy square feet of ore and fifty of charcoal with some wood for firing it, such kilns, according to Roy Willis, could reach, with the aid of bellows, a temperature of between 1,200°C. and 1,400°C. The iron thus smelted was then resmelted in a smaller furnace, for purposes of hardening into what was a form of steel; and forging followed. Though slow and laborious, the method was as good as any known before industrial times, and had been widely used throughout Europe and Asia, if with many variations of practice. Roy Willis estimates that some eleven thousand hoe blades were being produced annually after about 1800, half for Fipa farming use and half for trade, Fipa hoe blades being then used as a currency in the regional marketing system.

The origins of a Fipa state, a clan-structured community on its way toward functional unity of material interests and moral loyalties, is dated by Willis to soon after 1500. For various reasons that need no discussion here, this was generally a time when early forms of state in East Africa, usually in terms of a kingship, began to crystallize from segmentary lineages. What actually happened was dependent upon ecology, opportunity, and the accidents of human nature. But it seems clear that the Fipa, for their part, entered after 1500 on a long period of transition to what Willis has defined as an "exchange-based state": a unified power structure, that is, adjusted to the values and concerns of Fipa commodity production.

This developmental process is said to have lasted "anywhere from about 150 to 350 years," a period in which developmental details begin to elude us. The severe upheavals of the nineteenth century through East Africa—an onset of severe drought, spread of the tsetse fly and consequent sleeping sickness in people or comparable disease in cattle, and finally colonial en-croachment and then invasion—eventually consigned the Fipa and their neighbors, some of them sorely smitten by these various plagues, to German and eventually to British rule in what was to be the colony of Tanganyika (Tanzania after 1964). After that the history of Ufipa frays into silence.

Barring the absent detail, however, it remains clear that Ufipa became a viable state at least by 1700. Its development, even in the bare outline that we have, shows it as the outcome of a process in which tolerance of change was an essential feature. But what it did not acquire was a tolerance of dispossession. In this it was like other precolonial states. Degraded under colonial rule to the status of migrant workers, often as semislave laborers for colonial settlers near and far, the productive force of Ufipa dwindled and died. Ufipa's self-identity as a state, as the arena of a living community, withered and vanished. Not until 1953, with the late colonial rise of what were called "tribal unions" or "tribal associations," which then became the parent of na-tionalist associations, would Fipa people think it useful or mean-ingful to reassert their existence as a community distinct in themselves.

But if Ufipa was clearly a state, both stable and dynamic, did the Fipa constitute a nation? If not, were they on their way to becoming one before the disasters of a dispossession which their state could neither absorb nor survive? Where, in any case, runs the dividing line between nation and nation-state? Applying labels to historical communities along the track of nationalism soon gets you into trouble. We shall look at what nineteenth-century Europeans were making of the problem of labels, mostly a puzzle and confusion. But what, at least, was or is "national consciousness"? If the answer should be that national conscious-ness embodies a shared loyalty to a distinctive culture, language, set of beliefs and so forth, the evidence still gives no certain guide.

"England," according to J. R. Strayer, writing in 1963, "was clearly a nation-state in the fifteenth century, when France was not." And why not? Because "this was a time when a French prince (the Duke of Burgundy) could still hope to split off prov-inces from France and combine them with his holdings in the Low Countries to make a new kingdom."[9] This scarcely helps us. If France was not yet a nation-state because it was about to be reduced in size, losing French-speaking Burgundians but retaining Bretons and Basques and Occitans, what was the magic wand that had to be waved to convert France the nation into France the nation-state? The developmental answer, as we shall find, came with the rise of social strata capable of making the great revolution of functional unification which began in 1789. But those same social strata had yet to exist in the England of the fifteenth century, nonetheless held by Strayer to have already become a nation-state. Such labeling may raise good questions. It seldom provides good answers.

Of course, writers on nationalism during the nineteenth cen-tury never looked at the African evidence, remaining unaware of it or even of the possibility of its actually existing. Like Hegel, they thought that the African evidence belonged only to a time before history, and was altogether beneath their notice. It was in fact nothing of the kind. Consider only the case of labeling in relation to medieval empires.

After the collapse of the western Roman Empire toward`A.D. 500, much of it became enclosed within new "empires"; and I place the word between quotation marks simply to emphasize the difficulty of knowing just what these sprawling political formations really were. They were labeled at the time or soon after as *regna*, the plural of *regnum*, or kingdom. Now a kingdom ought surely to be in some proper sense a state: but no, according to Strayer, "the barbarian *regnum* was certainly not a state," not a state in any sense at all, although, Strayer hastens to add, "it is rather difficult to say just what it was." For while "the ruler often took an ethnic title (*rex Anglorum, rex Francorum*, and so on), most of the *regna* were not ethnic units. The usual pattern was a dominant warrior group." Having no ethnic boundaries, since these *regna* enclosed several or many ethnicities, "a *regnum* had to be defined in terms of its king or, better, its royal family."

If this is right, and surely it is, how extraordinary, then, that writers about Africa exactly contemporary with Strayer should tell us that Africans have known no effective and meaningful participation in their own politics. How odd that the Regius Professor of History at Oxford University, in that same year of 1963, should have told us that Africa's history was only a tale of barbarous tribal gyrations.[10] For the African evidence, if actually examined, provides an exact parallel with the European *regna*, and in almost exactly the same historical time.

Getting to grips with labeling, Ibn Khaldun, the great North

African historian of the late fourteenth century, came to the conclusion that "people cannot persist in a condition of anarchy, and need a person to restrain them. He is their ruler. Royal authority is an institution natural to mankind."[11] Hence the undoubtedly functional states of the Maghrib did not evolve into nations but remained *regna* remembered to this day by the names of their ruling dynasties: Almoravids, Almohads, Hafsids, and so on down a long line, including rulers of empires such as the Fatimids of Tunisia who seized all of Egypt at the end of the tenth century.

Applied to the big political formations south of the Sahara in medieval times, this fits exceedingly well. Ancient Ghana, Mali, Songhay, Kanem: each of these geographically huge but functionally strong state formations were precisely *regna* in the European medieval sense. Each was the product of an ambitious "core people"—Soninke in Ghana, Malinke in Mali, Songhay in Songhay, Kanuri in Kanem—and each was able, just like the Normans in the empire of the Franks or the Germans in the Holy Roman Empire, to enclose a vast area within its rule and to extract from it both tax and tribute. Each was open to developmental influence from outside its *regnum*, notably the influence of Islamic law and literacy, but none of them appears to have produced any idea of forming a national identity, much less a national consciousness.

It is important to emphasize that the object of the core peoples of these *regna*, whether in Europe or in Africa, was in no sense to advance the cultural unities out of which nations grow, but to enrich themselves from tribute and taxation. Of course, their rulers might argue, or might have argued if one could imagine the point being put to them, that in exchange for their unifying

93

warfare and profiteering they opened wide regions to the expansion and improvement of trade and production for trade. They did do this; and this undoubtedly could be a general gain.

Courts and cavalry in either case, royal hospitality and waste, princely power and its assertion, the support of scholarship and the advance of literacy and learning: all this and much else gave glory to these imperial rulers, in Africa as in Europe. But it all had to be paid for, and the laboring masses were those who paid, whether as serfs or slaves, feudal villeins or subject clans; and whenever one great dynasty declined and a successor took its place, the price had again to be paid in renewed subjection. "God having overthrown the emperor of Mali to the benefit of the emperor of Songhay," in the words of Mahmoud Kati, the seventeenth-century historian of Timbuktu, in his *Tarikh al-Fettash*, "the latter ravaged the empire of Mali, carried off its children into captivity, and seized all the goods of the vassal peoples." Compare European wars of much the same period.

A modern historian has put all this in familiar language. The "phase of domination" by medieval states in the Western and Central Sudan through all of seven centuries, Claude Meillassoux explains, "corresponded to that of the constitution and domination of a military class, which grew out of plundering warfare";[12] and it is this concept of "class," we shall increasingly find, that offers a key to the puzzle of this apparently so arbitrary "labeling."

But did these medieval *regna*, meanwhile, exercise a civilizing function on behalf of their subject peoples as well as their ruling peoples? The answer is yes. In Africa as in Europe (and one could of course extend the parallels to Asia), the core peoples

94

of the *regna* fostered trade and production for commerce, and therefore in due course technological and innovative change, and thus new arts and sciences: "the simultaneous propagation of military conquest, state administration, commerce and Islam, favoured the civilisation of the subjected peoples, and thus their incorporation as subjects of the political formations."[13]

But what the core peoples of the *regna* did not favor was nationalism. They could not have the slightest interest in promoting or provoking ethnic self-assertion, including their own. They simply stretched their rule over many ethnic groups, extracted tax and tribute, and left it at that. George Bernard Shaw in his play *Saint Joan*, first seen in New York in 1923, explained this *regnum* business in a brilliant mockery of the earl of Warwick's chauvinistic chaplain at the time of the Anglo-French wars of the fifteenth century. Besieging Orléans, held by the French, the English nobleman explains to his chaplain that Dunois, the French king's commander in Orléans, is a hard nut to crack:

Chaplain: He is only a Frenchman, my lord.
Nobleman: A Frenchman! Where did you pick up that expression? Are these Burgundians and Bretons and Picards and Gascons beginning to call themselves Frenchmen, just as our fellows are beginning to call themselves Englishmen? They actually talk of France and England as their countries. Theirs, if you please! What is to become of me and you if that way of thinking comes into fashion?

Chaplain: Why, my lord? Can it hurt us?
Nobleman: Men cannot serve two masters. If this cant of
serving their country once takes hold of them,
goodbye to the authority of their feudal lords,
and goodbye to the authority of the Church.

The *regna* therefore had little concern with "ethnic minorities." Once these many subject peoples toed the line of imperial policy and interest, the *regna* likewise had no interest in suppressing them or pretending that they did not exist. On the contrary, they seem to have given free rein to ethnic diversities, provided that the overall power of the *regnum* was not placed at risk. Several centuries have been required to conceive, although not yet to achieve, a comparable tolerance in large political formations, today in a very different set of circumstances and, as we begin to see, in necessarily federalistic terms. Nothing in this context remains more depressing, however, than the incapacity of European states at the end of the twentieth century to accommodate the reasonable expectations of ethnic diversity: as shown, to offer only one recent and demeaning example, by the Romanian inability to accommodate its ancient Hungarian minority in a supposedly democratic Romanian nation-state.

When the African *regna* in due course fell apart and disappeared from history, pretty well by the beginning of the seventeenth century, their subject peoples—just as in Europe—by no means followed them into the void. What became of them? They survived as well as they could, and often better than before. The examples are legion. The Dogon of the Bandiagara hills, south of the great middle bend of the Niger River (in what is Mali today), were "discovered" by ethnologists during the colonial period, but had clearly conserved their intricate and philosophically rich culture of belief and intuition from ancient times. This was an orally transmitted culture, be it noted, but one in no way less effective in its sociopsychological matrix than the literate though Muslim cultures of their former overlords.

Or what happened to the once-famous core peoples of the *regna*? They, too, survived, though in a new obscurity. The lordly Soninke, who had once and for centuries ruled the *regnum* of ancient Ghana with a pomp and circumstance that won the admiration even of Córdoba, that most civilized of medieval cities, might seem to have "vanished from history." But the chroniclers of the colonial partition, only "yesterday," found the Soninke safely tucked away in the colony of Senegal, along the south bank of the river of that name; and this is where they live today. If the Soninke sometimes ponder the glories of their imperial past, there is little to show that it keeps them awake at night. If they have new aspirations to nation-statehood, they have not so far said anything on the subject, being in this respect differently motivated—or advantaged?—than the "forgotten nationalities" of once-imperial Europe.

Yet even a superficial acquaintance with the Soninke today tells one that they remain in their own thinking a distinctive people and culture, possessing a vigorous "national conscious-ness," whatever this may precisely mean, and a valid though little-written language. Their case is one among many, it seems to me, that underline the cultural misery of the whole nation-statist project. For postcolonial nation-statism in policy and rhetoric has preferred to talk down "ethnic survivals" like the Soninke—every reader may supply his or her own example from a host of candidates—as deplorably illegitimate and best

97

forgotten, because, not having formed nation-states and there-fore not being admitted to be nations, they have no right or reason to remain alive.

So it is that the ideology of nation-statism, here in Africa as in Europe, becomes appallingly reductive, rather as though a wealth of cultures were really an impoverishment. Much ink of mockery has been spilled in deploring the polyglotism of the Tower of Babel, even while the beauties of imperial monoglo-tism, of "world language," leave so much to be desired. Here again we have one of the impoverishments left in legacy by the nineteenth century.

Tribalism and the
New Nationalism

IF THE ethnic diversities of Africa outlived the long medieval period of the *regna*, many subsequent revolutions and reorganizations, and finally the manifold upheavals of the nineteenth century, these diversities then found it relatively easy to live through the colonial period—as ethnic diversities, that is, though sorely often not as persons or constituent communities. The new nationalists of the 1950s would then embrace nationstatism as the only available escape from colonial domination. Striving to transform colonial territories into national territories, they would find Africa's wealth of ethnic cultures both distracting and hard to absorb into their schemes. They would fall back into the colonial mentality of regarding it as "tribalism," and, as such, retrogressive. This diversity, it seemed, had to be just another hangover from an unregenerate past. It should at least be on its way to museum shelves, and should be meanwhile handled as a temporary nuisance. That was to prove difficult. The nuisance was found, as in the earliest days of nation-statist debate in centers such as Cape Coast during the 1860s, to be stubbornly insistent. It refused to disappear into museums.

This was scarcely surprising: most of these precolonial political formations were communities with a venerable past rooted in popular acceptance. In the public mind they were living realities; they were identities to which people strongly held. Dismissing them as the regrettable phenomena of "tribalism" might comfort those, British or others, who preferred to think of precolonial Africa as a kind of savage backwoods, rather as the notion of a Scottish nation or a Welsh nation had long become an antiquarian absurdity to average English opinion. But that is not how the "tribesmen" were prepared to see it.

Out of this came confusion. For there was also at work, from quite early in the colonial dispossessions, another meaning for "tribalism." This was the new product of "divide-and-rule" policies, perhaps the only African political invention of those times that did or even could succeed, and was well promoted by the British and the French, major colonial powers, as a useful administrative instrument. Let related ethnic "units" band together and become "tribes"—a term probably applied in the African context by officials educated in the classical tradition of Caesar's Gallic wars—because, if they banded together, the costs of European administration would be that much less.[1]

Segments or even substantial communities in more or less closely related communities, though historically separate and distinct from one another, now declared themselves a single people; and new tribes, such as the Sukuma and Nyakusa, rose fully formed from the mysterious workings of "tradition." Not being worried by such workings, whatever Europeans supposed them to be, such coagulated clans and segments do not seem to have minded becoming "tribes" with exotic names—Sukuma, for example, is a word borrowed from the neighboring people of Unyamwezi—but rather pleased about it. A single agreed spokesman against the claims and demands of colonial power was easily seen to wield more argumentative clout than a mob of spokesmen from smaller units. And then, of course, there were appropriate personal ambitions. According to John Iliffe, whose description of this process in Tanganyika is exemplary, "many Africans had strong personal motives for creating new units which they could lead. Europeans believed Africans belonged to tribes: Africans built tribes to belong to." And the effort to create such "tribes," Iliffe goes on to remind us, "was as honest and constructive" in those circumstances of apparently permanent foreign rule as the later effort, when that appearance of permanence was gone, to create a Tanganyikan nation. "Both were attempts to build societies in which men could live well in the modern world."[2]

This was one situation. And as Africans from rural areas moved, ever more in the 1940s, toward the "melting pot" of periurban slums and shantytowns, this "tribalism" that was a genuine product of African diversity but also an invented weapon of self-defense, became a potent factor in opening the route to nationalism. "Tribal unions" and "tribal associations," or other such manifestations of solidarity, began to flourish in the 1940s, and were to be powerful influences in the building of nation-statist politics. Their nature, of course, meant that they were destined to become divisive of national unities. They would then play the role, after independence, of opposing "tribe" to "nation." But that was still for the future. For the present these "tribal unions" were able to rephrase and reabsorb

Africa's own history in times of great political change and challenge.

Elsewhere, contrasting situations developed. In West Africa, for example, the cultural diversities of African life were no fewer than in East Africa; if anything, they were more numerous. They were many hundreds, very old, and sometimes encased in venerable historical institutions. The Asante example, which we have briefly inspected, was a relatively recent one. The kingship of the ancient state of Benin in Nigeria (not to be confused with the modern republic of Benin) was several centuries older; so was the kingship of the Mossi. Others could rival them in antiquity. But "recaptive" politics—the politics of Freetown and Monrovia, or of educated (but not recaptive) groups in Accra and Cape Coast and other such places—were in no state of mind to accept these diversities as useful or constructive.

Broadly, the educated elites in West Africa—for a long time, it would be much the same in South Africa—saw Africa's own history as irrelevant and useless. The issue has been contradictory because so was their stance. They saw that the assertion of Africa's having a history of its own must be part of their case against colonialist racism. They presented this assertion in books they wrote about Africa's past glories. They lectured on the subject, composed brilliant and poetic evocations of great moments in Africa's past. If they were clergymen, they recalled the Christian African bishops of Byzantine descent. If they were lawyers, they praised the writings of classical Greece in praise of Homer's "blameless Ethiopians." If they were politicians, they did their best to square the circle.

But when it came down to brass tacks, to the question of who should take over from the British when the British withdrew, they demanded a more or less complete flattening of the ethnic landscape. All that history then belonged to what Attoh Ahuma, back in 1911 in his book *The Gold Coast Nation and National Consciousness*, had found no difficulty in calling the "savage backwoods." Deplorable in the past, it could do nothing for the present; and the future would forget it. As the gathering force of nation-statism in its guise of liberating ideology began to reap the fruits of argument and agitation around mid-century, what David Kimble has called the clash between "the inherited privileges of chieftaincy" and the "acquired privileges of education"—meaning Western education, and its derivatives—became acute and would soon become violent.[3]

Stereotyped as a conflict of rivalry between the makers of Progress and the upholders of Tradition, this contradiction was to be vividly dramatized in the political campaigning that climaxed and followed the struggle for indigenous power, but perhaps most clearly of all in the Gold Coast (modern Ghana) after 1947. To the upholders of Tradition, well able to speak their minds because they also had sometimes grazed in London's Inns of Court, the new nationalists led by Kwame Nkrumah were dangerous and irresponsible purveyors of destruction, "verandah boys" greedy for the spoils of office but not deserving any spoils, and often enough little better than crooks or con men. Great chiefs such as Nana Ofori Atta, splendidly equipped himself, found it obviously right that he should despise these would-be usurpers of an executive power which ought in all equity and good sense to revert to himself and his peers. Even greater chiefs, the king of Asante for one, gathered their robes about them and made ready to resist. Yet to dismiss these men as "tribalists" would be a misuse of language.

They, too, were caught in a contradiction of their own making. In their own context they were for African advancement, and some of their spokesmen, notably J. B. Danquah, valiantly argued the case for that advancement. On the other hand, they were the favored recipients, almost to the last days of British rule, of official approval and support. All through Nkrumah's severely testing campaign for independence, after 1947, he had to face the malice and intrigue of opponents such as Kofi Busia, always running to the British and then the Americans to complain against the new nationalists, while governors almost to the last saw these new nationalists as disgusting "trouble-makers."

Meanwhile, the British for their part were likewise caught in a contradiction of these years. In West Africa, up to the end of the 1940s, they redoubled their efforts to launch their colonies down that same slipway of chiefly rule which their own colonialism had previously done its best to undermine. Titled honors were duly handed around to suitable chiefly recipients. Red carpets were appropriately laid for chiefly feet. Hard-pressed district officers were urged to invent new ways in which the authority of chiefs, now that Britain was to withdraw, could be reinforced by prudent measures of administrative devolution, notably in the matter of "native tax" and "native treasuries." A painstaking survey of these matters commissioned by the British government from an acknowledged British authority, Lord Hailey, and afterward completed in several volumes, dealt with the new nationalism simply by ignoring it.[4]

So the cleavage between Africa's own history and Africa's borrowed nation-statism was made complete in West Africa, and widened elsewhere. For none of these "traditionalist" caperings, and British arguments in praise of them, could seem anything but obstructive and reactionary to the new nationalists. As the self-appointed champions of Progress, a cause they were also ready to suffer for—and sometimes fatally—they saw every such maneuver as one way or other of conserving an African inferiority of status, as a resurrection of incompetence, or as good evidence that any conceded independence was intended to be scarcely worth the name.

To the new nationalists, and increasingly when genuine "tribunes of the people"—for one example, Sékou Touré in French Guinea, Abdoulaye Diallou in Soudan (Mali) for another—joined their ranks and led their emergent parties, the challenge was to confront and disarm a hostile hierarchy of "ancestral powers" hand in hand with colonial policemen and their bosses. And here one has to bear in mind, against a certain historical hindsight which has liked to suggest that the British and the French were amiably ready to pack up and go, that the new nationalists had to meet, almost to the last moment, an acute and even harsh hostility. There was not much in those last years of colonial rule that was amiable about the attitude and actions of colonial officialdom. Whatever might be said in London and Paris, the officials "on the spot" had few warm feelings about the new nationalism.

One needs to bear in mind, furthermore, the general sterility and helplessness of imperial attitudes concerning the issues raised by winding up colonial empires. The British in West Africa brought a handful of the "educated elite" into legislative councils, but avoided as far as they could any who spoke in the language of the new nationalism, preferring "reasonable men" who would not rock the colonial boat. This indulgence in "advisory democracy" had almost no influence on the upheavals that

105

were about to take place. The French, for their part, simply fought a rearguard action in defense of a chiefly power which they thought, quite mistakenly as it was to prove, could be relied upon as a convenient partner. As the new nationalists in French Guinea were to show, such "native partners" were easily swept away, often leaving no trace behind.

Eager to get rid of colonial rule along the only route now open to them—the route of nation-statism on the European model—the new nationalists were in any case left to conduct their struggle on their own. Some of the best of them, during the 1950s, saw the dangers of this "neocolonialist" nation-statism. They argued and pressed for interterritorial federalism. They tried to devise ways of rejecting the carapace of the colonial frontiers. They formed ambitious interterritorial movements— for example, the multiterritorial Rassemblement Démocratique Africain in the French West and Equatorial territories, the Pan-African Freedom Movement in the British East and Central territories—but they formed them in vain. Neither the imperial powers nor ambitions unleashed among the new nationalists themselves were ready for such visionary initiatives, while the imperial powers, just in case the vision might become real, positively worked for their destruction.

Being left on their own, the new nationalists had to make the best of things. This was at least difficult, besides being often dangerous. It could mean being shot at by police or army. It could mean long terms of imprisonment. It could mean torture or quiet murder behind doors, as in the Portuguese colonies. It had often to defy a skeptical, mocking, or contemptuous outside world taught by decades of imperialist ideology that Africans were really, if the truth be told, primitive beings incapable of knowing what was best for themselves, let alone for anyone else.

Being a new nationalist made huge demands. He had to be a "modernizer" in every sense of the word. These new nationalists had to be fluent in writing as well as speaking at least one European language. They had to be widely read in the culture and history of that language. They had to know how to move with self-confidence, real or assumed, among the traps and idioms of European—and soon American—politics and manners. They had to reduce vague aspirations into coherent paragraphs of constitutional programming couched in the concepts of European law and precedent. They had to do a lot of other things besides.

The idea that old-fashioned, barely literate, and in any case many-wived traditional worthies could do these things with any hope of success seemed so obviously impossible as to preclude serious denial. All the same, it was denied. "As we have noted," wrote Obafemi Awolowo, the highly articulate Yoruba pioneer of west Nigerian nationalism in 1947, when the battle for independence was just beginning, "only an insignificant minority [of Nigerians] have any political awareness." This in itself was an astonishing statement, given Yoruba political history over the previous several centuries, but it was entirely characteristic of the pioneers of Progress in the recaptive tradition. And Awolowo went on to underline his point. "It is this minority that always clamours for change. . . . Are we to take our cue from this clamant minority?" Certainly we are, proclaimed Awolowo, himself a member of that minority and later to make a great political career with the new nationalism: "The answer is an emphatic 'Yes.' It must be realised now and for all time that this articulate minority are destined to rule the country. It is their heritage."[5]

But Awolowo, like others of his kind, was to find that matters were not so simple. When push came to shove, as it did in the 1950s, the ignorant "masses" who were in Awolowo's superior eyes indifferent as to "how they are governed or who governs them," were found indispensable to nationalism's success. Having formed their parties of national liberation, the educated elite had to chase their voters. And so they did, penetrating places never before seen, crossing rivers never before encountered, confronting languages never before learned, and all this with the help of local enthusiasts somehow recruited. They thus made contact with these "masses" quite often with only the assistance of aged Land Rovers able, with their four-wheeled drive, to go where no other wheeled vehicles had ever been, but only just able, and not seldom abandoned by the way.

One's memories of those years are of jubilant young men (as yet, rarely young women, although these came along as soon as the men would let them) setting out on endless journeys delayed and harassed by endless troubles and upsets, lack of petrol, spare parts, cash, and even food. Mostly these journeys have been long forgotten, but a few records survive. Thus it was that young men of the National Council of Nigeria and the Cameroons (NCNC) set out upon a journey of this kind that lasted eight whole months. By whatever transport they could find, on foot or horseback, in truck or "mammy wagon," their arrival was often "accompanied by brass bands, flute bands, cowhorn bands and dancers" in places never visited before. Meeting the "masses" in "schoolrooms, compounds, cinemas and churches, they touched the lives of hundreds of isolated communities in a way never known before."[6] There was no successful party of the new nationalism in those days that did not do as much or much the same, from the far north to the southern bastions of white settler rule; and even within those bastions they somehow managed to do it too.

Wherever there were well-implanted traditional authorities buttressed by colonial officials, the new nationalists had to provoke and exploit the often concealed realities of social conflict. So it was that the pioneers of the new nationalism had to react in hierarchical Northern Nigeria, where the British stood behind (and usually very close behind) the emirate princes. "All parties," declared the Northern Elements Progressive Union (NEPU, or Jam'iyya Namnan Sawaba) in its radical manifesto of 1950, "are but the expression of class interests, and as the interest of the Talakawa ["commoners" in Hausa usage] is diametrically opposed to the interest of all sections of the master class"—the Hausa-Fulani emirs and their henchmen—"the party seeking the emancipation of the Talakawa must naturally be hostile to the party of the oppressors."

To officials and visiting "experts" all this could sound like very desperate talk; and in those years of sharpening Cold War propaganda, it was often traced to Soviet or Communist influence, as surviving police archives, whether in English or in French (and no doubt in Portuguese and Spanish, but those archives I have not inspected), sufficiently though quite foolishly attest. There were no Russians in Africa in those years, save for one or two elderly "white" refugees from the revolution of 1917, and the relevant European Communist parties had only the flimsiest of contacts with tropical Africa. This was well known but failed to assuage the grim suspicions of the Cold War. In 1952 I visited the house in Kano of the then still youthful but already widely admired founder of Northern Nigeria's "commoners' party," NEPU, who was Mallam (afterward Alhaji) Aminu Kano, officially reputed to be "very radical," and was able to make this visit only when accompanied by a British district officer. This D.O. was a nice man, however, and agreed to my request that he remain outside. It was seldom like that. Visitors contacting nationalists in the 1950s were all too likely to find themselves asked to leave the territory, and not return. The P.I.—prohibited immigrant—list soon grew to formidable dimensions.

Misunderstandings therefore multiplied. Few of the new nationalists thought in terms of revolutionary change, and even if they talked of socialism or comparable horrors, it was rarely after giving thought to what these terms might mean or ask of them. What they wanted, in most cases, was simply the inheritance of which Awolowo had lately written. But for this, of course, they needed the pressure of the "masses," while the "masses," beyond any doubt, looked to independence for large if also vague social changes in their favor. Later on, when American support became possible as well as desirable, all talk of socialism was an embarrassment to nationalists striving for their colonial inheritance. Some of them invented an amiable creature called "African socialism," which meant precisely nothing but sounded good. Others, if they were francophone, followed the classicist Léopold Sédar Senghor, of Senegal, into the pleasant groves of *négritude*, which sounded even better and meant even less.

Even so, the substantial point was gained. The elites needed the masses, and took steps to recruit them. With or without flutes, gongs, and aged Land Rovers, the effort was successful. In the name of social change and improvement, the "masses" surged into politics. By the late 1950s the whole colonial continent, even in the solitudes of the vast mainland colonies of Portugal or the forgotten zones of Spain, trembled or thudded with hopes of social change, everyday change, that ranged from sober calculation to dreams of messianic glory.

At this point, as would be rapidly seen in the aftermath, things began to change. As long as the principal colonial powers had not withdrawn, the ideas and aims of the "social conflict" held their primacy over those of the "national conflict"; and "tribalism," in that context, retained its positive value. In Nigeria, for example, the Igbo National Union, as a "tribal association," played a crucial role in the formation (1944) of a party of nation-statist independence, the National Council of Nigeria and the Cameroons launched by Herbert Macaulay and Nnamdi Azikiwe. So did other such associations elsewhere, most notably in Nigeria the Action Group (1950) whose "tribal" strength derived from the Yoruba "national union," Egbe Omo Oduduwa (1948).

Such new political parties drew authentic and sometimes overwhelming popular support from their ethnic roots: the Egbe Omo Oduduwa, for example, wrote its inspiring call for Yoruba resurgence in the terms and language of foundation myths and beliefs that everyone had learned to respect at their mothers' knees. Such beliefs were powerful instruments in raising mass expectations of a better life after colonial rule was over.

But once colonial rule *was* over, or would obviously soon be over, the leaders of the new nationalism became the potential or actual leaders of their newly independent colony. From being instruments of pressure against foreign rulers, the new parties at once became instruments of rivalry within the nation-statist political arena. The competing interests of the "elites," as they began to be called by sociologists and others, took primacy over the combined interests of the "masses." The "social conflict," one may say, was subordinated to the "national conflict"; and "tribal unions" such as the Igbo National Union and the Yoruba Egbe were in a different posture. They were now divisive of that national unity, initially empowered by a social unity behind social aspirations, which the whole independence project was supposed to be about.

Not, of course, everywhere or to the same extent. In the Tanganyikan (Tanzanian) case, for example, the multiplicity of fairly numerous ethnic groups, coupled with the strongly unifying influence of a single major nationalist movement, the Tanganyika African National Union (TANU), was able to keep the "social conflict" near the center of the picture. Where the elitist politicians of multiparty Nigeria went for the spoils of office or each others' throats, usually the same target, those of Tanganyika, or most of them, remained more or less acutely aware of their duty to promote postcolonial social change. They functioned within a power-monopolist TANU, raised to national authority in 1961, as companions rather than as rivals; and this progressive outcome of one-party rule, afterward sorely abused when postcolonial poverty had duly opened every door to post-colonial corruption, was undoubtedly a great factor for good at the start of independence.

* * *

Events moved fast in the 1950s. Once the major colonial powers had digested the difficult thought that actual territorial possession was no longer useful to them, one phase of "tribalism" and its like shifted almost imperceptibly into another. In the case of Britain, for example, the many Nigerian students living there by the end of the 1940s had transformed their own union, the West African Students' Union (WASU), into an agitational pressure group in which all its members acted in the name of Nigeria. By late in the 1950s, with nationalist parties on the scene and increasingly in rivalry with one another, WASU's members suddenly became Yoruba or Igbo or Hausa and so on, much to the discomfort of British sympathizers, their nationalist friends having taught them to regard such ethnic loyalties as belonging to colonialist artifact.

But however fast things moved, and no matter what unexpected paths they took, two principles were now in any case established. The first principle, universally accepted like the second, was that advancement toward the nation-state was the only feasible route of escape from the colonial condition. The recaptive descendants of Freetown and Monrovia, like their Western-educated friends at Cape Coast, Accra, and Lagos, had clearly been right about this. For the British, and then the French, would hear of nothing else. Those who argued for inter-territorial federalism or its equivalent, pointing out the obstacles to progress adhering in the colonial frontiers, were ignored or pushed aside. Any such large and constructive reorganization of frontiers could never suit the imperial powers, eager still to retain "neocolonialist" levers of interest and influence. Nor could they suit the nationalist leaders, now increasingly impa-

113

tient for the fruits of power, and rightly aware that interterritorial reorganization must delay and perhaps threaten their enjoyment of these fruits. So the colonial territories and states had to be accepted, as they were: taken over, and renamed with the titles and prerogatives of as many new nation-states as there had been colonies.

The second principle, servant of the first, was that the "national conflict," embodied in the rivalries for executive power between contending groups or individuals among the "elites," must continue to take priority over a "social conflict" concerned with the interests of most of the inhabitants of these new nation-states. Anything else would slow up access to full political independence, sow frightful suspicions of "radicalism" in London and Paris, and therefore threaten the financial and other forms of aid upon which the "elites," once in executive power, found that they were advised to depend.

So these men and women, no few of whom had paid dearly for the success of their anticolonial agitations, pressed eagerly along this chosen path to power, feeling themselves beckoned by destiny and all the gods as well as urged on by families and dependents. And the frontiers of the colonial partition, however inappropriate to an independent Africa, became the sacred frontiers which it must be treason to question or deny.

It was difficult in that haste and hurly-burly of risk and ferment to see how little was being thought of and foreseen; and perhaps it was impossible. The prestige and power of the imperialist project and achievement had been so great, so immensely hard to confront and overcome, often so hopeless to contemplate; and the cards in the hands of the nationalists, save for stubbornness and courage, were few and feeble. After the

Second World War the weakness of the imperial powers had allowed the opening of gates to colonial freedom, but those powers were still very much present and well able to defend their interests. In later times it might seem to have been easy to challenge those powers, almost a going along with what was going to happen anyway. At the time it could be a hazardous enterprise, to be embarked on only by the rash or the blindly romantic, and all too possibly ending in ruin.

That so little was foreseen is easy to understand. Any questioning of nationalism, of the credentials of nation-statism as the only feasible route of escape, had to seem very close to betrayal of the anticolonial cause. To warn of nation-statism's likely disaster in the future of Africa, just as it had lately been in the past of much of Europe, was what no one, but no one anywhere, appears to have thought sensible until years later. Besides this, the record of nation-statism in recent Europe—above all in Central and Eastern Europe—was little known or not known at all: Africans who studied in Europe before 1939 seldom went to Central or Eastern Europe. If they had done so, the parallels in nation-statist experience could still not have struck them as interesting, for it was not until the 1970s that the nation-statist route of escape began to seem, just possibly, a dead end.

Lately, no doubt, nationalism has increasingly gotten itself a bad name, and the nation-statist project—the attempt to turn colonially formed territories into nation-statist territories—looks increasingly like a mistake, like a "shackle" on good sense and policy in Edem Kodjo's memorable phrase. That is easily acceptable in and for Europe in the wake of Fascism, Nazism, and Stalinism, under whose ideological impetus more crimes and horrors have been committed in the name of one or another kind of nationalist glory than will ever be counted or even remembered. But for the nationalists of Africa the matter had to look quite otherwise.

Men of their time, the pioneering nationalists were intensely conscious of the history they had lived through. They scrutinized the news with all the seriousness of those who have had to struggle hard for enlightenment and who, having found it, look only for that. They studied the portents and examined the entrails of Europe's nation-liberating struggles; and they found in them sure prophesies for colonial Africa and for the nations that Africa must build if it was to realize its destiny.

Their every experience had confirmed it. Whether or not they were the descendants of recaptives or of others like Edward Wilmot Blyden, the West Indian of Hausa parentage who became in the 1890s a beloved and famous spokesman for Africa's claims, they knew what happened to persons "without a nation."[7] With Blyden their experience of European racism easily confirmed for them that nationality has to be "an ordinance of nature; and no people can rise to an influential position among the nations without a distinct and efficient nationality." Colonized and despised Africa, as the Gold Coaster Attoh Ahuma would write in 1911, must "come into the open where nations are made": new nations, that is, which had yet to reach existence.

And this was a conviction that held firm through later years. It was a conviction formed in a nineteenth-century Africa whose intellectuals were acutely aware of the drive and promise of national liberation in contemporary Europe. Their self-assurance could scarcely have been otherwise. For they had lived through a time when nationalism glowed with the brilliance of a manifest destiny, and spoke with the tongues of angels. The legacy of this conviction, in a large sense the legacy of the 1860s, was to retain its force, a force that had come from Europe with the breadth and surge of a grandly liberating adventure.

It is time to look at that adventure, and the light it may cast on much later developments in Europe but, also, as we may find, in Africa.

The Rise of the Nation-State

As to the nature of nationalism and its embodiment in the nation-state, it has been customary among our historians to begin with the French Revolution of 1789 or with England's Glorious Revolution of a century earlier, because each in its way set the rising "middle classes" on their path to state power and economic primacy. From that standpoint, which has been generally accepted, those great events shaped the process by which nationalism was to become embodied in the nation-state, and whereby the structures of the resultant European nation-state, accepted as being entirely necessary to civilized progress, were to be awarded the priority of whatever was thought "right and natural."

Yet the actual process of embodiment of the pressures of nationalism in those nation-statist structures, and the passions that were thus engendered, are better seen and felt in later events, lesser perhaps but stirring and tremendous, that are also nearer to our own time. The nineteenth century in Europe, above all its middle years, were the nation-state's great gestation period; and the births that would follow were many. In 1919, after the Wilsonian nation-statist settlement at the end of the First World War, there were to be twenty-seven nation-states in Europe, with more to come. In the 1850s there had been the merest handful.

But the high adventure of nationalism on its way to state power was already, in those 1850s, an issue of the most vivid public concern, every bit as emotive as great ideological debates in more recent times about capitalism and socialism. And the same concern, in the context of my themes here, was certainly prevalent and hotly discussed among the political philosophers of Freetown and Cape Coast: those who became the fathers of the same nation-state–forming process in a future Africa. Horton and his friends, recaptive descendants or not, might be immensely far away from Europe in "journey time"; but they knew the place, watched it carefully, and kept their scouts and informants on the spot.

What does it all look like, glancing back? The affair of Sir James Lacaita and Lord John Russell is a little-known but excellent case to begin with. It can take us straight into the high temperatures of nineteenth-century nationalism; and there it can show us, at those temperatures, how political smelting of the crude ores of a longing for liberty among the oppressed, or else of liberal subversion when seen from the standpoint of the oppressors, was made to produce the abrasive metal of the nation-state, in this case the Italian nation-state.

The scene is Chesham Place in London on a wet July day in 1860. A visitor with a bad cold stands shivering and ringing the bell of a tall gray mansion. He is a gentleman of Apulia, in southern Italy, and by trade a former lawyer of Naples in the south Italian kingdom of that name. His name is Sir James Lacaita, his knighthood being for services rendered to Britain, which is his adopted country since the king of Naples drove him into exile from his native country. The bell he is ringing is that of the London house of Britain's foreign secretary, Lord John Russell. They are old friends and often meet, but today of all days there is a problem.

Mopping his nose as best he can, for his cold is at its climax, Sir James Lacaita is relieved when a servant answers the bell. But the servant, who also knows him well, feels unable to be helpful.

"Is Lord John at home?"

"Not at home, Sir James."

Lacaita receives this answer as though it were terrible news. He becomes a little frantic.

"Is he out or only busy?"

"He's engaged, most particular, Sir James, with the French ambassador . . ."

But this news is evidently even worse. Lacaita looks desperate.[1]

To savor the drama of the astonishing scene which then unfolded, and the hugely decisive events to which it was to contribute, a little background will be helpful. It has to do with the unification of an Italy then divided into half a dozen different sovereignties and state loyalties. As a country, Italy had not been unified since Roman times. Its situation in the 1850s was for the most part one of pitiful subordination to various foreign powers. The Austrian emperor held great provinces such as

Lombardy under heavily garrisoned direct rule. All the central provinces were divided into a cluster of small states subordinate to the temporal power of the pope in Rome, who, though Italian, ruled with the strong protection of the Austrian emperor and the emperor of the French, Louis Napoleon. South of these papal states was the large kingdom of Naples, including the island of Sicily; and King Ferdinand II of Naples, though Italian, was also protected by the emperors.

Italy was not a country, then, but an idea: the idea, precisely, of persons who longed for Italian unity and independence. Among these persons were the king of Savoy, largely that part of Italy known today simply as Piedmont, and his leading minister, Count Cavour. This little kingdom was well organized and independent, and the king and Cavour wanted to make it the core of a united Italy. But making it the core of an independent Italy was going to be difficult.

King Victor Emmanuel II of Savoy and Count Cavour saw that to achieve their aim they must somehow knock over their opponents one by one, beginning with the least dangerous of them, the Bourbon king of Naples. Yet to make headway with this aim they could, in practice, use only such men and methods as the king and Cavour could at need disavow; otherwise the Austrians or the French, or both, would turn and rend the whole endeavor. The man Cavour turned to, or rather turned a blind eye to, was Giuseppe Garibaldi, a former seaman of intensely patriotic loyalties who had made a great name for himself in old guerrilla wars in South America. Eleven years earlier, in 1849, Garibaldi had also led a bold expedition to liberate Rome from the pope and his French imperial protector. He had failed, but the exploits of this leader and his men, his Garibaldini, had inspired a passionate admiration in every liberal heart in Europe and America.

Now in 1860, in another desperate effort to set the liberation of all Italy in train, Garibaldi had secretly sailed with 1,150 volunteers—the famous "Thousand" as they were to be known—from the north Italian port of Genoa to liberate Sicily, far in the south, from the grip of the Bourbon kingdom's police and army. If Sicily could be liberated, southern Italy could be next; and if the Bourbon kingdom could be overthrown, then the unification of a liberated Italy might come within sight.

All this would come to pass, although only by a combination of reckless courage, shrewd calculation, and amazing strokes of favorable fortune. The Thousand sailed in purloined steamships with one antiquated cannon and a stock of almost useless firearms, got ashore in western Sicily by sheer effrontery and good luck, and went on to defeat the Bourbon armies in Sicily, vastly superior though these were in arms, training, and number of troops. These successes against all odds and expectations rang from one end of Europe to the other; and they were applauded in America. For these memorable victories had given Garibaldi and his men, somewhat reinforced from the kingdom of Savoy (in practice, from Piedmont), a full command of the whole island of Sicily, and brought them to the brink of the narrow strait, at Messina, that divides Sicily from the mainland of southern Italy. But could Garibaldi get his men across this water?

It seemed unlikely. Patrolling the decisive strait was a strong and active Bourbon navy. To evade those warships would be possible for a few men, but scarcely for many. Besides this, there was a great likelihood that the French emperor's navy would come to the assistance of his Bourbon client, King Ferdinand of Naples; and if this were to happen, then Garibaldi's chances must be reduced effectively to nil. Bottled up in Sicily, his slender forces would face eventual destruction.

But Cavour, back in the king of Savoy's north Italian city of Turin, thought of a stratagem to reduce the chances of French intervention against Garibaldi. Cavour's friend Lord John Russell had lately become England's foreign minister and was known to be in discreet sympathy with Cavour's aims and those of King Victor Emmanuel. On the advice of the British diplomatic representative in Turin, Cavour sent a message to his friend Sir James Lacaita in London, asking the latter to visit Russell secretly and explain the desperate nature of the moment. Cavour knew that the French emperor was actively thinking of sending the French navy to sink Garibaldi and all the Italian hopes vested in him. But he also knew that the emperor would probably not do this unless the British government were to agree with the intervention and join in it.

Russell on his own, though likely to want to oppose any such intervention against Garibaldi, could scarcely decide British policy, powerful though great ministers were in those days. But the famous William Ewart Gladstone was a leading member of the same British government, and Gladstone, if consulted, would be a most persuasive ally against intervention on behalf of Naples. Here we have to jump back ten years for a moment.

Gladstone in 1860 was not a newcomer to the problems of Naples. Ten years earlier, at first a tourist, he had sojourned in Naples. Though a staunch Conservative, having then not the slightest thought of its being possibly right to subvert the established imperial powers in Italy and liberate the country, he was outraged by the miseries and tortures of life in Bourbon Naples. Given chapter and verse on these by Italian friends, notably the Giacomo Lacaita who was later to be Sir James, Gladstone decided that he must see for himself. He asked for official permission to visit the Vicaria prison where it was known that criminal and political prisoners were indiscriminately held but, it was said, under relatively good conditions. Perhaps supposing that an English Conservative would be no likely or inconvenient witness, the Neapolitan government consented. It reckoned without the visitor.

Gladstone was moved to great disgust and protest by what he saw and heard in the Vicaria, and proceeded with his investigation. He next visited the island prison of Nisida, where prominent "politicals" were also held, and there he was shaken to the roots. When he published his impressions back in England, there were people who said that he exaggerated, and that prison conditions could never be as bestial as those that he described. But Gladstone had no doubt that he had told the truth, and that the truth must become widely known. It must be used to alleviate the sufferings he had witnessed.

In our own times we have become familiar with such sufferings, but in those days the impact on the public of what Gladstone had to tell was both profound and effective. "It is not," he said of the state and government of the Neapolitan Bourbon kingdom, "mere imperfection, not corruption in low quarters, not occasional severity that I am about to describe; it is incessant, systematic . . . violation of the law by the power appointed to watch over and maintain it. . . . It is the perfect prostitution of the judicial office." He thundered: "I have seen and heard the strong and too true expression used, 'This is the negation of God erected into a system of government.' " He was believed.[2]

In the years that followed, much more was learned and published in condemnation of the miseries of the kingdom of Naples, and British opinion grew well prepared to see in Garibaldi a liberating hero who deserved its ardent support. When Lacaita stood on the pavement of Chesham Place in July 1860 he knew all this. But he also knew that the French government was now embarked on a diplomatic effort to persuade the British government to oppose Garibaldi and, immediately, to prevent Garibaldi from getting across the Strait of Messina. So the whole chance for the liberation of Italy from dictators and secret police was at stake when Lacaita, having rung the bell at Chesham Place, was told that Russell was busy in conference with the French ambassador. The French had proposed a treaty bearing on intervention against Garibaldi: was this conference not the prelude to its signature? If so, Garibaldi and his cause were lost.

"He's engaged, most particular, Sir James, with the French ambassador," the servant told him. "I've turned away the Turkish ambassador, and I've strict orders to let in no one except the minister for Naples."

This was the crunch. "There's no time to lose," Lacaita was later said to have thought (as the story has come down to us from reliable witnesses), and then inquired:

"Is Lady John at home, then?"

"She's in bed, Sir James, ill."

Then Lacaita took out a card and wrote upon it, "For the love you bear the memory of your father," a man well known for his admiration of things Italian, "see me this instant," and sent up this strange message to the lady of the house. The lady at once received him in her bedroom, listened to his tale, and sent a message to her husband. Thinking to find his wife suddenly taken worse, the British foreign minister left the French ambassador in his study and rushed upstairs.

Lacaita assailed Russell with a flood of passionate appeal. If Garibaldi crossed the Strait of Messina now, Italy would be made. If he was stopped, reaction and ruin would prevail. Recovering from his surprise, Russell listened patiently, and said to the coughing and sneezing Lacaita, "Go to bed, and don't be so sure that I am going to sign the treaty yet." And the treaty was not signed, and Garibaldi got across the Strait of Messina, and months later the cause of a liberated and unified Italy was made secure.

The story of Lacaita's lucky visit to Chesham Place came out years later, but the exploits of the Garibaldini and their chief, outfacing every discouragement and risk, were heard and welcomed from one end of Europe to the other, and across the seas in North America and among the exiles of the southern pampas. Garibaldi himself seemed to epitomize everything that brave patriots can do in defense of their country and their cause; and the song that had been written for him and his men, before the hard-won battles of Calatafimi and Milazzo that opened the way to victory, rang with that note of high romance in which the national cause, burdened as it was with memories of those who had died for it, was heard and celebrated:

Si scopron le tombe, si levano i morti . . .

The tombs are uncovered, the dead come from far:
The ghosts of our martyrs are rising to war,

With swords in their hands, and with laurels of fame,
And dead hearts still glowing with Italy's name . . .

But the heroism of the Garibaldini was not the only force that
made Italy; there was also, and crucially important, the well-
trained army of the king of Savoy and his social and political
establishment. Victor Emmanuel and his royal army came in
and completed what Garibaldi had begun, and in doing so they
presented the full equivocation of nationalism: a cause devoted
to freedom, but also a cause capable of becoming the reverse.
After the unification of Italy in 1861 the new Italian nation-
state would turn quite shamelessly to colonial enterprises in
Africa. The very steamship company whose boats had carried
the Thousand to Sicily would be foremost in Italian colonialism; and Garibaldi himself would speak in favor of loading on
Africans the chains of servitude that Italy had struck from
itself. But in 1860, for a little while, the two aspects of
nationalism—the "national" and the "social"—were in happy
unison.

Nothing showed this better than the circumstances of Garibaldi's visit to England in 1864. Crowds of a size and fervor
never seen before came out to welcome him, because "to the
common people" of England "it was an unexampled privilege
to carry one of themselves in triumph through London streets."
The four-horse carriage in which he rode, wearing his famous
red shirt and gray blanket, "struggled in the course of six hours
through five miles of London streets, amid half a million of our
people who had turned out to greet him"; and everywhere he
went it was the same. The English people had found a hero, and
they knew what to do about it.

But, continued G. M. Trevelyan, the English historian of Garibaldi's campaigns, he had "won, no less, the hearts of the English upper classes, at that time heartily antagonistic to continental clericalism and despotism." The carriage that he rode in for his triumphal entry to London belonged to the duke of Sutherland, whose amiable wife afterward "drove [Garibaldi] into [the] School-yard at Eton, followed by boys and masters shouting after him as if he had just won them the match against Harrow." Titled ladies vied to have this guerrilla warrior as their guest. All the great men of the land were at one in praising him.[3]

This was the England much to be admired for helping to free Italy from rank reaction and clerical rule. But it was the same England that was about to fall on Africa with all the weight of its own imperialism; and a later generation of the English governing classes, asked to sympathize with the same cause of national liberation in African colonies, was going to take a different view of the matter. Then it would be found a scandalous evil that Englishmen or anyone else should toil and protest on behalf of "mischief makers" in Africa who sought to overturn the eternal verities of empire. Nationalism in Africa would be seen as a wretched subversion, and altogether a matter for the police.

In retrospect, the equivocation looks easy enough to explain, since this or that policy toward nationalism was an issue of *raison d'état* even if the nongoverning classes might see things otherwise. Yet there remains a mystery at the seat of all these vivid passions and clamors that filled so many years of the nineteenth century, and would duly fill many more in the twentieth. Where did European nationalism find its reservoirs of loyalty and conviction? How did it come about, in due course, that European nationalism would sponsor its reflection in Africa, and promote that curious but compellingly emotive contradiction in terms, the concept of "national liberation"? We can usefully turn back a little and consider the doctrine as it evolved in nineteenth-century Europe.

The process of forming nation-states in Europe, raising the number of these from perhaps half a dozen eventually to thirty or more, was generally thought and multifariously reported as the burgeoning of something called "national consciousness," a theme to which I must briefly return. The Divine Will, concerned not with sordid calculations of dynastic advantage but with the sovereign beauties of the "national principle," fount and foundation of all future community, was generally seen as urging each culture to realize itself as a nation, and then as a sovereign nation-state. This might be mysterious, because hard to explain as a necessity of social development; nonetheless, it remained the great and central fact of all morally viable political action. Here we may note that the democratic revolutions of the North American states took an altogether different and constructive federal course; but this great and hopeful result would still leave open, in its own way, space for the equivocations of North American nationalism in its dealings with South America.

In Europe by the end of the nineteenth century it appeared obvious that that continent's manifest supremacy of power derived from this God-directed work of forming nations from cultures, and nation-states from nations. That is what all the political philosophers had taught in the aftermath of the French

Revolution. This nationalism, in Elie Kedourie's words, was "a doctrine invented in Europe at the beginning of the nineteenth century."[4] Here was Europe, after 1800, in the throes of completely reforming itself and its loyalties by appeal to the absolute authority of the "national ideal," a concept that nobody in the Europe of earlier times had seriously considered or even heard of.

Seen thus, the grand adventure of individual courage and gamble—as, for example, Garibaldi's—acquired the merits and status of a glorious crusade; the acting-out of a moral imperative which drew its power from the unfolding potential of humanity's divinely gifted mission and, as such, an enterprise justified in whatever it might command men (or women) to do. European history in due course, most grimly in the murderous battles of the First World War or the Holocaust of the Second, would show where this kind of thing could lead. It had in fact been leading there for a long time.

In 1832, explained a new German nationalist called P. J. Siebenpfeiffer, the path of German nationalism—the welding together of the successor states in Germany of the defunct Holy Roman Empire of the German Nation—was already pointing to the concept of German domination. "The day will come," he said, "when sublime Germania shall stand on the bronze pedestal of liberty and justice, bearing in one hand the torch of enlightenment . . . and in the other the arbiter's balance." Then the last shall be first, as God has willed it, for "the people will beg [Germania] to settle their disputes: those very people"— the French, the British, the Russians, whoever—"who now show us that might is right, and kick us with the jackboot of scornful contempt."[5]

And in 1832 Siebenpfeiffer was already standing on well-trodden ground. More than thirty years earlier the German theologian Friedrich Schleiermacher had sketched the defining of that ground in words which other "rising nation-states" would echo in their own way. "How little worthy of respect," he exclaimed, "is the man who roams about hither and thither without the anchor of national ideal and love of fatherland; . . . how the greatest source of pride is lost by the woman that cannot feel that she also bore children for her fatherland, and brought them up for it, and that her house and all the petty things that fill up most of her time belong to a greater whole and take their place in the union of her people!"[6]

Such proclamations—and those written in Germany were exceptional only in their naïveté and fervor—must seem bizarre in the wake of twentieth-century nationalist holocausts and miseries. They were widely accepted at the time. They embodied the mysteries of "national consciousness" in a language and ideology that swept whole multitudes, "lower" or "upper" or "middle" in class affiliation, into reckless obedience. This was how God willed it. That was how things had to be. The dealings between and among different peoples were no longer to be measured by the slow and prudent fusion and erosion of interests and advantages, promoting a consensus that recognized the needs and rights of diversity. All such dealings were to be crammed within the iron shell of the sovereign nation-state, reduced to the service of that state (and its bureaucracy by appointment or inheritance), and concentrated on the advancement of its power against necessarily rival nation-states. Every tolerant rule of Mother Nature, allowing as she does for infinite variety within a life common to all, was to be condemned as inefficient, thrown out as an enfeeblement, and thrust behind "modern history" as an unregenerate dross of sin.

Such attitudes have remained influential. They have launched fearful policies of oppression. They have directed furious efforts to excuse the nature of this nationalist beast. They still inspire frenzied latter-day nationalists in every part of the world, not least in a Europe which should, above all, have learned better. They even live in the words of political philosophers who, certainly in themselves, have not had the slightest wish to promote or excuse nation-statist frenzies. A much-reprinted work by Hans Kohn, writing in the United States during the early 1940s, at a time when European frenzies of this kind plumbed new and unspeakable depths in the Germany of National Socialism and the Italy of Fascism, offers an explanation.

"Nationalism is first and foremost a state of mind," he tells us, "an act of consciousness."[7] Deriving in some evidently occult way from the existence of nationalities, it shares their impalpable nature. For nationalities "defy exact definition." We cannot quite say what they are. We cannot penetrate, it seems, the temples of their birth. But they come into existence, along with the distinctive languages which express them, and which give them the lineaments of everyday life. And with this gift of separate tongues, each to be developed into a supremacy and made "more real" by ejecting as impure words borrowed from abroad—so that *bank*, a typical example, this time Hungarian, has to become *pénztar*, and *bahnhof* has to be *pályaudvar*—the nationalities become ever more divisive. So the trouble starts. As Hans Kohn concludes, this is when "nationalism demands the nation-state." Then this "creation of the nation-state strengthens nationalism." And the gas chambers already loom ahead.

Of course, Hans Kohn was faithfully telling us what has in fact happened. However formed, nationalities in Europe did become nations, and the nations duly encased themselves in sovereign states, or at least in states intending to be sovereign; and these, one after another, have torn each other to pieces. Unfortunately for the prophets of the Siebenpfeiffer sort, they have done this without for a moment standing, at least when seen from their victims' view, on "the bronze pedestal of liberty and justice." More often, they have been wielding the scythe of indiscriminate slaughter. It is all the more surprising, in retrospect, that the fact of these nation-states should have been so often taken for granted to the point of supposing that they have existed from the dawn of time. A newly formed nation-state, moreover, seems at once to present itself, in some un-explained but altogether persuasive sense, as having always existed, and arrogates to itself an untouchable sanctity of rights and conduct.

The explanation, no doubt, is that this irresistible nation-statism took its rise in a period when economic development in Europe fostered and required the presence in society of acutely stratified classes. This has been the line of thought followed by materialist and other philosophers of various loyalties. In the years after Schleiermacher had instructed the German woman on the supreme blessing of being a servant, these philosophers were awkward heretics. They found the high-flown verbiage of Deutsch-Nationalismus, or its equivalents elsewhere, wanting in its intellectual credentials. To get at the origins of nationalism

they thought it more useful to ask the question *Cui bono?*—
Whose interests are being served? Nineteenth-century nationalism could best be understood, they argued, by perceiving it as
a struggle for state power by social classes crystallized, or in the
course of becoming crystallized, in the economic and technological developments following England's industrial and France's
political revolutions.

Looked at in this way, as it increasingly has been by nonmate-
rialists as well as materialists, the rise of nationalism in its
nineteenth-century context was the outcome of a combination
of effort between rising "middle classes," few in numbers and
weak in the power to impose themselves, and the multitudinous
masses of the "lower orders." After gaining power, of course,
the "middle orders" would abandon the "lower orders"—just
as, in the Italian case, most of the survivors of Garibaldi's Thousand were demobilized into poverty or unemployment—and
the equivocation would then explode into civil strife.

But that would be later: meanwhile, nationalism could advance boldly under the banners of populist democracy. Indispensable to nation-statist success in all the many upheavals of
the nineteenth century, as E. J. Hobsbawm has insisted, were
the agitations and uprisings of peasants and urban workers.
These were "lower orders" which had until now played no role
on the widening stage of statist claims and conflicts. But now it
was the "labouring poor" who died on the democratic barricades
of Europe's great "year of revolutions," in 1848, against aristocratic and tyrannical power.[8] It was "workmen of the towns"
who filled half the ranks of Garibaldi's Thousand twelve years
later,[9] while Garibaldi himself was by origin a lowly seaman of
Nice when it was still Nizza. Was not this climactic year "the

springtime of the peoples"? Yes indeed. But who exactly were "the peoples"?

Broadly, the lawyers and doctors and students wanted national power, while the "lower orders" wanted social power; and the two aims for a while could march together because the "middle strata" could never win without the massive supporting pressure of the "lower orders." This is why we find that all the political revolutions which reduced Europe to nation-states were "in fact or immediate anticipation, social revolutions of the labouring poor."[10] In the desperate Berlin uprising of 1848 only some 15 representatives of the educated classes were among the 300 or so who died in the fighting. In the much bigger Milan uprising of that year, aimed at the overthrow of Austrian imperial power, there were, notes Hobsbawm, "only twelve students, white-collar workers or landlords among the 350 dead of the insurrection."

This is the background against which one sees the relevance of an apparently crazy claim advanced in 1847, but much noticed only later, by a youthful Karl Marx and his friend Friedrich Engels: that "a spectre is haunting Europe, the spectre of Communism." The specter was real, even if the label was fantasy. Moreover, wrote those two young men, "all the powers of old Europe have"—as indeed they had—"entered into a holy alliance to exorcise this spectre: Pope and Tsar, Metternich and Guizot, French Radicals and German police spies. Where is the party in opposition [to ruling powers] that has not been described as communistic by its opponents?" We can all offer much more recent examples from the "holy alliance" of the Cold War years.

What prevailed after 1848 was "old prejudice and old reaction": the real alliance, not the specter. The "labouring poor" scared the life out of the lawyers and their kind, and the democratic constitutions shriveled away. There were some gains for the poor. "Old reaction" had to make a few concessions, at least on a temporary basis. Hungarian landlords, assembled in their parliament of 1848, heard or thought they heard the thundering march of those uprisen slaves to whom Sándor Petöfi had dedicated his famous vow: "This we swear, this we swear, slaves we will no longer be." Hungarian serfdom was hastily abolished. But all the democratic revolutions of 1848 were crushed. The nation-states that came eventually to birth were to be the political work of "middle strata" who prudently survived aristocratic reprisals, while the "labouring poor" paid the price of defeat in persecution, exile, or renewed subjection. Nation-state Europe began in the bloodshed that would stay with nation-state Europe. As was dryly remarked at the time, the goddess of history would surely drink the nectar of progressive change, but only "from the skulls of the slain."

This triumph of the "middle strata," empowered with the surging rise of capitalist economies and technological expansion, was the achievement of the remainder of the nineteenth century. Obstructions were thrust in its way by papal or aristocratic reaction. Wars, banditries, and various outbursts of human folly added to these obstructions. None of them was more than a temporary nuisance. The great caravan of bourgeois supremacy rattled onward through it all. The culture and command of bourgeois Europe took power and primacy in all the arts and exercises of everyday life.

Solidly implanted in their new mansions, the "middle strata" of the capitals of Europe, as of provincial cities aping the capitals, looked from their tall windows at a world that seemed, after the 1850s, eternally theirs to rule. Admired by Church and State, they forgot the skulduggery of their recent ancestors and forgave themselves their wealth. Balzac's *comédie humaine* of the 1830s, so acidly dramatic in its novelistic ironies and all-embracing in its social travels, gave way after the 1850s to increasingly comfortable five-volume canters through the pastures of the privileged and rich; and the "middle strata," drawing aside their skirts from the "labouring poor," saw that God was in his heaven and all was right with the world:

> The rich man in his castle, the poor man at his gate:
> God made the rich and lowly, and ordered their estate.

The arts were tamed, speculative thought thrust out of sight, things-as-they-were raised to the unchangeable. And to great majorities at the time, it seemed no more than the workings of the Divine Will and dispensation.

So it came about that the doctrine of nation-statism, here too, became enshrined as the supreme problem-solving formula for peoples emerging from the dead hand of tyrannical and foreign rule, whether Austrian or Russian or Turkish or other.

When this happened, the ideologists of this enormous success were going to put the doctrinal cart before the horse. They were going to say that it was a preexisting and dominant "national consciousness" which had demanded this enshrinement in the nation-state; whereas in fact the power that made enshrinement possible, the power of the "lower orders" in their multitudes and willingness to fight and die, was almost always fixed on social and not on national objectives.

But the "middle strata," some of whom also did their share of fighting and dying, needed to seat their legitimacy as rulers on something more solid and respectable than class ambition. This "something," moreover, had already begun to exist, if vaguely, as a "national consciousness" in their own narrow ranks. They understandably projected the same consciousness across their nation-state. They presented their nation-state as the product of a national consciousness rather than a class consciousness. In this way the emergent state seemed to be the product of nationalism, whereas in truth it was nearly always the other way around. As it was going to be in Africa in the twentieth century, it was the European state in the nineteenth that demanded the nation.

Having managed to win free from old and wicked empires, poets and constitution makers hastened to invest the new nation-states in the garments of manifest destiny, rather as though, in some ineffable reality, these nation-states had "always" existed. Were they not the gift of an eternal force of freedom? And freedom, Garibaldi had promised in the furies of battle for the Italian nation-state, would not betray "those who want her": *Libertà non tradisce i volenti!* The promise was going to be promptly broken, but the sentiment and the sense behind it retained their power to inspire. They seemed to descend from the shrines of truth itself.

The breaking of the promise of freedom was the outcome, as is easily understood now, of the victory of the "national" over the "social." This was going to form the central problematic of these European nation-states. It would equally form the central problematic of Africa's new states after the 1950s, however different the conditions and appearances might be. Here is where the parallels take hold and yield conclusions.

They do so, of course, on a considerably different time scale. When in about 1690 Priest Anokye assembled the lords of the Akan, proclaimed the destiny that was now Asante, and provided divine blessings for their new kingdom, there was altogether absent any sharp sense of there being possibly a difference, a conflict, between the good of the nation and that of the people. But when the nation, after a century and a half or slightly more, had gathered such wealth and power in the hands of the king and his chiefs as their ancestors had never dreamed of, this sense of difference, of opposed interests, was clearly on the near horizon. Sharpening awareness of this conflict of interests would then be delayed and blunted by the distractions of foreign dispossession; and would become obvious and painful only in the wake of those distractions, perhaps only in the 1970s.

But in the nineteenth-century Europe of new or prospective nation-states, this fact of conflict and this awareness of opposed interests became almost immediately apparent. With the turning wheels of industrialism and an ever more ingenious and daring use and abuse of finance capital, events moved fast, fractures split wide, protest flared into violence, "things fell apart." The parallels with colonized Africa still hold good, but within a much-hastened time scale.

It will be useful to probe into all this a little more closely. Here, then, are two European examples for the period between about 1850 and the end of the First World War when the old European internal empires, whether Russian, Austro-

Hungarian, or Ottoman, perished and gave new space for nations: for the emergence, as it was sometimes said, of "forgotten
nationalities" smothered till now beneath those empires. One
example is Romania; the other is a richly illustrative region of
the country that in 1919 became Yugoslavia, the kingdom of
the South Slavs. This region is called the Vojvodina.

Of the detailed route by which the kingdom of Romania
emerged in 1880 as a formally independent nation-state recognized by the ruling powers of Europe—in effect, Germany,
Russia, Austria, France, and Britain—little need be said here.
This largely followed the liberation from Turkish rule—an indirect rule exercised by Greeks known as Phanariots—of the ancient provinces of Moldavia and Wallachia; and this took place
in the wake of various wars in which, give or take a few disasters,
Austria and Russia prevailed. What was called "the concert
of Europe," meaning the chief military and economic powers,
managed with some hiccups to absorb this new kingdom on the
remote banks of the lower Danube River into its structure of
diplomatic compromise. And the new rulers of this Romania at
once proceeded to discover prestigious ancestors so as to lend
it—and therefore themselves—a veneer of "natural right." The
Romans had once formed a province in these lower Danube
lands, and the literate Romanian language reconstructed in the
nineteenth century could be shown to have a clear relationship
with Latin. After the Romans, true enough, there had come a
long series of "barbarian invasions" by peoples of the East—
Goths and then Slavs, Avars and Serbs and Croats—but the
influence of Byzantine Christianity together with the "Roman

heritage" was able to compose a respectable legacy of civilization.

The vast majority of the population of Moldavia and Wallachia, when Romania was born from those lands, were peasants for whom the concept of nationalism and the fact of "national consciousness" had no meaning or existence. In so far as they possessed a political consciousness, this was an understanding confined within their village boundaries. Viewed from a nationalist standpoint, the peasants had no politics: they were, in the words of a British observer in 1820, in this respect "a dead and helpless mass." This observer was a British consul, a certain William Wilkinson who explained what this meant and why it was so. He thought there was no other people anywhere so burdened by despotic oppression as were the peasants of Wallachia and Moldavia, nor any who would bear half that weight of oppression "with the same patience and seeming resignation."

"The habitual depression of their minds has become a sort of natural stupor and apathy, which renders them equally indifferent to the enjoyments of life and insensible to happiness," Wilkinson concluded.[11] This was the kind of thing that European visitors to a somewhat later Africa were going to write or say about a great many Africans they found; but in the case of the nineteenth-century Wallachia and Moldavia that became Romania in 1880, there was some excuse. In contrast with the culture and everyday life of most African peasants in that period, those of Romania were sunk to a parlous condition of helpless misery and ignorance. Bonded serfs or "lost communities" without any legal or even customary rights, possessing not so much as a tradition of having once owned such rights, these

Romanian rural people lived on the margins of a land-owning princely culture which had long abandoned them to squalor and inertia.

To the outside eye, and evidently to their own as well, these peasants had no civic existence, nor any ties save those of blind obedience to the persons or powers that stood above them. Their ways were obscure, ignored, or despised by the landlords and city folk who lived from the profits of peasant labor. No known society in any part of Africa was thus abused and subjected. In Asante (to stay with the same example as before) much labor was performed by persons called slaves and having slave status, but that was a status, however humble, entirely different from the status of Romanian serf. In Asante a slave who worked well could expect to inherit some of his master's property and marry his master's daughter if feelings worked that way; he was, in practice, a junior member of the master's family, and even female slaves had some comparable rights. No such relationships were as much as thinkable in nineteenth-century Romania.

To the rising Romanian "middle strata," sparse handfuls of educated men looking to nationalism as a way to escape foreign rule, the peasantry in its mass could scarcely be said to be there at all. These "middle strata" were at first pitifully weak in self-confidence as in numbers, and were made weaker still, after about 1840, by their indulgence in a ferociously anti-Jewish mentality of prejudice and hate. The Jews of Romania, as it happened, were for various reasons connected with Jewish history, a community of unusual enlightenment and love of education. These attitudes were rewarded in everyday life with cultural and economic success. And this in turn made them a convenient target for the envy of an idle and indigent landowning "class," called boyars, who, when the need arose, found little problem in working up peasant envies as well. None of this seems to have existed to any serious degree before the middle of the century, but it existed ever more sharply after that, and increasingly deprived the "middle strata," through their own perversity, of valuable allies usually far more literate and industrious than they were themselves.[12]

That was one handicap on progress. There was another: the "middle strata" active in pioneering Romanian nationalism scarcely knew their own country. Often obliged to live in exile, with Paris the brilliant sun of their ambition, they consumed the midnight oil in philosophical debate and constitution-making ingenuity which had and could have almost no connection with sordid reality. They longed for democratic freedom, but freedom, as they conceived it, for a nation that was really constituted only by themselves. In 1842 their dominant spokesmen—speaking mostly for boyars who were squires and small land-owners rather than great magnates—managed for the first time to elect themselves a leader; and this prince, educated in Paris and "already infected with romantic nationalism," looked forward to grand and revolutionary democratic upheavals.[13] Like their fellow "middle strata" in most of continental Europe, the prince and his friends were greatly inspired by hope but rather little by realism. When democratic tumult duly arrived in 1848, citizens' barricades against imperial cavalry and mercenary mus-keteers mostly collapsed as soon as built, save in the extraordinary case of Milan; and imperial powers were easily restored.

Then it was found, in the case of Romania, that the peasants certainly did exist and that nothing, furthermore, was going to be achieved without the peasants. For it was the peasants, initially those of Transylvania (then under Hungarian rule, but with a large Romanian population), who carried the "middle strata" to brief but eventually decisive power. The peasants rose in multitudes, ragged but much feared, wielding knives and pitchforks, and demanded justice. But what they meant by justice was found to have almost nothing to do with the ideas of the prince and his nationalist friends. The schemes of comfortable Romanian landowners, plotting to extract state power from foreign kings and potentates, seemed utterly unimportant to the peasants—in the measure, that is to say, that the peasants so much as heard of such schemes. Peasant needs were otherwise. As R. W. Seton-Watson's classic history of nineteenth-century Romania has it, "their whole aspirations centred on a single word, Land."[14] They wanted an end to their serfdom, which they said they felt as an outrageous slavery. Even more, they wanted to own the land they worked; they wanted to use the fruits of their labor for their own good.

Peasant anger simmered while the landlords promised, or seemed to promise, those eagerly desired concessions. At this point there is a record of a meeting of boyars deputed to discuss land reform with peasant spokesmen. And then quite suddenly, as it were, the "savage backwoods" of Romania are heard to speak their mind with pith and point. What difference, a peasant asks, is there "between a boyar and a thief?" If a boyar, says this man, "could have laid his hands on the sun, he would have seized it and sold to the peasants, for money, the light and the heat of God." No doubt an extremist view, but evidently well nourished, for the man goes on: "Your lands would bring you nothing if we were not there to fill your granaries with produce, and your houses with gold and silver. These riches are not the fruit of the work of your arms. They are made by the sweat of our brows under the blows of your whips, and that of your government.''[15]

It might be so; but none of this would matter much to the trajectory of this nationalism. The rural multitudes could have their shout. But the rural multitudes would never be able to produce, from their own illiterate and savage ranks, leaders who could seize and hold control of the nation-state about to be born. Obafemi Awolowo would say it of Nigeria in 1947: it was the articulate and literate minority who could and would do that, for "it is their heritage." And that was how, in 1880, it was the Bratianus and the Sturdzas and their kind who would then be able to show, like their African descendants little more than half a century later, what they could do for and with the nation.

Having won their national struggle, as they thought, they at once lost all serious thought about the social struggle. In its natural resources Romania was among the splendidly fertile countries of Europe; a prosperous Romanian agriculture must have smiled upon an energetic farming population. But the desolate hand of an old imperialism cast a long shadow; and Seton-Watson could only conclude of that Romania of 1880 that "the peasant was sunk in misery and neglect, and had no say in the government of a country of which he was the real backbone."

Thus abandoned while the victorious "middle strata" sang their anthems of liberty and progress, and bought their clothes in Paris or wished they could, and waited for any chance there might be to demonstrate that Romania was well abreast of the latest Western styles, the peasants retreated from the scene. They give the impression of having turned their backs on a new state power whose authority they did not share, whose rulers they did not trust, and from whose politics they expected no benefit. They saw their self-proclaimed liberators, it seems, rather as though these were a new version of old oppressors, no doubt less dangerous than Turks or Russians but also no friendlier. Such written testimony comes to us mainly from educated Romanians living in cities, but it speaks a stern language. In 1904 a liberal academic in Bucharest warns of "a volcano trembling under our feet," and of a day coming "when fire will devour the palaces, the granaries and all the property of those who exploit the peasantry." Two years later another academic is urging that there must be land reform in favor of the peasants, "or the question will be solved by a dreadful *jacquerie.*"

Nothing is done; instead, the *jacquerie* punctually arrives one year later. This peasant revolt of 1907 was a vast and desperate affair; but it failed. True to the style and form of the nineteenth century, the "romantic nationalists" in power came smartly to earth and called out the troops. And the troops were severely practical: they shot and bayoneted and disemboweled or otherwise destroyed a great number of peasants and burned whole villages to the ground. When good national order was restored, the toll of peasant dead was found to be about 10,000 persons.

Reports of all this crossed Europe, and were thought disgraceful in salons where the harvests of the guillotine, just over a hundred years before, were no longer much remembered. In England, or at any rate in London where news of a country as remote as Romania could at times be heard, there were those who felt that the poor peasants ought to be pitied as the victims of foreign incompetence: what else but irresponsible oppression could be looked for from a bunch of Romanian lawyers schooled, moreover, in Paris? A long time would have to pass, people said, before these new countries now released from the clutches of tsar and Turk could hope to achieve any reasonable level of civilization. Peasants should meanwhile not be slaughtered in thousands, but then one had to bear in mind that these were rude and rough countries. Strong rulers might well be required; they must in any case be tolerated. That the nation-state formula might somehow be astray, and much to blame, occurred to no one at this time.

Even so, there were doubts about nationalism, or at least about other people's nationalism. As early as 1844, an article in the then prestigious British literary journal, *Fraser's Magazine*, had already opined in the light of various upheavals in distant lands that "nationalism is another word for egotism." One sees what the writer was getting at; but there was more to be said. The Romanian nationalists, like others of their kind, saw generally in nationalism the only way to rescue their peoples from disunity and despair. They believed that divinity had chosen them as the rulers of the future; and this was only what the barest evidence seemed to support. Much that they said may come through as insincere rhetoric couched in rococo prose; much that they did cost them life or health or fortune. Garibaldi's famous exhortation to the handful still alive with him beneath the last crest of the hill at Calatafimi, when Bourbon fire poured down on them and seemed unstoppable, may sound impossibly romantic: "Italians, here we make Italy or we die!" But they took that crest and they made Italy, and only afterward did they carry down their dead.

To other circumstances less than heroic they had to bring the same spirit of stubborn persistence; and this was all the more true after the mid-century uprisings were crushed. Years of poverty in exile opened before them when hope was quenched and little remained save a dwindling will to survive. The bourgeois nation-states would eventually be built on a proper understanding of finance and commerce, to which the decorative arts were asked to bring suitable tributes and even, now and then, bohemian scandal. But somewhere in their foundations, buried deep and at moments wistfully remembered, lay the dreams and aspirations of youth "lost on the barricades."

Yet "the fate of the survivors was almost more grievous." The comment is Alexander Herzen's, written in years when defeat and demoralization seemed everywhere to prevail among those exiles. The illegitimate son of a great Russian nobleman, Herzen had early turned to protest against the tsarist autocracy, had been sent to the Urals, and had then gone to Western Europe as a permanent exile. He must have been an obvious model for the awkwardly protesting Pierre Bezukhov in Tolstoy's *War and Peace*. His extraordinary memoirs of political dissent, and of the dissenters themselves, have given us one of the great human documents of the century.[16] Herzen lived in the buzz and scurry of exile plots and conspiracies, and knew their authors from the inside. Escaping from police or prison, the exiles gathered in the relative freedom of Geneva, or fled in silence into England, or ran the gauntlet in a far from friendly France, or simply hid in cracks and crevices wherever "old reaction" still reigned supreme.

Their plight was what we know from political exiles of our own time. Somehow they had to keep faith with themselves while parrying the blows of implacable misfortune. If they grew strange and unmanageable, who could be surprised? "While absorbed in dissensions among themselves, in personal disputes, in melancholy self-delusion, and consumed with unbridled vanity," wrote Herzen without any obvious forcing of the tone, the political exiles "kept dwelling on their unexpected days of triumph, and were unwilling to take off their faded laurels. . . . Misfortunes, idleness and poverty induced intolerance, obstinacy, nervous irritability," and they "broke up into little groups, rallying not round principles but round names and hatreds. . . ." Yet "with all that, ideas did not move a step forward, thought slumbered."[17] All of them gave way in more or less severity, with Herzen among them, to the onset of a disease from which political exiles can scarcely ever escape, *dementia emigrantis*, the manic misery of those who must live on hope deferred, and meanwhile hate their fellow exiles because, from sheer frustration, they have come to hate themselves.

The experience of this nationalism in the formative years of its rise in Europe was and perhaps had to be a thing of extremes, ranging from petty miseries to moments of heaven-storming triumph. And if so much of that experience now looks shabby and even ignominious, it remains that nothing in its record can be understood without heeding the resonance of its call to freedom. That was a call sounded always in notes of different value. But centrally among those values, this inspiration of nationalism as a promise of liberation had to include the enjoyment and enlargement of one's own culture and language, of one's own inmost identity. In the Europe of those days this came to mean one enlargement above all: that of literacy. To write in one's own language was to demonstrate an equality that could underpin all other freedoms, and prove a legitimacy of cultural development that nothing else could sufficiently attest.

It is easy nowadays to forget how new was this popular accent on literacy. Here among the insurgent peoples, the "forgotten" or "forbidden" nationalities under imperialist rule, the dominant civilization had been cast in Latin or else in one or other of the languages of imperial dominion. Nationalism had to begin by insisting on the cause of national literacy. And in this field there was almost everything to be done. Only a fortunate handful of peoples, French or English or Dutch or German, or new North Americans across the ocean, possessed a substantial number of literates. Most other Europeans were almost or completely nonliterate. Many of those who conducted business and public affairs did not even speak their own language, much less write it, but French or English or else Latin. The flowering of national languages and national literatures thus became, after the mid-century, an integral and influential aspect of the whole process of escape from imperialism. The Kenyan writer Ngugi wa Thiongo's insistence in our own time on the importance and value for Africans of writing in one's own language (in his case Kikuyu) has its origins here.

Language as a necessary defense against alienation, against loss of identity, can also illustrate the Janus-dialectic of the nation-forming process. To return for a moment to the Hungarians, they were a people installed in Europe by their raiding medieval ancestors. Coming from the east, they had settled on lands along the reaches of the middle Danube River and established their homeland in these plains, reaching from the pleasant western hills of their *alföld* to the horse-breeding levels of their *puszta* east of the river. Warring with Germans, Slavs, and Turks, they conserved their spoken language, an Asian tongue called Magyar, amid a sea of surrounding peoples who spoke languages of European ancestry. But their ruling class, noble families grown rich on quasi-feudal enclosures of land and marketable wealth, looked to Vienna and preferred to speak German, while usually writing in Latin whenever writing had to be done.

Having gathered strength early in the nineteenth century, Hungarian nationalism insisted on the resurrection of Magyar in a literate form. Under the insistence of new nationalist agitators, Lajos Kossuth prominent among them, they turned the writing and speaking of Magyar into a test of patriotism; and modernized Magyar became an official language, although Hungary would remain until 1918 a part of the great Habsburg empire ruled from Vienna. But what was sauce for the gander could not be admitted to be sauce for the goose. The many non-Hungarian peoples who were ruled within the empire from Budapest, above all the South Slavs along the middle Danube and the Romanians within Transylvania (also part of the empire then), were not to enjoy the same advancement. They certainly had their own languages, but these could not be recognized.

No one on this issue was more intransigent that Kossuth himself, prime example of liberator turned oppressor. Having struggled for Hungarian rights within the empire, Kossuth would in no way admit the "forbidden nationalities" to the same freedom. For him, standing at the source of Hungary's nation-statism, "the non-Hungarians were culturally inferior and must be so treated: it was intolerable that they should have the same status of equality with the ruling Hungarian nation. The suggestion that Romanians, Slovaks, or Serbs were nations, with a national culture of their own, was simply ridiculous."[18] Submerged in the grand onrush of imperial history, they had better stay submerged. As for the Jews, that awkward nationality so hard to deny or to admit, they had better be removed from sight; anti-Jewish persecution became violent after about mid-century.

The submerged peoples, each in its own fashion, thought otherwise. Surprising only the front-runners in these national stakes, the more strenuously the Hungarian nationalists "clamoured for Magyarisation, the more the Slovaks and Serbs and Romanians distrusted the Hungarians, and the fiercer became their own nationalism."[19] Strong words were said and shouted, and war followed. The case of the Serbs of the Vojvodina north of the Danube, inhabiting the broad plains of ancient Pannonia, has well displayed the drama. And drama it was. The briefly triumphant Hungarian "bourgeois revolution" of 1848—the one that abolished Hungarian serfdom—passed at once to anti-Serb repression. Many perished. The little Vojvodina capital of Novi Sad (Ujvidék in Magyar) was reduced to a population of few more than 7,000 from the 20,000 or so of previous years, and would not reach 20,000 again until late in the 1870s.[20]

But this Vojvodina peasantry was in a very different condition, whether of body or mind, from that of nascent Romania. It looked back across the nineteenth century to a cultural heritage received from the Serbs of the long-independent kingdom of Serbia south of the Danube, and it would now draw fresh inspiration from a Serbian cultural renaissance. Moreover, this was a peasantry of fairly recent formation, and in circumstances much to its own advantage. Under the neglect and indifference of Ottoman Turkish rule, these wide and well-watered plains had fared badly. Settlements had been small, impoverished, and widely scattered. After the coming of the Turks and the fall of the medieval Serbian kingdom, explains a local historian, "these regions knew the passage of many armies fighting wars without number. Villages were abandoned, people thrust down into poverty and hunger. Travellers who came here in the Turkish time spoke vividly of this misery."[21] Both in the Bačka region west of the Tisza River and then in the Banat region to the east, after 1637 this land of farming plenty is described as a wilderness.

Having supplanted the Turks, the imperial Austrians embarked on a policy of peasant settlement in these impoverished and empty lands. They sent in German peasants after 1720, Hungarian peasants a little later, then Slovaks and Ruthenes and others. Meanwhile, the small existing Serbian population grew rapidly as it was joined by Serbian refugees from lands immediately south of the Danube: from Serbia itself and from Srem, the old Sirmium of the Roman Empire, both still threatened by the Turks. The number of these Serbian refugees moving north across the Danube was again increased after 1739, when Turkish armies retook Belgrade, the capital in Serbia. The majority population of the Vojvodina remained Serbian, and Novi Sad, as a provincial capital, grew into a city of Serbs.

Here, then, was a mosaic of ethnic diversities created by the push and pull of conflicts and rivalries enclosed within the Austro-Hungarian Empire but, generally, living under conditions notably better than those of the Romanian multitudes to the east. Here there had been no quasi-feudal expropriation of rights to land and its produce, or treading down of the poor and defenseless. These Vojvodina peasants farmed their lands as free peoples expected by Austrian imperial policy to act, if necessary, as the guardians of a military frontier against Turkish threats from south of the Danube. They knew their own value, and they respected it. Long after, during the great partisan risings against Nazi German occupation in the Second World War, the peasants of the Vojvodina would be among the first to raise fighting units. Provoked after 1848 by an imperious Hungarian attempt to "Magyarize" the culture of the Vojvodina, the Serbs here, as a majority population, embarked on community self-defense.

They had already begun to form "ethnic movements" of a "help each other" kind in which we can recognize the near equivalent of the "tribal associations" in a later colonial Africa. Their initial aim, in short, was not for national independence or even political autonomy, but intraethnic solidarity and mutual aid. In the one case as in the other, this took the characteristic forms of social dancing, music making and expressions of a folkloric style: the wearing of "traditional dress," whether genuinely handed down from the past or simply invented, and the organization of ties of friendship within communities. Nothing much specifically political, much less nationalist, might have evolved without the provocation offered by Hungarian claims to primacy and domination.

These developments were aspects of the social struggle. They arose from issues concerned with the competition for land, for equalities of marketing, generally for the defense or advancement of one's everyday culture against Hungarian or Austrian hegemony. They formed the reverse of a "melting pot," if the metaphor be allowed: people held strongly to their own communities, and if someone "married out," the case was not all that common. Right down to the Second World War, when much altogether changed, ethnically diverse communities in the Vojvodina kept to themselves, conserving their languages, their habits, their styles of village settlement and much else. If a hierarchy of ethnic "values" slowly emerged, with the German peasants invariably claiming primacy for whatever was done *bei uns* and the Hungarian peasants trying vainly to overtake the Germans, this was a ranking tolerated by the Slav communities but never accepted as having an inherent worth.

This social struggle was going to assume a consciously national form as and when the communities could produce educated men: persons who were at home in the ideology of nationalism as an anti-imperialism, as an anticolonialism, and eager to wield this ideology as a weapon of political advancement. When this began to happen in the Vojvodina, a preliterate people, such as this Serbian peasantry then was, discovered the need for an entirely new vehicle of written communication. Serbian possessed no written form save an antiquated "church Slavonic" that nobody used in current speech, and few outside the monasteries could understand. Everyday Serbian speech might be well enough served by adding German and Hungarian words to lexically deprived dialects. But the cultural nationalists, the modernizers, now required the development of a written Serbian based on everyday speech but capable of handling all the new range of political ideas and aims, artistic forms as well as technological innovations, that could express a Serbian "national consciousness."

Peasant Serbian in the Vojvodina might have a rich vocabulary of spoken terms for rural things—something like forty different words for the parts of a peasant cart (as I myself can painfully recall from 1943, being then expected to know them)—but what the new nationalists required was a written vocabulary of urban as well as rural things, and therefore an agreed spelling as well as an agreed syntax. Hence the enormous importance of the handful of scholarly men in these cultures who set themselves to enlarge and standardize national languages. Later on, in the African case (or the Latin American case), this was going to happen in anticolonialist nationalism wherever indigenous languages had acquired wide currency among neighboring peoples—as with kiSwahili in East Africa and Hausa in West Africa—or in rare cases of new literacy such as the writing of Somali in an alphabetic script. But it was not going to happen, apart from a few missionary endeavors, with the vast majority of African languages. All too often, Africa's nationalists were going to have to find their way ahead in languages not their own.

The Serbs, for their part, were fortunate. They produced innovators such as Dositej Obradović (1743–1811), who was "the first popular Serb author who refused to write in the old Slavonic language and used the spoken language," being thus "the first awakener of his people . . . the first with the vision of a modern [Serbian] nation." With Obradović came others in this cultural realm, above all Vuk Stefanović Karadžić (1787–1864), who went further in developing spoken Serbian into a literary language, publishing grammars and dictionaries, simplifying spelling, and unifying syntax.[22]

This evolving cultural nationalism was spurred on by Hungarian imperial attempts at suppressing it, and these attempts, in their turn, were themselves spurred on by Austrian efforts, within the empire, at extending the supremacy of the German language over Hungarian in public and literary life. The Serbs responded by defying or evading Hungarian laws which tended to the suppression of the Serbian language. As early as 1825, this led to the appearance of a literary journal for the South Slavs, the *Srpski Letopis,* and in following years of the first functioning instrument of Serbian cultural self-assertion. This was a publishing venture called *Matica Srpska* (The Serbian Beehive), which then moved its offices from Budapest, where it had been founded, to more hospitable quarters in Novi Sad.

The rest almost followed of itself, and much the same could be said of other "submerged nationalities" in those old empires where ethnic diversity now began to give vehement expression to a wealth of cultural development. Among Croats, Slovenes, Slovaks, Czechs, and a panoply of others, there emerged above the mournful seas of imperial orthodoxy a splendid cultural landscape hitherto lost or hidden. What happened in the modest streets of Novi Sad, along the middle Danube, happened elsewhere. In 1863 there was formed in Novi Sad a Serbian national theater with the aim of dramatizing, for the stage, parts of the Serbian *narodne pesme,* popular heroic songs composed long before and known to everyone. There was as yet no theater, and the players had to borrow hotel rooms as best they could, rather like the Yoruba actors and playwrights of the late colonial period in Nigeria. But they persisted, and in 1872 they acquired a permanent building for themselves.

These, too, were the years of emergent nationalist politics. Pioneers such as Svetozar Miletić arrived on the scene. In 1869 there appeared the first Serbian political party in the Vojvodina, a nationalist party which called for equality of rights and status among all the region's nationalities. This again was part of a broad trend: in 1848, for example, the Slovaks who were equally

under Hungarian rule within the Austrian empire asked—
vainly, as it would soon transpire—for a "parliament of nations": a parliament of all the nations in the empire, whose
identities and language should have equal status with each other,
with each nation having its own system of education and an
assembly of its own, using its own language. The Serbs, meanwhile, hoped for unification with Serbia, and this they finally
achieved in 1918 with the collapse of the Austrian empire. Serbian troops moved northward over the Danube, and the Vojvodina became part of a newly proclaimed kingdom: not of Serbia
but of Triune Yugoslavia, the kingdom of the Serbs, Croats, and
Slovenes. What befell them we shall see in the sequel.

It may be useful, meanwhile, to insist on the point that this
South Slav nationalism, like others, was by origin in no sense a
mysterious "demanding of the nation," but a practical reaction,
increasingly a mass reaction, against the consequences of imperialist rule. In a substantive sense it was a reaction against
the colonial status of second-rate citizenship or, as with the
Romanian peasants, of no citizenship. It was a demand not for
nationhood but for elementary justice. The demand for the
nation came only when justice was repeatedly denied, mocked,
or trodden into the ground.

But when that demand did come, it was the rural multitudes
who gave it effective force. Obradović and Karadžić and their
like—famous names in European history—were men of high
vision as well as sterling courage, as were men like Svetozar
Miletić who clothed their aspirations in political form, nationalist form. But they could never have prevailed without the power
of wide communities. Later on, of course, and usually provoked
by imperialist repression, these communities did acquire a "na-

tional consciousness"; and the new European nation-states lining up for recognition in 1919, as new African nation-states were to line up forty years or so later, would then appear as though they were the fruits of this consciousness, and as though they possessed a legitimacy founded in the noble history of a distant past.

No doubt there were some grounds for that claim: nothing in the entangled history of nationalism is all that simple. The ideology of nineteenth-century Polish nationalism was largely the product of a nobility which could draw on a long historical heritage and claim precedence over neighboring nationalisms. Given the absence of a law of property inheritance by primogeniture, sons and daughters of noble families all received aristocratic titles so that this noble class, the Polish *szlachta*, grew into a substantial fraction of the whole Polish-speaking community of Poland. It had an emphatic consciousness of Polish nationhood. Even so, one may doubt how far the bulk of Polish persons, peasants in the large majority, would have shared the sentiments of the *szlachta*, any more than the bulk of Hungarian peasants would have felt their hearts beat as one with their *meltoságosurok* who owned the land and colonized the towns and steered the public life of Hungary. Their own traditions of loyalty were likely to be of a very different kind.

With this peculiar chemistry of nation-state formation there was smuggled out of hearing, or simply censored out of sight, the dynamic element which so decisively transformed the social struggle of the masses into the national struggle of the "middle strata" (or the "educated elites," or however one prefers to label them). This element was the process of conflict, of class conflict as it would emerge, between the objectives of the few who could

159

understand and use state power, and the many, once power was thus seized, against whom it was going to be used.

That confrontation would become violent and even ruthless in its methods, whether in European cases or in African cases (or other such cases elsewhere in the world). But its development was gradual and often hard to perceive. In the South Slav case, the osmosis of "social" into "national" went by various and subtle routes including linguistic innovation. The word *naród* meant and means "people": in the process of nationalization, however, it much more compellingly came to mean "nation" as well. Even the internationalist appeal of socialism could also speak and act, as it would in Piłsudski's Poland of the 1920s, in the language of patriotic nationalism.

Little more than twenty-five years divided the birth of these European nation-states from the claims of anticolonial nationalism in Africa, while the interval of time between the respective pioneers of the nation-state-forming project in Eastern Europe and in Africa was shorter still. But such has been the culturally compartmentalizing power of imperialism that little or none of all this experience was shared, or even could be shared. Educated Africans in the period before the Second World War, so far as their writings and records show, had little or no awareness of what was happening to European peoples under imperialism. Nor would they have had any sufficient means of analyzing those events, even if they had possessed awareness of them.

African nationalist thinkers in the 1940s and 1950s, true enough, looked carefully ahead and sometimes shrewdly guessed at the traps that might lie hidden there. The European nationalists had done the same, but no more perceived the full horror of those traps than would their African companions later on. Dositej Obradović had certainly not envisaged a Serbian nationalism that would turn patriotism into an all-purpose chauvinism and duly ruin every political structure to which it put its hand. The early nationalists of Croatia would assuredly have drawn back in loathing if they could have foreseen the murderous brutalities of the so-called Croatian Independent State, Nezavisna Država Hrvatska, set up in 1941 by Croat servants of German Nazism and Italian Fascism. Not even Lajos Kossuth in his most nationalistic mood would have thought so much as possible the mass murder of the Jews of the Vojvodina by Hungarians in and after that same terrible year of 1941.* But the traps were there, lying ahead; and in due course they were sprung.

Here we may turn to Africa again, and consider what happened there, during and after the Second World War, when the many began to find a great need for social justice in their everyday lives, and the few showed how that need could be given political form and force.

---

*One more appalling chapter of the Holocaust that still remains to be told in detail: in 1940 there were about 26,000 Jews living in the Vojvodina; in 1945 only 3,285 survived, according to official Vojvodina estimates assembled after the war. See *Vojvodina u Borbi* (Novi Sad, 1963), passim.

The Challenge of Nationalism

THE ACTIVISTS of the 1950s plunged into their chosen road of nationalism, seeing this as the only available guarantee of a route open to progress. They accepted the aim of building nation-states on the British model (or, later, on the French) because, as it seemed to them and as they were strongly advised, there could exist no other useful objective. Nkrumah's advice that they should seek the political kingdom, and all would then be added to them, expressed a central maxim of which the truth appeared self-evident: once sovereignty was seized by Africans no matter under what conditions, the road to freedom and development would be theirs to follow.

That this acceptance of the postcolonial nation-state meant acceptance of the legacy of the colonial partition, and of the moral and political practices of colonial rule in its institutional dimensions, was a handicap which the more perceptive of the activists well perceived. They foresaw some of its possible perils, and they warned against these perils. In accepting the British government's offer of 1951 to make him leader of a Gold Coast

(Ghana) government pledged to an eventual African independence—a long step forward at the time—Nkrumah told his voters that "there is a great risk in accepting office under this new constitution which still makes us half-slaves and half-free." There would be a great need for "vigilance and moral courage" to withstand the consequent temptations of "temporary personal advantage." This was because "bribery and corruption, both moral and factual, have eaten into the whole fabric of our society and these must be stamped out if we are to achieve any progress."[1]

No doubt it was inevitable that such warnings fell on deaf ears. Along with the nation-state as necessary aim and achievement, the legacy of the partition was transferred practically intact, partly because it seemed impossible to reject any significant part of that legacy, and partly, as one is bound to think in retrospect, because there was as yet no sufficient understanding of what the legacy implied. There were political thinkers, true enough, who understood that the colonial partition had inserted the continent into a framework of purely artificial and often positively harmful frontiers. There were others who perceived that a petty-bourgeois nationalism was bound to remain a nationalism subordinate to external powers organized on a capital-owning and capital-commanding basis. But they were few, and their voices feeble in the great resounding chorus of anticolonial agitations that was now heard on every side.

This chorus had little to say on the subject of nationalism. As a mobilizing and emotively compelling slogan, nationalism had small meaning in the Africa of the 1950s. Its history was as little known as its credentials. Outside the boundaries of thought in a few old nations like Asante, nobody was thinking about the implications of nationhood. The implications that counted were those that linked the slogans of nationalism to a removal of the colonial incubus, to the arrival in Africa of that dispensation of *uhuru*, of freedom, so warmly praised in the wartime propaganda of British imperial agencies. The war had become a *vita vya uhuru*, a war for freedom, and if *uhuru* meant anticolonial nationalism, then let it be so. The already veteran anticolonialist of Nigeria and later president Nnamdi Azikiwe put the matter well when speaking in Washington in 1949. Asked what forces had impelled the struggle of Africans for anticolonial independence, Azikiwe replied by quoting a comment of Eleanor Roosevelt's made during the Second World War. She had affirmed that "we are fighting a war today so that individuals all over the world may have freedom. This means an equal chance for every man to have food and shelter and a minimum of such things as spell happiness. Otherwise we fight for nothing of real value."

In its essence, this 1950s nationalism had far less to do with any national cause than with demands of a social nature and content. "One thing's certain," wrote Jacques Rabemananjara, the Malagasy nationalist, in 1958, "in today's political vocabulary the word nationalism means, generally, the unanimous movement of coloured peoples against Western domination. What does it matter if the word doesn't really describe the phenomenon to which we like to apply it?"[2] What fired the activists, in short, was never an imagined spectacle of the beauties of the sovereign nation-state, but the promise that the coming of the nation-state would strike away the chains of foreign rule and all that these had meant in social and moral deprivation. It has been in this large sense that the language of European

nationalism, as applied to Africa, had been consistently misleading. Their poverty of thought about the implications of
accepting the sovereign nation-state on the European pattern
may be held against the activists; but this poverty was not
without its advantages.

Generally, they remained free of the kind of millenarian romanticism which so monstrously inflamed the nationalists of
Europe in the nineteenth century, above all in the German-
speaking states. The violence and death so accurately forecast
in the strange but influential writings of Heinrich von Kleist
(1777–1811), portending dogmas of the "national will" that
were going to end in mass murder, had no echo here. There
might be good reason to fear that there would be nationalists
in a future Europe who "will know nothing of reverence for
anything," as the poet Heine warned against Kleistian thoughts,
and "who will ravage without mercy, and riot with sword and
axe";[3] and this prophecy was to be horribly realized a century
later. Nationalism in Africa, or whatever was labeled as such,
has since then led to plenty of horrors and miseries. But there
is nothing in the African nationalist documentation, nor in one's
memories of what was otherwise said or advised, to give any
ground for grim disasters. African nationalism was the product
not of a Kleistian chauvinism but of a mixture of antiracism
and, which amounted in practice to the same thing, of anticolonialism. "Let freedom come," and freedom would bring its own
good solutions.

This pragmatism, or if one prefers it this poverty of ideological thought, was the natural and direct fruit of African nationalism's being, all through its early and introductory phases, the
impulse and achievement of what can broadly be called the

165

"social struggle." Like the European movements of the 1840s, it was always the "labouring poor" whose involvement and effort in the 1950s gave the tribunes of the "national struggle," who were the educated elite in one manifestation or another, their ground to stand on. Without the mass pressure that surged into the streets of colonial cities and made its impact felt even in remote corners of the bush, the educated elite would have remained upon the sidelines of everyday life, genially teased and tolerated by colonial officials of a liberal sort, or else jeeringly ignored and pushed aside by officials of another kind.

As it was, the activists were given power by the pressure of a social struggle, with the ambitions of nationalism very much in second place; and this simplicity of "basic idea," in the familiar terminologies of European nationalism, may be seen as a blessing. It certainly helped to obscure the implications of the nation-statist legacy, but it also meant that African nationalism stayed quite largely immune to the eruptive territorial ambitions and rivalries that have sunk European nation-statism so often into pits of internecine bloodshed. With some minor exceptions, arising largely from claims determined by the arbitrary and inappropriate nature of the imposed frontiers, the record of the modern African nation-state over its forty or so years of life has not led to interstate warfare and, for reasons inherent in its nature that will become clear, is quite unlikely to do so in the future. In all essentials of mobilizing efficacy, African nationalism for long remained close to the social struggles that had given it scope for development.

And so long as this was so, of course, the activists of those times could feel that they need not fear the constricting embrace of a purely nationalist project. They could look beyond that project to the consummation of social struggles which should be far more liberating for their peoples. "Self-government will not necessarily lead to a paradise overnight," commented a Nigerian nationalist as early as 1950, "nor will it turn African nationalist leaders into angels. But it will have ended the rule of one race over another, with all the humiliation and exploitation which that implies. It can also pave the way for the internal social revolution that is required within each country" of a decolonized Africa.[4] The thought was not even a controversial one, as between left and right: all notable nationalists thought and said much the same thing, even if they often put it differently. The same meeting in England which heard the Nigerian I have just referred to was also warned by the staunchly conservative nationalist Dr. Kamuzu Banda of Nyasaland (later president of Malawi). He said, also in 1950, that imminent self-government "in Central Africa today would mean delivering the Africans into the hands of white minorities inspired by the same *Herrenvolk* ideas as the South African Nationalists," by which, of course, he was referring to the Afrikaner white National Party of apartheid. The immediate need was not self-government "but a quickening of educational and political development."

There was already, in short, a lively understanding of the critical nature of any "transfer of power" that might be in prospect for the 1950s and after. If the imperial governments really wished to move beyond the colonial structures, and the severely restricted political life that was narrowly possible within those structures, they must pay rapid and large attention to social advancement in schools, trade unions, and cooperative associations of rural producers. Only by thus reforming the social structures of colonialism could there then be a transfer of power to colonized majorities, rather than a mere adjustment of imperial attitudes to educated minorities and to the personal or collective ambitions of these elites. Still strongly influenced by the pressure of the struggle for social change, nationalists thinking along these lines could have no use for obscure imaginings. Optimists in an anti-Hobbesian sense, they looked to the coming of the nation-state as the harbinger of all democratic benefits that people could wish for. There should be education for all, health services for all, opportunities for all; and these blessings would bind up the wounds of the colonial past and present, and bring a new life that must in every positive sense become a modern life. Why indulge in messianic ideologies of the "national will," whatever that might be? A little decent pragmatism would do quite well instead.

Accepting the nation-state that was offered to them, the pioneering nationalists saw no useful alternative and asked no further questions about its credentials or potentials.

And would the great "transferring powers," Britain and then France, have had useful answers to such questions, supposing that these had been posed? It seems not. The authoritative Lord Hailey in his majestic many-volumed survey of Africa and its administrative problems, published at various times between 1938 and 1950, had almost nothing to say about the nation-state and its potentials for good or evil. Lesser authorities did no better, and even those European parties of the left sympathetic to African aspirations, notably the British Labour Party, had little to offer save bromides of goodwill. For this they can scarcely be blamed, if only because knowledge of African realities, in those late colonial times, was in practice restricted to persons able to travel to distant colonies and then able, moreover, to gain access to administrative information. As such persons were never welcome, their coming was rare and their access rarer still.

Even so, in retrospect, it is bound to seem strange that the whole project of nation-statism, of promoting nationalism as a means of promoting nation-states, was so little inspected by British authorities. The French, of course, could and did argue that they were not promoting nation-statism in "their Africa," but the elevation of their colonies to membership in *la plus grande France*, so that the only nationalism that could count in those colonies would have to be French nationalism. But the British in authority ardently believed in the project of African nation-statism. "The objectives of our colonial policy have been summed up in a number of different formulae," affirmed Sir Hilton Poynton, a former administrative head of the British Colonial Office, speaking in 1978 after a long and successful career, "but the shortest and simplest is 'Nation-building.' "[5] And by this, Sir Hilton clearly meant the "building" of separate nation-states as the successors and inheritors of colonial states.

But would a multiplication of new nation-states be helpful to peace and progress? Nobody seems to have asked, much less answered. And yet the great "transferring powers" were singularly well placed to know that nationalism could "ravage without mercy and riot with sword or axe," as well as with weapons far more dreadful than any known in Heine's time. After all, Europe had just emerged from the latest horrors of nation-statist violence sung to the tunes of Hitler's favorite marching song: "Today Germany is ours, tomorrow the whole wide world." But all that seems to have been forgotten, or at any rate forgotten in African contexts; and in so far as the British took notice of nationalism in Africa, they followed their policy in India and treated it as a subversion better handled by the police until, toward the eleventh hour, they declared that promoting nationalism had been their policy all along.

In 1930, for one example among a legion, could the Gambian nationalist E. F. Small be accepted as honorary Liberian consul at the Gambian capital of Bathurst? Better not, for the man was "worse than an agitator," in fact, a "self-appointed champion of non-existing grievances felt by an imaginary body of citizens."[6] Small would later be one of the active forerunners of Gambian independence, and thus of the Gambian nation-state, and was eager then to gain as much international experience as he could, but meanwhile—or therefore?—he was dangerous. Explaining Small's unsuitability for honorary consulship, Acting Governor Workman wrote to Lord Passfield, then colonial secretary in London, that while "I am not aware whether Small has definitely joined the Communist Party [presumably in Britain, for there was none in West Africa], his attendance at meetings of the European Congress of Working Peasants in Berlin, and his correspondence with the League Against Imperialism, sufficiently indicate his attitude." This was quite enough, and Small was turned down, even though the evidence suggests that he was almost as far from being a Communist as from being a Working Peasant.

French colonial authorities had the same approach to African askers of unwanted questions. An indignant report in the Paris colonial police files, undated but evidently of 1929, notes that "nothing had been reported, to date, allowing one to conclude that the Marxist doctrine has been established in native circles. There nonetheless exists an annoying [*facheux*] state of mind among the half-civilized along the West [African] Coast. In daily contact with Europeans, they have acquired ideas about equality that sometimes take the form of demands expressed in an unacceptable tone [*sur un ton déplacé*]."[7] The natives, in short, were tending to get above themselves, and "the Marxist doctrine" was bound to be at the root of the trouble.

Hence there were abundant warnings and gnashings of teeth on the subject of international Communism, archenemy of civilized nationhood, but none at all, so far as the records indicate, against nation-statism. A few years later large segments of French society would reach the conclusion that while German and Italian nationalisms, now reorganized as Nazism and Fascism, were undesirable, anything smacking of Communism must be infinitely worse; if a choice between these had to be made (as it would have to be in 1940), then it must be for compromise (and then surrender) to German and Italian nationalisms. As to catastrophic potentials in nation-statism, little or nothing would be said in any African context, perhaps because memories of the French disasters of the Second World War were felt by the 1950s, and rather understandably, to be better not revived. It remains to add that the cause of Communism, in French as in British Africa, never won more than a handful of adherents.

Brought at last to accepting African nationalism—and therefore its development into African nation-statism—the "transferring powers" still had little interest in debating its potentials. As it happened, African nation-statism almost entirely escaped the turbulent hysterias of Europe: it was far too much concerned with earthy practicalities to be fired by metaphysical yearnings of the Kleistian sort. Yet one might still have expected the great trustee to draw the attention of his wards—and it was in these terms that British authority saw the colonial relationship—to the quaking ground on which they now proposed to tread. No such warning seems to have come to hand. On the contrary, after 1950 the British in power persisted with a remarkable complacency in shepherding the British colonies, not into a society of interrelated states such as the pioneering nationalists desired for their continent, but into an accumulation of newly invented and entirely separate nation-states, a very different thing.

This was thought to be in line with what were considered to be British national interests, as somewhat later another proliferation would be seen as being in line with French national interests; and the great question became, not whether this might be the best outcome, but how to ensure that the outcome continued to match with British (or French) interests. That being so, what was needed was to spot and promote candidates for suitably convenient African nation-statist leadership. American policy in Africa would in due course follow the same approach. Nothing could be more natural; but it helps to explain why alternatives to nation-statism were never discussed. Such candidates, duly tried and tested, should be *interlocuteurs valables*, in the handy French term that now came widely into use: in practice, persons worth negotiating with because, at the end of the day, they would accept the primacy of British or French or eventually American interests. But what was further desirable was that candidates should possess and retain great influence in their respective countries.

It was in this respect that the project so often failed. When it came to choosing *interlocuteurs* who could and did really speak for their peoples, and who were therefore likely to dominate the political scene after the "transfers of power," but for whom the primacy of external interests was not acceptable, the process went sorely astray from an imperial standpoint. This is a fact which also has its bearing on the poverty of political debate. Senior colonial officials during the 1950s were by far the best-informed actors on that scene. But once it came to weighing up the credentials of anticolonial Africans, and the ideas for the future that those Africans might have and mean to promote, the narrowness of these officials' powers of judgment became painfully apparent. Plunged with the advent of anticolonial nationalism into an unfamiliar world of politics, these senior officials had entered terrain they neither understood nor were qualified to measure.

This was found surprising, but should not have been. Much more often than not, senior officials tended to be shrewd and even genial observers of humanity. Their long experience, usually begun "at the bottom" of the ladder of promotion, discouraged snap judgments, just as their responsibilities inclined them to think twice. Several had a deep interest in Africa; a few were amateur historians or archaeologists whose work provided a valued groundwork for the scholarly professionalism of later years. Most were highly conscientious in their duty. Yet all their training and preparation had been military or administrative. Of practical politics they knew nothing, and on the whole desired to know nothing, for politics savored of public bars and brawls or, at least, of irresponsible know-it-alls on lightning visits from "home." Politics were what the police brought to

173

the side door of Government House, leaving the stench outside. Of the politics of African independence, when in due course it arrived, the colonial "men at the top" had no more useful notion than the "man in the street at home"—often much less, in fact, for the "man in the street at home" was at least familiar with the democratic process.

What is bound to be surprising, in retrospect, is that an administrative apparatus pledged to "nation building," and to the instruction of Africans on "how to do it," should have been content with its political incompetence. Yet those in control of the "transfers of power" were in practice precisely those least able to measure the dangers ahead, and to advocate alternatives that might avoid such dangers or diminish them. It may be said that this was not their job, and that is true, especially when "decolonization" became a kind of *sauve qui peut* among administrations about to be disbanded. But political incompetence on the European side has as much a part in the story of decolonization as anything that can be attributed to the African side.

Some of the young entrants to the colonial service, during the 1950s before recruitment to it petered out, were later to have distinguished academic careers; but most of them would probably agree with remarks made by A.H.M. Kirk-Greene, who was one of them, about the deficiencies of their political preparation. He pointed out years later that "the colonial cadet was seldom if ever taught on his training course how to relate or interact with the representatives of that new phenomenon of the 1950s, the political party." More seriously, since bright young men and women learn fast if pointed in the right direction, they appear to have been invariably pointed in the wrong direction. " 'Politics' for the average British colonial administrator," writes Kirk-Greene in his fascinating retrospective of 1978, "was something of a dirty word, with 'politician' not far removed from 'trouble-maker.' "[8]

Or not really removed at all. On that same retrospective occasion, a conference of former colonial officials held at Oxford University, another notable senior official who had been deputy governor of Tanganyika (which became in 1964, with Zanzibar, the Union of Tanzania) recalled traveling there in 1957 with the then governor, Sir Edward Twining. Nineteen fifty-seven was just four years before Tanganyika became independent. It was a time, in short, when the credentials and potentials of African nation-statism, and those who would lead it, must have been, one might have thought, of the highest interest to colonial governors and their kind. During their travels together, the two men did indeed discuss the various persons and personalities who came within Governor Twining's interest and purview. Africans likely to become important as independence for Tanganyika now approached were considered in their talk, just as one would expect. So "Twining mentioned in passing a certain Julius Nyerere: 'a bit of a trouble-maker, I think,' he added. He told me [the official, that is, who was about to become deputy governor] that he [Twining] had let it be known among all his senior officers that he thought it would be best if they avoided contact with him [that is, with Nyerere] as far as possible, and did not receive him in their offices." But Nyerere was already the manifest high-flyer among Tanganyikan nationalists and, in 1961 at independence, would at once become their uncontested leader and spokesman. Yet it could not be said that Twining was an irresponsible or idle governor; on the contrary, he was then and afterward much praised, while the deputy governor in question told the Oxford conference that he regarded Twining as "a very great governor."[9]

If very great governors could not spot the difference between a "trouble-maker" and a future statesman of outstanding moral force and political sagacity, officials down the line were placed under a severe handicap. Again at that same conference of former officials, a senior officer in northern Nigeria told of his own initiation, as he put it, into the way that he should handle African politicians or persons of political importance. "One day the D[istrict] O[fficer] told me to get some practice and interview a local politician who had come to the Divisional Office. This was in one of the emirates [of Northern Nigeria]. The government messenger would be present to help me out. Learning from how I had seen the DO talk to political party members on previous occasions, I duly barked at the man, though by now my own knees were shaking as much as I hoped the politician's were. He slunk out of the office. 'Well,' I said triumphantly to the messenger, 'Will you tell the DO I did pretty well?' 'Not in the least,' came the reply, 'You forgot to order him to take his shoes off when coming into the DO's office.' "[10]

Given that the speaker could look back on a long career when recalling in 1978 this "initiation" into politics, the incident would have occurred during or soon after the Second World War, at a time, that is, when the advent of party politics in Africa was still some ten years ahead, at any rate in Northern Nigeria. Later, no doubt, politicians were no longer told to take their shoes off when visiting Britain's representative. But the British officials who made judgments and took decisions, while receiving local politicians with their shoes on, were officials whose training still belonged to the shoes-off period when politics had reeked in their nostrils. They found the adjustment understandably hard to make, added to which, in the new shoes-on period of "transfer of power" which began in the 1950s, one has the impression that senior officials generally nourished a more or less acrid resentment against Africans claiming to be competent in the mysteries of government. And this state of relationships "on the ground," more negative in some colonies, less so in others, goes some way to excusing the really extraordinary absence of any far-ranging debate, as between governors and governed, on the nature of the nation-statist future that now lay ahead.

If there was so little hard discussion about the future and its possible alternatives, this was essentially because there was no clear plan for imperial withdrawal. The imperial government generally in place in London was Conservative during most of the years before decolonization, and its personnel, like its voters, generally assumed that the empire was "forever." Colonial officials and advisers, better informed about reality, might have begun to canvass the idea that some of the colonies, at any rate in West Africa where there were no white settler minorities to muddy the waters, should probably move toward independence. But the day for that would still be distant. "Somewhere in West Africa within a century, within half a century, a new African state will be born," said an official report in 1945,[11] and there should be preparation for this improbable emergence. Little was made except, in the 1950s, under the pressure of events; and even this little was invariably couched in terms of a strategy of delay. "All the steps presented in a public relations manner as steps towards granting African independence," as was said somewhat later, "were in fact all steps argued for in private and

177

taken on the ground that it was essential to do this to prolong colonial rule."[12] As for the French, they opposed every such step in their African empire until the very last.

What the "nation builders" of the British Colonial Office understood as a duty was the need to ensure "continuity" in any steps that might be promoted with African self-government in view. Given their assumptions, this was entirely understandable: one assumption was that they knew better the needs of the future than any African could possibly know them; another was that Britain's empire, however "reformed," would still have much to give the motherland. The first assumption, as it were, fed into the second. That being so, constitutional reform in the colonies "was seen," in the retrospective view of Dennis Austin, the well-known historian of Ghana and the Gold Coast, "as enabling colonial rule to be more effective, not as hastening its demise."[13] This explains the otherwise surprising fact that colonial government became more and not less intensive. Far from enlarging conditions for African direct experience in the problems of government, "between 1947 and 1957 recruitment into the colonial service increased by more than 59 percent," but the recruitment was of British, not African, personnel. Up to the very eve of its actually happening, in other words, "the prospect of independence for each and every territory was quite remote."

And so it remained. As late as 1959 the British colonial secretary, Lennox Boyd, could still declare that in respect of East Africa he was "unable to envisage a time when it will be possible for any British government to surrender their ultimate responsibilities for the destinies and well-being of Kenya," something that was nonetheless going to happen only four years later.[14]

We have seen the similar nature of official attitudes toward the nationalists of Tanganyika next door. The evidence lay all around.

Back in 1947, arguing for gradualist "reform," Colonial Office liberals had put the case for the development of African local government in provincial councils and the like; these would "prepare the ground" for wider concessions of power at some unstated point in the years ahead. To this modest proposal Sir Philip Mitchell, then governor of Kenya, answered with a rejection out of hand, berating the London liberals for their ignorance and naïveté. "How primitive the state of these people is," he wrote to them about the Kenya Africans he governed, "and how deplorable the spiritual, moral and social chaos in which they are adrift are things which can perhaps only be fully realised by those who are in close personal touch with the realities of the situation."[15] The "vulgarity of such rhetoric," in a comment of Cranford Pratt's, "was avoided by the other East African governors, but they nevertheless expressed their general agreement with Mitchell. They had no sense that they were, or would soon be, under any nationalist pressure."[16]

Even when that pressure got through to eminent governors and officials, the notion that a truly postcolonial continent might be desirable was never on any imperial agenda. In his 1947 dispatch to London, rejecting provincial councils, Mitchell also wrote that "we are not here to create a succession of Bulgarias, but to develop and civilise this continent as part of what I may call Western European civilisation and economics." Yet it rapidly became clear in the 1950s, with the setting in of what Dennis Austin has called "the rush to decolonise," that the creation of "Bulgarias"—of suitably subordinate nation-states—was precisely what the colonial governments were "here" for, even while it certainly never occurred to anyone in power that the "neocolonialist" nation-state network they had in mind could be properly comparable with Moscow's network.

What Mitchell thought a mere illusion was precisely what came about. By 1963 each of the three major East African territories had declared for independence as so many "Bulgarias": Tanganyika in 1961, Uganda in 1962, and Kenya in 1963. Nyasaland, as Malawi, followed suit in 1964, and so did Northern Rhodesia as Zambia. Elsewhere the French, having lost their war in Algeria after awarding independence to Morocco and Tunisia (in 1956), backed away from all previous schemes and forecasts; in 1960, almost overnight, they recognized the independence of fourteen sub-Saharan colonies.

This gave rise to understandable African rejoicing as huge inherent problems were swallowed or thrust aside. In the realm of Islam, for example, canon law might continue to recognize only one and indivisible *Umma Muhamadiyya*, one family of Islam; but separate and separatist nation-state-forming movements nonetheless made headway against it. They had to do this, in the prominent Arabist G. E. von Grunebaum's striking phrase, "as hostile children of the West,"[17] and would eventually provoke an Islamic "fundamentalism" of explosive and therefore blind reaction. But they still marched forward as though meanwhile they were the manifest legatees of all that was desirable and right.

It is consequently fruitless to believe that the end of political empire was a program arranged and designed to give colonized peoples "the best possible start" to their independence. Much was said and done, true enough, to present the imperial withdrawal as a process planned and prepared in advance, and any subsequent mishaps and miseries were to be explained as entirely the fault of Africans failing to carry out "the plan." But the full extent of any plan, most obviously in the French empire, was to conserve as much as possible of the colonial legacy; and even that much of a plan, when perceived, looks like mere opportunism.

In the great example of Nigeria, for instance, local historians well qualified to judge have reached the conclusion that "no conscious British initiative to liquidate the empire was apparent at the Nigerian end."[18] Successive steps and constitutions transferring power simply went with the winds and tides of momentary pressure. The spokesmen of nation-statism were given their head, earlier in the nonsettler colonies, later in those with significantly large white settler minorities. They were then left to make the best they could of the "existing units of territory" in such ways as to ensure that these units remained separate from each other, no matter what arguments there might be, or might have been, for restructuring or federalizing them. Against the 1950s leaders of nationalism, the real count is not that they failed to foresee the traps and snares that lay ahead, but that they all too easily accepted what was offered to them. They accepted the colonial legacy—whether of frontiers or of bureaucratic dictatorship—on the rash assumption that they could master it. But as things turned out, it mastered them.

Critics have said that the pioneering nationalists of the 1950s should have better considered where they were heading and should have understood that nation-states fashioned from the structures and relationships of colonial states, and thereby pro-

181

duced from European and not from African history, were bound to be heading for trouble. This is asking a great deal of men and women to whom the lessons and examples of European history had been invariably presented as the sum and summit of all useful experience; moreover, as far as the crucial economic structures and relationships were concerned, these in the 1950s were little understood anywhere. Thoughtful analysts in Europe such as the late Henry Collins might draw attention to the long-term consequences of adverse terms of trade for African producers.[19] But these were awkwardly objective analysts from whom the orthodox did not take their cue. Their voices were heard with difficulty or else not heard at all.

Such considerations apart, it is a misreading of the history of those years to suppose that the nationalists, or at any rate the best of them, nourished any great illusions as to the obstructive nature of the colonial legacy they were going to accept. Its economic implications may have largely escaped them, just as these escaped their imperial rulers; but they thoroughly understood its political and moral implications, for it was from those implications that they, as the objects of colonial rule, had suffered. At the same time it needs to be recalled that any informed "looking ahead" was difficult or impossible if only because, to the very last, colonial governments in all the empires hugged closely to their chests whatever sound information their administrative files might contain. They camouflaged their social and economic problems with clouds of condescending propaganda. Or they simply denied that these problems existed. They preferred among the nationalists the boneheads to the brilliant, or at least the convenient to the awkwardly questioning. And they generally behaved as though every arrangement for decolonization must be expected in any case to end in tears.

No doubt one should bear in mind the poverty of nationalist analysis and the shortage of long-term thinking: what Amílcar Cabral, early in the 1960s, would deplore as a lack of ideological thought. It counted for much, and it confirmed the eventual crisis of the nation-statist project. Once again, though, one has to remember the compelling weight and influence of that project. Like it or not, the leading nationalists found themselves obliged by imperialist policies, fashioned in London and Paris, "to seek independence within the existing power unit" of their colony, rather than in any more rational or historically logical territorial unit, in the view of the late James Coleman, among the earliest and best of the American observers of the period. This followed on "the realities of the power structure" and the "practical necessity" which these imposed.[20] Each colony must accept its own separate and sovereign independence: each, however improbably, must become its own nation-state, or at least pretend to become it.

Some among the leading nationalists, as I have indicated earlier, demurred. They argued for a different destination in multistate sovereignties of a regional or subregional nature. This would be widely forgotten in the futile anarchy that began to develop in the 1970s, and the anarchy would be laid at the doors of a purely African irresponsibility or incompetence. There would certainly be much of both, but not during the 1950s. It might be "trouble-making" for Julius Nyerere, years before national flags were hoisted over new sovereign states, to look ahead and recommend steps in preparation for an East

African federation of Uganda, Kenya, and Tanganyika. And it might be "idealist chatter" for nationalist movements in 1958 to launch a regional organization, the Pan-African Freedom Movement of East and Central Africa, aiming first at independence and then at federation. But these were nonetheless political initiatives of foresight and imagination. Nothing came of them. But with active official support and promotion, something might have come of them. That something, one can argue, might have averted a measure of the sorrows which came after.

It might be visionary in 1946 for nationalist delegates from twelve French colonies in West and Equatorial regions to meet in congress, at Bamako, and form a political movement dedicated to the realization of two large independent federations instead of twelve nation-states. It might be utopian for the constitution of independent Ghana (1957) and its near neighbor independent Guinea (1958) to allow for reductions of national sovereignty in favor of federal union; and certainly nothing came of that. Yet, again, something might have come of it if the British and the French had backed such tentative moves toward a restructuring of frontiers. But the British and the French could see no advantage in doing anything of that sort.

In reality, and in the light of all that has happened since, it appears that these gestures to federalism of one degree or another were neither visionary nor utopian—up to the point, that is, at which the separate sovereignties were fixed and declared, each with its attendant group of beneficiaries-in-waiting. After that point, as Nyerere duly warned, any reorganization of the territorial map would become ever more difficult and even impossible. Each group of beneficiaries-in-waiting would then stand firm on its own sovereignty. Each would shout loudly against any threat to the attendant rewards—or spoils—of power and office. This of course is what was going to happen. But the fact remains that it did not happen while the trend toward federation had strength and influence.

And it did not happen then because the social aspects of anticolonial struggle still had command of the national aspects. Down the line of agitation and organization, among the mass of rural and urban supporters of the anticolonial movements, there was small sign of any developing loyalty or attachment to this or that colony-turned-nation. What the multitudes wanted, by all the evidence, was not a flag for the people or an anthem for the people, nearly so much as they wanted bread for the people, and health and schools for the people, while caring precious little, as these same multitudes would over-whelmingly prove in the years ahead, about winning frontiers for the people. The jubilant crowds celebrating independence were not inspired by a "national consciousness" that "demanded the nation," any more than were the Romanian peasants and their coevals in the nation-states crystallized some decades ear-lier from Europe's old internal empires. They were inspired by the hope of more and better food and shelter.

As long as the "social" held its lead over the "national," this continued to be so. But it did not continue to hold that lead for long. Once the national sovereignties were declared, the arena was fixed for rivalry over the resources within that arena; and the rivalry was bound to become abrasive, and therefore divi-sive, if only because the resources were in short supply. This divisive rivalry was then discovered to be "tribalism": that is, the reinforcement of kinship or other local-scale alliances competing against other such alliances. It may of course be

185

argued that a "race for the spoils" must have occurred in any case, and to some extent this must be true in newly formed states still weak in their structures. No conceivable postcolonial dispensation could ever have worked without a great deal of stress and strain, given Africa's condition after a century of violent dispossession. But the argument is itself weak. This postcolonial "tribalism" flourished less because the states were weak than because their organization into separatist nation-states gave full rein to elitist rivalries.

With separate and rival independences, the social soon ceased to prevail over the national in the dynamics of postcolonialism. With this, the rules of the game were changed and, once changed, could not be changed back again. Not for another thirty years or so would the sacred and immutable nature of this nation-statism begin to be seriously questioned. Meanwhile, the concert of beneficiaries, no longer in waiting, would make sure that its spokesmen, appropriately assembled after 1963 in an Organization of African Unity which, in practice, guaranteed disunity, were all assured of due access to power and privilege. The elites identified by Awolowo back in 1946 had only to proceed upon their way and assume their "birthright."

Of the other European empires in Africa there is nothing useful to be said in this context. Neither the Belgian nor the Portuguese nor the Spanish political establishments gave a single serious thought to issues of decolonization until these issues were thrust upon them at five minutes to midnight, or later still. Billed as Belgium's great national success and pride, the vast Congo territory was supposed to continue to be governed, as before, until some point in the future so remote as to be realistically unthinkable, or at any rate thought about. The

Portuguese and Spanish regimes were organs of systemic repression at home, and duly reproduced the same miseries in Africa, allowing few civic rights to their own citizens and none worth having to their "natives." Alternatives of policy or method could never be a matter for debate among them, but only a provocation of the political police.

All this was no doubt inherent in the difficulty of hauling the societies of Portugal and Spain into the twentieth century. But what may still remain surprising was the truly shameless self-righteousness with which the late colonial years were allowed to slide past, the bland complacency or outright cowardice of governors' reports or the gruesome fantasies of ministerial utterance: in short, the absence among those Iberian tyrants of any sense that history can be more than habitual stagnation. There, with a vengeance, the "national" had long since triumphed over the "social," and the donkey's bray of an extremist nationalism was just about all that was left.

With an end to these empires in Africa—a lengthy process, however, from the decolonization of Libya in 1951 to that of Namibia in 1990—there came about a refiguring of the continental map that was closely comparable in its structure, however greatly different in style and incident, with the refiguring of the map of Central and Eastern Europe after 1918, at the end of the Austrian, tsarist Russian, and Ottoman empires.

The peace treaties of Versailles and elsewhere likewise transformed the collapsed internal European empires into a plurality of nation-states. As it would be in Africa some forty years later, in each of these the euphorias of national liberation were splendidly rhetorical. But one may well think that resultant problems were a good deal more difficult for the decolonized African peoples than for those of Europe. The new states of Central and Eastern Europe were often in some sense old states as well, states shaped and inspired by preimperialist and native histories of their own. That might not be true of all of them. But all of them could discover, in their cultures, the notion of a statelike identity, even those who, like the Slovaks or the Albanians, had lived for centuries under a more or less dismissive foreign rule.

Poles and Bulgarians and others could claim with reason that their new independences of 1919 were restorations of what had been taken from them by force, and demand guarantees that an old life could begin again. But the old states in Africa were swallowed entirely into new states as though these old states had never existed save as quaint survivals from the "savage backwoods" of a deplorable past. And this was done, as we have seen, to a point at which the concept or sense of nationalism, of nation-statism, was boosted as "Europe's last gift to Africa."[21]

One can't but think that Europe's "last gift," in fact, was in the nature of bad or incompetent advice. Nationalists about to take power, or already in the earliest years of having taken power, were obliged to apply for guidance to experts or specialists from the various "motherlands" of Europe. Specialists thereupon arrived, naturally with strong opinions of their own, and proceeded to apply their nostrums whether or not they had deeply thought about the problems these were supposed to solve. On top of this, the nationalists inherited a disconcerting situation in which what was said was rather seldom what was meant.

In Britain's case, for example, aid for "colonial development and welfare" was held to be a pledge of disinterested help. However mutilated by her immense war effort, Britain would come to the aid of her colonized peoples, would invest structural capital now that they were setting out on their own, and would stand by with disinterested counsel. The major investments, as it came about, were in projects intended primarily to meet British import needs. Perhaps by national bias, I doubt if the insistence on British generosity betokened insincerity. But it certainly betokened a naïve ignorance of reality and it led, as in the fruitless case of "Tanganyika groundnuts," to unavoidable incompetence and waste of assets, undertaken as it was in complete disregard of ecological realities, not least rainfall.

As for official and business France, the Cambridge economist David Fieldhouse tells us that "the essential feature of the post-1945 French imperial economy was that the French government was using the power of the state to enable the colonies to buy a range of French consumer goods for which there would have been no alternative overseas market"; and, he adds perhaps more damningly, to buy "capital goods which [the colonies] could probably have bought more cheaply elsewhere."[22] This artificial pushing of French exports might seem forgivable at a time when France was struggling to recover from four years of enemy occupation and spoliation, but it was done, in practice, by large injections of French taxpayers' money. These enabled the colonies to balance their budgets, according to Fieldhouse, "by artificially increasing the price that colonial producers could get in France," another effect of which was to enable colonial producers "to pay for the equally inflated price of French exports." The French taxpayer as distinct from the French investor was obliged to foot a massively "uneconomic" bill, sustaining

French enterprises "which might otherwise have been forced to modernise or get out of business." Whether African populations actually gained, on balance, is another question. One certainty, however, is that the colonial trading pattern thus reinforced was one in which African populations, in the little polities of francophone Africa, were to become increasingly at the mercy of export-import terms of trade settled on the world market without reference to African needs or potentials.

More generally, events in the 1950s revealed what had not been understood before: that the colonial legacy in its structural framework was not, as imperialist propaganda had invariably insisted, a blessing of benevolent paternalism but a coil of problems pregnant with serious (if as yet unadmitted) crises of malfunction. The "transfer of power," in short, was above all a transfer of crisis. For the 1940s had confirmed, especially during the harsh years of the Second World War, a "flight from the countryside" launched initially in the Depression years of the 1930s; and this implacable shift of population from countryside to urban periphery would soon be quickened and enlarged beyond all control by a rapidly rising rate of population growth. As the countryside increasingly emptied, the newly "urbanized" were consigned to shantytowns in places of largely waterless desolation on the fringes of European quarters; and "urban unemployment," meaning in practice a fight for survival at the lowest possible levels of subsistence, became the curse that would afterward spread an epidemic scourge of relentless poverty.

Here was a crisis of structural change that nothing seemed able to cope with. Thoughtful colonial officials saw it and were appalled but felt themselves, as much evidence confirms, like

King Canute and the advancing tide: they might order it to turn back and ebb, and this they were regularly instructed to do, but were perfectly aware that the waters would not listen. In the vast but otherwise not untypical case of the Belgian Congo, an enormous territory enclosing the whole central part of the continent, as many as one in six Africans were already living in 1946 outside the rural areas that had produced them;[23] by 1953 the proportion was one in four, and soon afterward it would be larger still. Africa was ceasing to be a rural continent, or rather, a continent in which rural interests were accepted as paramount.

What the nationalists of the 1950s inherited was thus a crisis of social disintegration. By 1955 it was already palpable: "There is no doubt of the disintegration," I wrote in *The African Awakening*. "It is patent in a thousand ways, in the breakdown of tribal customs, in the astonishing inflation of bride-price, in a vast spread of prostitution. It has painful results for African agriculture. It speeds the ruin of village life."[24] These observations were really an understatement, but the major consequence came clear a little later. By the early 1960s there had appeared on the scene a deepening structural malfunction—between an impoverished countryside and an indigent "urbanism"—that was to bulk ever more largely on the agenda of the 1970s.

Increasingly, it was going to be the urban areas that would settle the priorities of governmental policy: a still largely rural continent was going to become, steadily, the victim of irresistibly expanding urban populations. The consequences of this for continental food production were already seen as a possible danger for the future, even if the probable size of this danger was not yet evident. "Already, by the 1960s, Black Africa was having to import substantial quantities of basic foods . . . with

191

a total cereal importation of 1,177,000 tons in 1961–63."[25] Then it began to be said that Africa was in a crisis of "overpopulation." Yet Africa even in the 1980s, with some 450 million inhabitants, or at least triple the population of a century earlier, would still be relatively underpopulated when compared with other continents. What looked like a crisis of "overpopulation" was really a crisis of underproduction of food and maldistribution of goods. The reasons for this imbalance and incompetence cannot be explained without grappling with the colonial legacy.

Outside in the wide and "well-informed" world, such things were of course noticed. They could scarcely not be. But they were generally seen as aspects of a naturally difficult but unavoidable period of "transition." It was thus explained in Western Europe, and also for a long time in North America where, one might have thought, the problems inherent in preferring nation-statism to federalism might have been well perceived. Everywhere it was in any case assumed that the essential healthiness of the colonial economies—and all the colonial powers, even the Portuguese, had long assured themselves and each other of this essential healthiness—would maximize the gains of independence: how otherwise, after all, would the bounties of colonial rule become manifest? All that was required was prudent continuity.

In this advocacy of prudent continuity the general influence of the United States, whether by policy preference or academic recommendation, was in this period an unexpected source of coming disaster, not in terms of any direct administrative or military intervention along colonial lines of action, nor in terms of any lack of financial aid, for America was in this and in some other respects a generous and benign source of aid. What was increasingly destructive of new thought and initiative after 1950 was a growing tendency for official America, and certainly academic America, to see Africa's needs in terms of the global preferences of U.S. policy: in terms, that is, of America's fear of whatever might be seen or interpreted as radical innovation.

That the colonial powers opposed radical innovation, whether political or social or economic, could be no surprise to anyone; it was what they had always done in knee-jerk defense of their imperial interests. But that the United States should do this was something new, or certainly was received as something new, to which leading nationalists reacted with a puzzled obedience. It left them with a sense of disorientation. Wasn't America the great radical innovator of the nineteenth century? Weren't America's policies of innovation at the root of America's immense success and power as a civilization? Surely the answers were yes; and yet it was now seen, in practice, that continuity with colonial policy was America's preferred option. This would be confirmed most painfully later on, in America's long campaign of subversion against an Angolan republic classed as "radical"; but it was a clear enough tendency even in the late 1950s. Continuity in policy might mean continuity in underlying dislocations, evidenced already by falling food production, by a deepening conflict of interests between town and country and, soon enough, by a failure of existing political structures to cope with instabilities now increasingly flagrant. Yet the stronger claims of what was then known as "Cold War policy," essentially arising from U.S.-Soviet rivalries or what were perceived as such, continued to forbid any far-reaching innovation.

In so far as American policy-makers listened to European advice, and one may think that they listened more often than was wise, this was the European message they received. As late as 1961, with "Cold War policy" a dominant influence in London, a senior British Foreign Office official and adviser could affirm with every confidence that "in spite of our substantial commercial and other interests in Africa, the latter's chief political importance for the West derived from the Cold War."[26] What this came to mean, in practice, was a resolute determination to oppose and if possible prevent any development, whether political or economic, that could seem likely to undermine Africa's subordination to the "world market": that is, to the continued postcolonial primacy of the relationships of the colonial era. Only this adequately explains the almost frantic efforts that were made, from the time of Ghana's independence in 1957, to harry, isolate, and destroy any influence that went in a contrary direction.

This was done in the name of "keeping the Russians out." Whatever threatened or could seem to threaten continuity with the relationships of the later colonial era was labeled as a product of Soviet subversion. But the Russians, no matter how much they may have wished to upset Western ploys and policies, were in no position to do it. This was partly because Moscow was able to know almost nothing at first hand about Africa until the early 1960s, and even then it had to go through a learning period. But more important, Moscow's own policy was no less neocolonialist in its content, whether in terms of the commercial deals they now began to make, or in those of their "aid" agreements, or in their presumptions about the future. Africa, to save itself, would have to march along the "socialist" road laid down by an all-knowing authority in Moscow: even while the wiser heads in Moscow, some of them in the newly formed

Africa Institute of the Soviet Academy of Sciences, now began to see that realities in Africa were not at all the same as Moscow's textbooks said they were.

The real weakness of the Soviet position in Africa, and toward Africa, was never admitted at this time, either in the East or in the West. It could not be admitted in the East because this would have questioned the infallibility of Stalinist doctrine. And it could not be admitted in the West because admitting it would have undermined the assumptions of the Cold War and, in doing that, would have given fresh latitude for African questioning of the postcolonial dispensation. Once again, in other words, there was little ground for any open-minded debate on basic issues of decolonization. Later on, moving from its initial enterprise of investigating Africa, Soviet policy usually became a compromise between a more or less completely imperialist-minded KGB, operating as the subversive arm of Moscow's ambitions, and the requirements of a Stalinist theoretical orthodoxy which possessed no clear contact with the facts of everyday life. Even that degree of social idealism which had survived Stalinism, in other words, was vitiated by bureaucratic self-interest. All this helps explain the jagged shifts and contradictions in Moscow's dealings with Africa. Defense of an Angolan republic against the military aggressions of a racist South African government and army went hand in hand, in the very same years, with the buttressing of an Ethiopian militarist dictatorship which could only do immense damage to the whole of the Horn of Africa.

This is looking ahead a little from the beginnings of postcolonial independence. Meanwhile, as the old imperial flags came down, the mood was not euphoric but it was certainly optimistic. And there were many reasons for optimism. The old empires were falling fast and would not be restored. The social freedoms that had provided the real magnet behind nationalism were making themselves increasingly felt; and the grim silence of the colonial years was already shattered by a hubbub of plans and schemes for a more favorable future. People even talked of a "new Africa," and yet it did not sound absurd. A whole continent seemed to have come alive again, vividly real, bursting with creative energies, claiming its heritage in the human family, and unfolding ever more varied or surprising aspects of itself. The world became a larger and a happier place.

It was going to stay like that for a while. In a large sense it has continued like that: in the sense that not even the worst news has been able to cancel out the tremendous central gain of anticolonial independence, perhaps the only gain at the end of the day, which has sprung from the reaffirmation of Africa's humanity.

The Black Man's Burden

THE YEARS of the 1960s were a time of exciting self-discovery for all those persons in Africa—and they were by now a significant minority—for whom the nation-statist project not only promised a real social and political development, but did so with the force of an irrepressible encouragement. The barriers of colonial racism were thoroughly cast down, or were in the course of being so, and the sense of liberation from a grossly limiting bondage was real and expansive, even among those for whom the ideas of nationalism had small attraction.

Probably there was no single moment after which this optimism began to seem naïve, or perhaps as much as a little shameful, and was replaced by "disappointment" or "disillusionment" in the headline jargon of newspaper currency. In some countries that "moment" had well passed by early in the 1970s: in Nigeria, certainly, with the miseries of the civil war of 1967–70, in Ghana with self-destructions that ensued upon the overthrow of the Nkrumah regime in 1966, in Uganda with the spread of kinship "tribalism," and so on elsewhere. But in other countries the notion of "disillusionment" in the 1970s could only seem absurd, and in truth was absurd. In the colonies of Portugal, for example, the 1960s seemed then, and I think will be so remembered, as a time of extraordinary and sometimes heroic achievement by nationalist pioneers who would win their anticolonial wars in 1974–75. In various circumstances the same was true of other white settler colonies, and it was certainly true of South Africa, where savage repression was already beginning to be the prelude to the emergence of new and more effective means of anticolonial struggle. The optimism of the 1960s had much to nourish it.

Looking back, one can easily see that this optimism nonetheless rested, and had to rest, on uncertain ground. There continued, for one thing, the general situation that had characterized the late colonial period, signaled above all by an insufficient analysis of everyday reality. There was much sociological or politicoscientific research and writing which intended to come to grips with that reality. But its practitioners were usually hampered, if they were orthodox adherents of the philosophies of "free enterprise," by the unwritten but often mandatory assumptions of the Cold War or, if they were Marxists of one kind or another, by comparable but opposite assumptions. With some partial exceptions, no peasant societies in Africa had been studied except in an anthropological dimension not concerned with developmental potentials; and it may not be an exaggeration to say that no such potentials were thought to exist in peasant societies. The newly sprawling towns, true enough, were beginning to be studied—by K. A. Busia, in a rare example even as early as 1950—but as problems for administrative correction rather than as real harbingers of structural change.[1]

Among the Western orthodox, perhaps most damagingly of all, there was little or no will or ability to come to grips with the facts of the colonial legacies from invasion and dispossession.

Given this inability, there was a generally accepted belief that the invasions and dispossessions, however morally regrettable they might be thought to have been, had at least made "development" possible for the first time. What was needed now was simply to democratize the colonial legacies and all would be well. This belief that "development" was now at last possible, the detritus of Africa's unregenerate past having been thoroughly if brutally swept away, may explain a good deal about the general conviction—whether among nationalist leaders, or among the burgeoning ranks of specialist advisers and planners now piling in from Europe or America—that rapid expansions of wealth and mass consumption were not only attainable but could be of an almost automatic nature. I agree with Fieldhouse in thinking that a basic proposition about the 1960s must be that "almost everyone expected too much." The very success and impetus of anticolonial struggles certainly gave strength to this expectation.

Historians may have had their doubts. If so, they were not listened to. Progress must depend, as every kind of plan and published perspective rapidly insisted, upon "modernization"; and "modernization," as it at once appeared, had to mean the wholesale import of non-African scenarios and solutions. The old recaptive–Cape Coast perspective was agreed to have got it right: Africa would prosper upon condition of rejecting itself. The future was not to grow out of the past, organically and developmentally, but from an entirely alien dispensation. And the cultural contradiction in this, it must be said, was barely so much as noticed. While triumphal slogans of "Africa for the Africans" rang out from the rooftops, innovations were to be forms of self-alienation. Being such, their sociocultural penetration was to remain persistently shallow: as would be seen most tragically when warlord mayhem burst upon the scene in later years. The republic of Liberia may have been "civilized"—in perhaps the most tragic example—by a century and more of imported scenarios and solutions. But that same republic, in the 1980s, would duly produce scenes of unprecedented barbarism.

This has been a degradation which seemed unthinkable in the early years of postcolonial independence. As African reassertion thrust away the psychological and practical hang-ups created by invasion and dispossession over many decades, the progress of the "outside world" came flooding in, and the results were impressive. The new universities might be extreme forms of the British model, "ivory towers" of elitism suitably removed from the proletarian hubbub of city streets, and garbed in gowns and "high table" ritual; but still they were valid universities where none, save for the odd exception, had ever existed before. And they were fed by new secondary schools using new textbooks and teaching new lessons. Technical and vocational training became available for the first time. Literacy in English or French began to be the possession of large numbers of young people. Books and newspapers became a common thing. All this understandably nourished optimism.

Cities began to acquire some semblance of urbanity. Paved roads became many. Automobiles multiplied. Public services of valuable kinds, whether in health or the means of marketing goods and the provision of amenities, steadily improved. Businesses and banks began to emerge on native foundations and encouraged the belief that an independent African capitalism might be possible and even easy to achieve. Qualified men and women came forward to represent their professions at home and abroad, and often did it with notable distinction. That all this should increasingly divide the elites or beneficiaries from the bulk of the population seemed unavoidable, and seemed, moreover, not to matter. A "new Africa" had been prophesied, and a "new Africa" was surely on the threshold. The later notion that "independence had failed" would have seemed absurd if anyone had cared to advance it, but no one save colonial-minded nostalgics did advance it. The few had expected an easy ride to levels of "high mass consumption," and they might be disappointed. The many had hoped for no such thing but simply for some direct and practical improvement, or for chances of improvement, and they saw reason to feel moderately satisfied. If there was beginning to be noise and tumult, even this could seem a vast improvement on the silence of the colonial years.

So there was much to suggest that the nation-statist formula and pattern were proving a success. The presidential and bureaucratic self-inflations and cavortings were still to come; meanwhile, the introduction of Africa to world forums in the shape of nation-states, easily named and more or less easily identified, was a considerable and even necessary convenience. The "developed world," at least, was accustomed to peoples who belonged to nations, and it could only seem right and natural that Africans should now have built nations to belong to, even if the claim of these new nations to be nation-states on the European pattern had yet to be made good. But Rome was not built in a day, and time would do its work. What was meanwhile impressive, and increasingly felt to be so, was that these new nation-states appeared to have few serious quarrels among themselves. After the Organization of African Unity began its work in 1963, this favorable impression deepened. For apart from a few intractable territorial disputes, which could be regarded as exceptional, the new nation-states had settled easily into their colonial frontiers, however artificial and irrational these frontiers might once have been. This great proliferation of national sovereignties was apparently not going to be a source of strife, but rather the reverse.

I thought so myself, even while I should have known better. On the day the Gold Coast Colony and Protectorate became the sovereign nation-state of Ghana in 1957, I happened to be sitting in the marketplace of the city of Kumase. Seated beside me was a handsome man with the dignity of years and self-respect, shining black of skin as Africans seldom are, who, upon our falling into conversation, told me that he was an ivory trader from Douala in Cameroun. His business, he said, was far-ranging and took him as far as the upper waters of the Senegal River in the country of that name, almost half a continent distant from Douala. How many frontiers he had been obliged to cross in selling his ivory, how many customs posts and officials he had needed to evade! But now, I commented, all that will be different. Now the despised colonial frontiers are proper national frontiers, or soon will be, and people will respect them and the laws of sovereignty. "You will have to adjust your methods of trade." I remember his smile of pity for my innocence, but he simply said, "Ah, do you think so?"

His skepticism was to prove well justified. The official frontiers would be unofficially ignored, and with every good reason in historical equity. For the colonial frontiers had been carved through ancient zones of regional trade, and men had naturally found ways of evading their obstruction. This is what was going to happen again, and massively as the years went by. No matter how convenient it would be for nationalist elites and beneficiaries to present themselves as presiding over solidly constructed states, these states were going to be very leaky vessels. Smuggling, in many cases, was going to be an overwhelming factor in many of the new national economies. The point is worth insisting on.

"Like most frontiers in Africa today," comments Jean Suret-Canale, the leading historian of the republic of Guinea, formerly the French colony of that name, "those inherited by Guinea from the colonial partition are completely arbitrary. They do not reflect the limits of natural regions, nor the limits of separate ethnic groups. They were shaped in their detail by the chances of conquest or of compromise between colonial powers."[2] These Guinea frontiers might acquire a certain rationale along their central axis between the port of Conakry and the internal market center of Kankan; but large zones on either side of this north-south spine were, he adds, simply tacked on without really belonging to it. These tacked-on zones during the colonial period had been "ends of the world" where nothing happened or was supposed to happen, save that law and order insisted on the utter quiescence of their numerous inhabitants: which meant, in practice, their stagnation.

But then, after the Second World War and a shifting of the colonial logjam, there had come the "opening" of these peripheral zones with roads capable of taking motor vehicles, and the peripheral zones were drawn within the reach of economic development. Yet the centers of that economic development for these peripheral zones were not within the frontiers of Guinea:

they were Dakar, Senegal, for the westerly among them and, for the easterly, Monrovia, Liberia, or Abidjan in the Ivory Coast.

Rational development of the economy of the new nation-state of Guinea, regarded as a sovereign "unit of development," had to be accordingly difficult. To sever these peripheral zones from their natural but external partners asked, in practice, for the impossible. For "what control can be expected of a handful of customs officers deprived of motor vehicles or, if they have any, obliged to use them on the one road that goes through their frontier post: and this when they have to operate along hundreds of kilometres of frontier crossed only by footpaths?"[3] Nor could stiff disciplines of monetary control be much help. "After 1960," continues Suret-Canale, "inconvertibility of the Guinea currency," introduced in order to achieve control of smuggling, "lends a new force to illegal trade: capital savings which can no longer make their escape in cash simply do it in kind," and again there could be, in practice, no efficient check on this. Then why not call on the remedy of patriotism, and apply to the nationalist loyalties of all these numerous peoples in zones peripheral or otherwise? And this of course was tried: in Guinea, for example, by applying to village committees and youth organizations and local militias, and asking them to destroy those very networks of smuggling upon which their local welfare was known to depend. Reams of exhortation were written and spoken on the subject. But the thing could not be done. And Guinea, in this respect, was a widely and increasingly typical example.

The years of independence showed rapidly that the arbitrary nature of the colonial frontiers was in no primary sense a reason for structural frustration: they could be ignored, and usually they were. The roots of nation-statist discord lay elsewhere.

Once in power, the nationalist elites had to face a painful contradiction between theory and fact. Theory supposed that the surging tides of anticolonial nationalism, unquestionably democratic as they were in sentiment and composition, would flow quietly into "party-political" compartments provided by the approved parliamentary models of Britain and France. These compartments would be expected to contain and represent the diverse group-interests of the body politic, and resolve their different claims by appropriate alliance between parties or compromise between parties. Governments would rise and fall according to the rules of parliamentary tolerance. Human frailties might interrupt the due unfolding of events, but would be held reasonably in check by consensus of the general interest. That is what theory said.

But fact said otherwise. Fact said that the British and French models derived from, and were inseparable from, a society already divided into established social classes. Above all, these models were dependent for their effectiveness upon the hegemony of widely spread "middle strata" capable of dominating society and its economic sources of wealth; and these indispensable "middle strata"—whether "high bourgeois" or "middle bourgeois" or even "petty bourgeois"—were precisely what the histories of Britain and France had produced over the past 150 years. Latterly, these histories had also produced another class, the "working class." They had found great difficulty in fitting this "new class" into the parliamentary compromise; but this, too, they had more or less managed to achieve. Parliamentary government might shudder and tremble from time to time, but could survive and prevail.

Fact in Africa therefore had to quarrel with theory. For the history of Africa over the previous 150 years, or much more, had not produced a society divided into easily recognizable and operable social classes. This might have been about to begin to happen in precolonial states, or nation-states such as Asante where economic development, as we have seen, was in the early stages of promoting private capitalist enterprise. But such cases were rare, and in any case their degree of "class crystallization" was immature. What African history had much more clearly promoted, above all where trade with Europe had become a widely controlling influence, were regional and territorial rivalries or combinations of interest.

These regional or territorial interests were what now flowed into the "party-political" compartments of the parliamentary structure. Often, though not always, they assumed an ethnic guise, especially wherever ethnic groupings or nationalities were numerous and economically expansive. Largely by European misinterpretation, the resultant conflict or combination of interests was labeled tribalism: Europeans had supposed that Africans lived in "tribes"—a word of no certain meaning—and that "tribal loyalties" were the only, and primitive, stuff of African politics. Colonial rule had worked on this assumption, dividing Africans into "tribes" even when these "tribes" had to be invented. But appearances were misleading.

What rapidly developed was not the politics of tribalism, but something different and more divisive. This was the politics of clientelism. What tribalism had supposed was that each "tribe" recognized a common interest represented by common spokespersons, and there was thus the possibility of a "tribal unity" produced by agreement between "tribal representatives." But clientelism—the "Tammany Hall approach"—almost at once led to a dogfight for the spoils of political power, for it meant, as Chris Allen has neatly explained, that "politicians at regional and national level gained and reproduced the support of local leaders by allocating to them state resources over which [these politicans] had influence or control. Each attempted to maximise this support and his access to resources in competition with rival politicians."[4]

This kind of race for the spoils of power or of political office (usually the same thing) became the motive force of these supposedly parliamentary systems. That had once been equally the case in Britain and France: but in those cases the crystallization of society into nonregional and nonterritorial social classes, together with the structures of interclass compromise promoted by the passage of time and the hegemonic influence of capitalism, enabled the British and the French to build a multiparty system with a nationally legitimate character. This was to prove so little feasible in Africa that a Nigerian parliamentary constitution of 1990, seeking a way out of military rule but despairing of the multiparty systems of the clientelist dogfight, actually provided for Nigeria to have, by government decree, only two political parties: one to be in power, and one to be in opposition, with the presumption (far from widely shared) that Box would duly and peaceably alternate with Cox. Generally, the nation-states of Africa have had to endure clientelist "single-party rule" with all its openings to dictatorship, or else "multiparty rule," which has simply led to other forms of clientelist corruption.

Inherent conflicts of theory and fact were worsened by another contradiction for which the nationalists were in no way responsible, and about which they could in any case do little. Theory, as the new nation-states took shape, said that government was to be democratic. The people would meet, discuss, and decide; and government would reflect all this. But fact again said something altogether different: it said that for as long as these countries had been colonies, government had always been by rigid dictatorship. Fact said that colonial powers had invariably ruled by decree, and decree had been administered by an authoritarian bureaucracy to which any thought of people's participation was damnable subversion.

Fact went on to say that the new nation-states inherited the dictatorship and not the democracy, and that anyone who thought it wasn't so had better have his head examined. The systems that were "taken over" might vary in detail and culture, but all of them—from the British and French through to the Belgian and Portuguese and Spanish—supposed that the actual work of government, and all the crucial decisions depending on it and from it, would be exercised by a bureaucracy trained and tested in authoritarian habits and practices. And this acute rigidity was made all the more immovable by another fact: that no colonial government had ever, anywhere, devolved any noticeable quantity of power to democratic forms of local government. Chiefly hierarchies had here and there been given powers of local government, as in Northern Nigeria: but never as organs of democracy.

So the practical outcome, the factual outcome, had to be authoritarian even when the nationalists wished it to be democratic. Bureaucracy ruled together with clientelism, and gradually became much the same thing. With all this the actual political content of these nation-states narrowed into groups and persons with command over, or at least access to, income-yielding resources—against all those other groups and persons, a numerical majority, who could be milked of such resources. And this in turn meant, as things worked out, a deepening opposition between the interests of the cities and the interests of the rural areas. Effective political power sat in the cities, whether as the seat of clientelist leaders or as clients of those leaders, and this trend became ever stronger as the cities grew ever larger. In these circumstances, authoritarian state power went together with expanding bureaucracies: that is, with hugely increasing quantities of persons who in one way or another looked to the state for patronage; and the ideal became not so much to occupy a job as to occupy a wage.

The urban tail increasingly wagged the rural dog. States which relied for their notional solvency on foreign subventions all the more readily accepted the result. In the little equatorial republic of Congo—"Congo-Brazzaville" to distinguish it from its much bigger neighbor "Congo-Kinshasa" (ex–Belgian Congo, and later Zaire)—the size of the state-paid bureaucracy grew continuously. The case was typical. All such persons more or less clustered idly in the capital city or one of its satellites, together with armed forces far larger than required to meet any conceivable threat to the state. And all of these, directly or indirectly, lived off "foreign aid" and the surplus extracted from an increasingly impoverished rural community, whose interests were shoved ever more painfully to the end of the line.[5]

* * *

Patently obvious in the 1970s, and due to become excruciating in the 1980s, the results were destructive of the national unity that had been expected to produce a balanced progress. No matter what experiments were attempted, either as "capitalist" or as "socialist" or a mixture of the two, this evolving conflict of interests between city and countryside led to declining food production, whether through city-countryside terms of trade that advantaged the city consumer against the village producer, or through plain neglect of state investment in useful infrastructure such as rural feeder roads and the like. This was seen, condemned, and regretted. But the record shows how extremely difficult it was to reverse the trend.

For again the trend was part of the colonial inheritance. Ghana provided the classic example when still a colony. Through the mechanism of a state marketing board, the British in Ghana (then Gold Coast) had regularly milked the producers of cocoa, the country's most valuable export product, of a large part of their surplus: in other words, they had paid cocoa farmers notably less than the value of the cocoa when exported to the world market. This had been justified on the grounds that the difference between the price paid by the state marketing board to the farmer and the price received by the board from foreign buyers would be held in a "reserve" which could be drawn upon by the farmers whenever the world price fell in value. In practice, the "reserve" was simply added to Britain's sterling assets in London. But now it was said, after Ghana achieved internal self-government in 1951, that the accumulation of a "reserve" from cocoa sales should be maintained, but used for the benefit of infrastructural modernization, for "national development," no-

THE BLACK MAN'S BURDEN

tably in the promotion of urban industry. The farmers, in short, would continue to be milked of their surplus.

This could be wise policy, given the urgent need for infrastructural modernization after the ravaging colonial years, provided that it were moderately done, provided that the goose that laid the golden eggs of cocoa were kept in robust good health. But the newly autonomous government and its foreign (mainly British) advisers appear to have seen no virtue in such moderation. They continued as before. Between 1947 and 1954, for example, payments to cocoa farmers amounted in total to no more than 48.6 percent of the sums actually received for cocoa sold abroad. What the farmers were getting for their work amounted, in practice, to 37 percent of average world prices. Not being fools, the farmers objected. They agitated for a better price. But they did not receive it. In a crucial decision of 1954, the prelude to years of upheaval and eventual devastation of what had been the world's greatest cocoa-producing agriculture, the government insisted on freezing the price paid to farmers at 72 shillings a load, or less than half the price the farmers had asked for.[6]

It was a decision that was to symbolize the continuing and costly triumph of the "city" over the "village." Part of that price has had to be paid in a reliance on imports of foreign food into a continent which had always been self-sufficient in food. Disgusted by the state's indifference or hostility—that is, the city's indifference or hostility—countless rural producers have turned their backs on the state. They have contented themselves with growing food for purely local consumption. Or they have gone massively into the transfrontier smuggling trade.

So it came about that a reasonable and even necessary policy of accumulating development capital from rural surpluses—necessary because there were usually no other surpluses of significant size—was turned into a disaster; and this in the 1970s became a general condition. Even apparently contrary cases illustrate it. In another West African republic, that of Senegal, groundnuts had long played the role of Ghana's cocoa: they were the country's greatest export asset, and the monocultural basis of the state's economy. After independence in 1960 the Senegalese state was careful to ensure that the interests of those who delivered the groundnuts should be well protected. But these deliverers, in an effective sense, were not the producers of the nuts. In Ghana the producers were a multitude of small and middle farmers, each owning land as individual operators or members of a family network; in Senegal, by contrast, the producers were often landless farmers working as ill-paid labor for landlords, the latter being also religious personalities (*marabouts*) or other influential entrepreneurs. Looking after the sellers of nuts to the coast did not mean the same thing as looking after the actual producers. The actual producers were not looked after. They were systematically exploited and abused. They, too, replied by turning their backs on the state and its exactions.

A severe rural crisis erupted in deepening anger and frustration. According to the historian Boubacar Barry, "In 1970 the rural areas [of Senegal] were on the verge of an uprising as a result of vexations perpetrated by the administrators [the agents, that is, of the state bureaucracy in one form or another] on peasants virtually unable to pay their debts"—unable to pay because of low prices paid to them for their product, added to drought and a cycle of bad harvests.[7] Ten years later, in 1980–81, the same crisis, still unresolved, had become acute.

"Famine settled in throughout the countryside, where the peasants systematically refused to pay their debts [debts, that is, incurred for the purchase of productive necessities]" and boycotted the purchase of fertilizer and equipment offered under the agricultural program, while refusing to market their crops through the official channel, writes Fieldhouse.[8] By this time the Senegalese economy was virtually stagnant and debt-ridden. In short, the groundnut producers upon whom the health of the nation-state economy depended turned to producing food for their own needs, or else grew groundnuts for sale on what now became known as the "parallel economy."

Smuggling of produce within frontiers and across frontiers became an almost universal rural response to the antirural discriminations of the official and city-based economy. All competent sources of information appear to agree on this. The volume of "parallel" and illegal—or, more bluntly, smuggling—trade naturally varied from republic to republic. In many cases it was very large. Peasant incomes in the small but naturally fertile republic of Benin (formerly Dahomey) fell continuously during the 1970s: in real terms, according to official figures, by as much as 2.6 percent a year. But who knows what the official figures were worth? They could take no official account of "unofficial" trade; and "unofficial" trade, according to well-advised estimates for 1982–84, reached the astonishing but believable proportion of *nine-tenths of all the trade* of the republic of Benin.[9]

In some large cases, such as Zaire, the position was no different. To the large and wealthy autonomous state of Kano in the Nigerian Federation, during 1988, there came the blessing of a bumper wheat harvest. It was thought to have produced some 285,000 tons. But the Nigerian Flour Milling Association affirmed that only some 15,000 tons, or 6 percent of this harvest, had reached the country's official mills.[10] "What happened to the rest," remarked one well-informed observer, "is anybody's guess." No doubt; but anybody's guess was almost certainly that the missing 94 percent of the wheat went quietly through illegal channels, a circumstance which surely surprised nobody and caused no surge of guilt.

Most of the smugglers will have been otherwise law-abiding and respectable citizens. For what this meant was not that Nigerians had become perversely given to economic crime; as it happens, they are a people with an ancient and sophisticated respect for law and contract. It meant that the Nigerian nation-state had lost its legitimacy in the eyes of a significantly large number of its people, perhaps even a majority if one takes account of the multifarious operations of the "parallel economy."

Here, in short, was another factor prompting disintegration. At the outset of independence there had been a narrow gap in trust and confidence between the bulk of the population and the beneficiaries or leaders of anticolonial nationalism. The social aspects of the anticolonial struggle still retained primacy of influence over all those aspects concerned with nation-statist self-identification. The welfare and advancement of the majority, one may even say, was still consciously accepted as an aim of policy more important than the interests of that necessarily small minority with access to political power and the economic fruits of political power. The gap existed but could be bridged if an attempt were made to bridge it. Now, after ten or twenty years, the gap had widened to an abyss: on one side, a great mass of resentful and impoverished rural people and, on the other, a small minority with quantities of wealth. Into that abyss there had plunged, more or less helplessly, the legitimacy and credit of the state which had allowed this gap to yawn.

No simple explanation of such phenomena can ever be adequate. In this enormous invitation to disaster there were many contributory strands of action or inaction. But they all came together, visibly in the 1980s, in destruction of the accountability of the state upon which the nation was supposedly built. One of these strands was the territorial awkwardness of the state formed by the colonial partition and "transferred" to African hands. Another, in this legacy, was the contradiction between continued state dictatorship and the expectations of state democracy. A third was the growth of illegal trade, itself a product of the contradiction between the interests of the few and the interests of the many: in general terms, between the city and the countryside. There were other factors of disintegration, all working in the same direction. One of these was what may be called the ecological inheritance, a second was the international context.

The ecological inheritance became much heavier, during the 1970s, with the arrival of cyclical drought in the savannah zones and the commercial devastation of tropical hardwoods in the rain forests. The effects of drought and commercial devastation are impossible yet to quantify, but all sources agree that each has already brought serious degradation. Much of Africa was now to be in peril of imminent desertification; and there were no signs as yet of any important reversals of the trend. With civil wars raging, large populations in the pastoralist cultures were subjected to an almost genocidal scourge of natural and man-made impoverishment. There would be no way by the early twenty-first century to recapture the human realities of the Africa even of the colonial years, let alone the precolonial years, save by reading books about them. Whole cultures will have vanished in the meantime.

This being so, one still needs to bear in mind that the ecological inheritance could never have been less than difficult. Africa was "tamed" by its historical peoples, over many centuries, against great handicaps not generally present in other continents, whether in terms of thin soils, difficult rainfall incidence, a multitude of pests and fevers, and much else that made survival difficult. No policies of "development," no matter how honest and intelligent, could have transformed every large zone of Africa into a smiling garden of high agrarian production. The trouble after independence, in this dimension, was that the plans aiming at "development" were neither honest nor intelligent, at least in the vital sense of being an efficient product of disinterested field research. And this, more often than not, seems to have been the consequence of relying on specialists and experts whose training and perception were the fruit of non-African experience, and who, moreover, were usually working for bureaucracies which have demanded quick results.

It took some twenty years after about 1950 to make serious headway with the proposition that African farmers aren't fools. Even then, the thought that they are fools has lingered in many learned heads and leapt with alacrity into the writings of a host of visiting "observers." The thought is far from new. The general assumption and attitudes of textbooks of the colonial era—of course, there were exceptions—was that African farmers had not understood, and by themselves could probably never understand, the potentials of their soils and situations. So the key to agricultural enlargement—to self-sufficiency in food, territorial solvency, and eventually nationalist success—was held to lie in the transfer to Africa of non-African farming experience and technology.

Here and there, this proved right, as in the import of improved maize strains to Kenya, but more often it proved wrong, sometimes disastrously wrong, as in the notorious case of attempted cotton planting in the middle Niger "delta."

Nothing better showed a general European contempt for African practical experience than this particular case of "colonial development." A huge public investment was designed by the French colonial authorities to grow cotton in the delta region upstream from Timbuktu where cotton had never been grown before. Nothing that the "hands-on" wisdom of Europe could advise was to be overlooked. Just to make sure, peasants from neighboring lands were hauled in and "settled" in villages placed under military discipline, with obligatory labor from dawn to sundown. This went on most of the years between the two world wars. By 1939 it had become clear that the plans were bad and the money wasted. What European wisdom had failed to undertake were serious studies of soils and local methods of cultivation. After 1945 all further attempts to produce cotton were abandoned, and then it was conceded, as local farmers might have told them in the first place (if the farmers had been asked), that irrigation in these ecological circumstances, "after producing less than average yields, eventually sterilised the soil by washing it out."[11]

By the 1980s there came at last the beginning of a reversal of this European contempt for African practical knowledge: it began to be accepted that African farmers might know better out of their own experience, even out of their own technology, and possess a hardheaded regard for their own best interests. As the ecologist Paul Richards has put it, "Practices such as 'minimum tillage' and 'intercropping' are now seen not as evidence of the 'backwardness' of African agriculture, but as principles with considerable development potential," and "are even beginning to attract the attention of commercial agriculture in temperate lands."[12]

Although the ecological inheritance has in many ways been adverse, Africans have often found ways of dealing with it. But Africans have had no such success in dealing with adverse factors in the international context.

Once one begins to peer into the relationships between the peoples of Africa and the colonial powers, or more generally the industrialized powers whether or not directly owning or having owned colonies, one is into a realm of high mystification. Against every likelihood of human nature, the view was steadily advanced in all established media that the cost of the "white man's burden" had been met, and generously, by the white man: Britain and France, above all, had disbursed their wealth in favor of the poor benighted blacks. But the often reliable statistical records of empire indicate that this had never been true. They also show that it became ever less true as time went on, so that after the Second World War these great imperial states, in the words of David Fieldhouse, "squeezed and exploited their colonies in Africa in ways never seen before."[13]

Fieldhouse also found it useful in his *Black Africa, 1945–1980* to remind his readers of the facts behind the myths of European generosity. If post-1945 France sent some of its taxpayers' money to Africa, the advantage accrued to its manufacturers and exporters; the British, for their part, were unreservedly mean. A "rough calculation suggests that between 1945 and 1951, Britain extracted some £140 millions from its colonies, putting in only about £40 millions under the Colonial Development and Welfare Acts," the latter being parliamentary measures of greatly cried-up generosity for whose hypocrisy the founding fathers of the British Labour Party (then forming the imperial government) must have been revolving in their graves.

Elsewhere, there was less hypocrisy, least of all perhaps in Belgium. Again it has been Fieldhouse who has well summarized Belgium's exploitation of its vast possessions in the Congo Basin. By late in the 1950s, the threshold of Belgian political withdrawal, about 1 percent of the inhabitants of the Belgian Congo (Zaire today) were of non-African origin and loyalty. But "95 percent of total assets, 82 percent of the largest units of production and 88 percent of private savings belonged to foreigners. . . . Here then was a society in which about 110,000 whites and a very few large overseas firms controlled almost the entire modern economy."[14]

The point of recalling these facts is not to rebut the myth of imperial generosity or to lament its dishonesty, useless exercises today and often no longer necessary. The point is to emphasize that the extraction of wealth from an already impoverished Africa was in no way halted by the "transfer of power." A transfer of poverty continued as before, even while the means of transfer were modified or camouflaged. When the boom in raw material prices collapsed with the ending of the Korean War in the 1950s, the direct political control of territories in Africa could be safely passed to the colonized while at the same time ensuring that these territories remained subject to the overall financial and commercial domination of what was now, during the Cold War, called the West, meaning essentially the United States and its European partners or dependents. Mystification resumed.

It might be far better for Africa to "belong" to the West than to the East, although this was a proposition during the Cold War more often asserted than proved; but "belonging" to the West was no bed of roses. Generally and with exceptions, the international terms of trade continued to move against the interests of African producers and exporters. In 1975, for example, a ton of African copper could buy 115 barrels of oil, but in 1980 only 58 barrels; a ton of African cocoa could buy 148 barrels of oil in 1975, but in 1980 only 63 barrels; a ton of African coffee could buy 148 barrels of oil in 1975, but in 1980 only 82 barrels; and so on down the line. Great conferences were called by United Nations organs with a view to reversing or reducing this adverse trend and its consequent extraction of African wealth for the benefit of non-African buyers and spenders.

None of these portentous and costly conferences produced so much as a sliver of material benefit for Africa. At the seventh, held in 1987, it was revealed that the fall of Africa's export prices during the year before had cost Africa no less than $19 billion, while the cost of manufactured goods imported by Africa had risen by 14 percent. Yet everything continued as before. In 1990 there came the sixth successive year in which the world's low-income countries—the ex-colonial countries, the so-called Third World—again increased their net transfer of wealth to the "developed world": that is, to the ex-imperialist and other industrialized countries. And still there was no sign of change.

When the economies of "actually existing socialism" in Central and Eastern Europe and the Soviet Union went flagrantly into crisis in 1989, there was much self-congratulation in the West and happy talk about the virtues of free-enterprise capitalism. It was less noticed that these were virtues of which Africa had so far known little or nothing.

While the outside world stood by and continued stolidly to take its cut of Africa's productive wealth, giving back less and less in grants, aid, or better prices, the scope for political redress correspondingly narrowed. As the new nation-states lost their legitimacy in the eyes of widening ranks of citizens, and hunger spread with less and less means of relieving it, there came what everyone could see, or at least could feel or apprehend, to be a steady decline in the moral and political values of those who led or claimed to lead these nation-states. The facts show that this apprehension was by no means always justified, for there were leaders and political movements or national parties that remained true to the proposition that honesty and hard work could still save the day. But deepening impoverishment piled tremendous handicaps on every effort at honesty and hard work. Even among those who still hoped for the best, and strove for the general good rather than the individual racket—and there were still many such in this Africa of collapsing expectations— a growing sense of fatal isolation took hope by the throat and gradually choked it into the lassitudes of despair.

What could anyone do? Their economies would not work, their institutions fell from one dilapidation into another, their peoples were in dissidence when not in seething revolt. Meanwhile, the West assembled learned conferences and dictated new policies that in substance were no different from old policies;

while the East barked its slogans and presented whenever it could the solutions of "actually existing socialism," solutions which, as for example in Mozambique, not only solved nothing but were now seen to have created still worse problems than before. The time would even arrive, after 1977, when Soviet policy would attempt with great and costly effort to install in a supposedly "revolutionary" Ethiopia those very policies and institutions of centralized dictatorship that a reforming leader, Mikhail Gorbachev, was about to denounce as disastrous to the Soviet Union itself.

It seems generally true that the decline in moral and political value of those who claimed to speak for Africa was both rapid and widespread. Again there were notable exceptions, as the work and reputation of a man like President Julius Nyerere were enough to show. Yet it was characteristic of those gloomy years of the 1970s that new policies and aims introduced to Tanzania under Nyerere's inspiration, seeking to find ways of mobilizing mass support for self-reorganization, were generally mocked by other African governments as "utopian" or "idealist," rather as though "reality" in this Africa could never do more than serve a narrow and reckless self-interest. Nyerere's "experiments" on behalf of a general good were an object of "outside" scorn while the actual workings of the terms of trade, worldwide, ensured that none of these experiments could do more than limp, or even work at all.

Exceptions apart, this was now a time when the devil could and did take hold of the hindmost, and shake the living daylights out of hope or wish. In such circumstances even the best of persons seldom show to much advantage. Several tried until they ended up in exile, prison, or death in "unexplained circumstances"; others were less heroic but perhaps more useful—the argument around that point was as difficult here as it has ever been anywhere else—and weathered the storm in silence or compromise. Meanwhile, they were all nagged or bullied by complacent persons and institutions, distantly abroad, who called for "more democracy" as though democracy were a patent medicine to be uncorked and poured at will.

They could agree that there was everything to be said for more democracy. But the democracy in question, neatly bottled by a host of academic propagandists, was invariably presented as the parliamentary democracy distilled from the fruits of a mature capitalism that was said to "rule the West" and did indeed, now and then, rule the West. But it could rule this Africa only on the supposition, just as invariably advanced by the aforesaid institutions and persons, that the colonial powers had promoted a simulacrum of the West's governing conditions. They had, alas, done nothing of the kind.

What they had done, much more often, was to destroy or downgrade Africa's own institutions and cultures which, through an immensely long history, had taught how to provide forms of public control over executives, forms of public comment against executives, forms of public distrust of executives— in short, forms of democratic behavior—and which had given Africa's peoples, or many of them, a confident sense of possessing *and exercising* a real control over their own lives. The institutions of that past sovereignty could not be restored. The cultures which had produced them, though often still alive after the batterings of colonial dispossession, were in any case sorely lacking in self-belief. What remained possible now could only be difficult experiment or renewed subjection.

The notion that a past Africa had developed forms of democratic behavior rather than forms of barbarism, or the notion
that these precolonial forms of public participation might now
be concepts useful to the evolution of postcolonial forms of
democracy, could only seem foolish or sentimental to the opin-
ion-makers of Western orthodoxy. Their political science has
seldom taught them any African history, and when it has, it
has taught them a history that seems entirely severed from
modern potentials. As for the bulk of commentators on this
Africa of uproar and confusion, asked to utter instant wisdom
on matters of complexity, they were usually lost in a sea of
ignorance. When they saw a difficult experiment—as in Tanzania during the later 1960s, as in anticolonial movements of the
Portuguese colonies during the early 1970s, as now and then
elsewhere—they fell back on slogans drawn either from an old
Eurocentrism or the Cold War, so that Africans and African
movements that had seldom or never heard more of Communism than the names of Marx and Lenin, or even less, were
solemnly denounced as potent agents of red revolution. But
much more seriously, in looking at Africa these commentators
also saw something else; and this was really there. They saw
nation-states harried by purely internal subversions and distractions. They saw clientelist "tribalism"; and this they saw as a
final proof that nothing in Africa's past could be useful to
Africa's future.

Now "traditional" Africa had certainly produced modes of
loyalty and self-defense that may be called tribal if you are
determined not to call them national. Far from being subversive
of established order, they were more generally constructors or
guardians of established order. But in periods of breakdown or

224

severe disorder, these modes of loyalty and self-defense under-
went a change that was both a reduction and an extension.
They drew back into the defense of individuals or clusters of
individuals while at the same time extending their effectiveness
in many ways subversive of the state. One can make a comparison between this use of kinship in political contexts, ever more
active in postcolonial Africa, with the use of smuggling in economic contexts: each, in its way, acts as a compensation against
the weakness or the incapacity of state institutions unable to
protect citizens and advance their interests. One could regret
this, but regretting it was only a way of saying that citizens
should quiescently accept hunger or injustice.

The "tribalism" that now disturbed these states was partly,
as we have seen, a convenient invention of the colonial period:
gathering Africans into invented tribes could make colonial administration easier, or at least cheaper, while from an African
standpoint, being so gathered could produce a stronger bar-
gaining voice. But we may remember that it was also something
else, and much older—as old, at any rate, as the major period
of the slave trade in the eighteenth century or earlier. The
Nigerian historian Peter Ekeh has argued convincingly that the
spread and reinforcement of kinship ties and manipulations—
in short, forms of clientelism—became a dominant mode of
political life in Africa in that historical period, the major slaving
years, whenever the state either failed to defend citizens from
violence and enslavement or became the wrecker of community
life. He draws a comparison between the rise of feudalism in
medieval Europe and the rise of this African "tribalism." For
"if in Europe the response to the failure of the state to provide
security for the individual was the institution of feudalism, in

Africa the response to the violation of the citizenry by the state, in its sponsorship of the slave trade, was the entrenchment of kinship corporations."[15]

Leaving aside the issue of feudal comparisons, Ekeh's thesis seems powerfully instructive: an early product of that deeper understanding of Africa's history which the advance of historiography, written now from inside its subject rather than from outside, will increasingly give us. It has, in any case, a very modern application.

The slave-trading African state, as it evolved after about 1650, became dependent for its viability on external sources: whether to export captives for enslavement, or to import the firearms that slaving raids (or defense against them) invariably required. It was in this dimension a protocolonial state. In most cases this coastal or near-coastal dependency was already far advanced by early in the eighteenth century. But as it advanced, together with the state's violence or its incapacity to prevent violence, the state "grew apart from society," in Ekeh's words, to a point at which citizens sought other forms of self-defense. As the slaving state became increasingly a predator, "kinship systems were strengthened and elaborated as a means of providing protection against the dangers of the violence created by the slave trade." In just the same way, much later, the predatory nature of the postcolonial or neocolonial state in Africa (but not only in Africa, as the Stalinist state in Eastern Europe would show at much the same time) has provoked self-defense by kinship ties or their bureaucratic equivalents and, with this, a corresponding subversion of the state by smuggling and related kinds of economic crime.

True enough, this line of thought leaves questions open for

investigation. What in practice was the status of kinship corporations before the slaving centuries made them so generally useful, even indispensable? What can be their power of survival if a form of state should emerge that is competent to defend its citizens, and stand for them rather than against them? But in present reality there is no doubt that kinship corporations or their equivalent, rather than any other form of political self-organization, are what generally count for most in everyday life. The hostility or sheer incompetence of the state has ensured as much. So the big problem about building democracy can be no more a matter of counting the number of political parties on the electoral scene than of counting the quantity of angels on the point of a pin.

When in due course the pirates who had seized power in the vast country of Zaire, in central Africa, became due for expulsion and in 1991, meanwhile, there was some let-up in dictatorial terror, it was found that the new "multiparty" state proclaimed in 1990 had fostered overnight no fewer than 230 "political parties," not a single one of which had any of the organizational and mobilizing capacity that a political party is supposed to have. This was a reversion to kinship corporations under the thinnest guise, and was going to solve precisely nothing. The real solution would have to lie elsewhere. It would be to devise and uphold a state such as citizens will accept and respect as the valid and therefore worthwhile representative of their interests and protector of their rights.

Kinship corporations cannot produce a democratic state, whether or not they are disguised as political parties. They are bound to be the enemies of the state if only because it is the state that has allowed them into the political arena through its

227

failures in effectiveness. Being the enemies of the state, kinship corporations hasten its downfall. They point, more often than not, to a collapse of civil society and the response of *sauve qui peut*. They open the gate to fearful abuse of the common interest. They have led in Africa to terrible destructions. If the worst of these were still reserved for the 1980s, a decade that may be truly called "the decade of the AK-47," they nonetheless reached a sorry level in the 1970s. Uganda, Chad, Burundi, and quite a few other lands, were submerged in tides of violence which revealed time and again that the "tribalism" of kinship corporations and their equivalents could act as an agent of mutual havoc that nothing seemed able to contain.

Soldiers evidently incapable of tolerance or mercy rode to power as the champions of this or that "ethnic group," even when actual ethnic differences had little or nothing to do with their coercions and plunderings. Politicians harvested the spoils of kinship manipulation with an ingenuity of crime and corruption that rivaled anything of this kind ever managed elsewhere. Presidents outrageously enriched themselves; governments mocked the most elementary justice; officeholders turned themselves into licensed profiteers. Gradually, through the 1970s, a mood of soured exasperation crept across every public scene.

We shall see that this was just what was happening in Central and Eastern Europe where, if the appearances were different, the decisive circumstances were essentially the same. And in Africa, too, dissidents and patriots emerged, and sometimes survived. They, too, tried whenever possible to take hold of this caricature of nation-statehood and make it function as its prophets had believed it could. Some of the soldiers were among them, and among these—exceptionally, in this case, during the

1980s—was a military ruler of the Federation of Nigeria, General and then President Ibrahim Babangida. He was one of those not-so-few Nigerian soldiers who stood historically in the position of other patriots such as Murtala Muhamed and Olusegun Obasanjo. These were men who had worked to keep the federation together even during and after the worst excesses of "tribalism" in the Nigerian civil war of 1967 to 1970. They were pledged to the conviction that military rule had no developmental value; at best, it could hold the ring until politicians were ready and able to behave as statesmen. Repeatedly since 1966, when governments had begun to be overturned, Nigerian soldiers returned the state to civilian hands. They were as repeatedly disappointed in their hopes.

Another of those disappointments was to occur in 1983. Soldiers again removed an existing civilian government. They did this, said Babangida in the aftermath, because that civilian government had "ruined the economy of the country, generated national dissension and instability, and engaged in massive rigging of elections with the attendant violence and insecurity of lives and property." He continued with a bitterness laced with exasperation. He said that "if Nigeria's political class had learned anything after thirteen years of military rule, it must have been how to mismanage the economy in a more damaging fashion, rig elections in a more brazen manner, and cause widespread disaffection among the general population on an unprecedented scale."[16]

The more incompetent the state, in short, the wider grew the gap between the state and society, including the gap between town and countryside; and the wider this gap became, the more frantic and unbridled were the subversions of "tribalism," as people sought for self-defense in kinship ties or their equivalents. The circle of negation seemed complete.

The political sociology of much of Africa, after the 1960s, thus began to acquire a mournful guise of repetitive failure. This was increasingly ascribed to a failure of persons rather than of institutions. The reality, as the facts have urged, was rather that the nature of society had failed to meet the requirements of the parliamentary models by which the new nation-states were supposed to operate. No strongly hegemonic "middle strata" had emerged, or even, outside small clusters of capitalists in several cities, begun to emerge; nor did it seem at all probable, given the ambience of the world economy, that any such hegemonic strata could emerge in a foreseeable future. The hopeful millionaires of Lagos in Nigeria, or Nairobi in Kenya, or others elsewhere and of older provenance, as in Cairo and Tunis, had evidently come too late to the feast, swamped by new multitudes of the poor while hampered in their every effort at becoming a "true economic bourgeoisie."

The soldiers repeatedly "took over," the worst as pirate warlords and the best as standing in for a bourgeoisie which stubbornly refused to appear; and the political record, as General Babangida cuttingly observed, became a succession of disasters. In this installation of "solutions by coup d'état," there were several that were probably decisive in the downfall of a nationalism which no longer placed the struggle for social improvement at the center of its project. One of these "turning points," early on, was almost certainly the overthrow and murder of Patrice Lumumba in the first months of Zaire's independence; after that, as we shall see a little further on, the nation-state of Zaire became a mere fantasy of what the term has been supposed to mean. Another such "turning-point," once again in response to the pressures of the Cold War, was undoubtedly the overthrow in 1966 of the regime in Ghana headed by Kwame Nkrumah: decisive, in this sense, not because that regime had been a model of success (though one may think it far less of a failure than its critics have alleged), but because its overthrow opened the door, as was soon proved, to the habits of violent excess.

With clientelism now feeding voraciously on the fragility of states—states that could so easily be overthrown or subverted by generals or colonels, and soon enough by sergeants and corporals—there seemed no limit to its ravages. From internal self-government in 1951 to independence in 1957 and on to Nkrumah's overthrow by soldiers in 1966, a period of fifteen years, Ghana had lived under a nationalism which, with whatever errors and miscalculations, had maintained a strong respect for the advancement of a social struggle under a rule of law and of constitutional restraint. It may be said that the project was unrealistic in the general conditions under which that project had to be attempted, but this is argument by hindsight. No competent Ghanaian at the time, not even those who were foremost in opposing the policies of the Nkrumah regime, seems to have thought that the social project was bound to fail. They disagreed on the methods and the personalities, a rather different matter.

After 1966, however, the strong legitimacy of this national project rooted in social improvement—and through fifteen years when not a single political execution had taken place—faltered rapidly and fell away. Between 1966 and the early 1980s, when some of Nkrumah's socially based ideas and objectives began once again to win support, this small but self-destructive country moved through no fewer than nine transitory regimes. With each of these regimes up to the early eighties, the overall social and economic situation grew worse and executive violence increased. Those years could be seen as a continued "defense of the West," aided now by a host of Western speculators and contractors counting avidly on borrowed money, or else they could be seen, as others saw them, as a sociopolitical wasteland in which nothing advanced the people's cause. The country that had not unreasonably claimed to have led Africa out of the direct grip of colonial rule was steadily reduced to bankrupt misery and political irrelevance, until it had to join, shamefacedly, Africa's ever-lengthening line of suppliants and beggars. Ghana persistently relegated itself to the paracolonial status of "Third World" dependency.

Could there be a way out of the impasse? If the solutions of capitalism meant turning one's back on a nationalism centered on the social struggle for improvement, and were in any case hamstrung by the absence of a "true economic bourgeoisie," what about the solutions of socialism? The trouble with them, of course, was that a "true economic working class" had likewise failed to appear. Rural multitudes had poured into cities and become proletarians in the sense of possessing nothing. But this was not at all the same thing as saying that in doing this they acquired a proletarian consciousness of class and category, and would or could unite around that consciousness. Trade unions in many of these countries had played a leading role in anticolonial agitation and the demand for social justice. They sometimes continued to exist and worked to mobilize their forces. But nowhere were they able to achieve the solidarity and coherence that could have moved them toward empowering socialist political movements.

In spite of this unpromising prospect for the socialization of these economies, some of them in the 1970s continued to claim a socialist project described as Marxist, or Marxist-Leninist, or merely "African"—in the latter case, rather as though the laws of political economy failed to operate in countries that were "black," giving way instead to a magic labeled *négritude*. If anything, and the process was marvelous to behold, the illusions of achieving "high mass consumption" by way of an imported capitalism on the Western model were far outdone by the illusions of doing it by way of an imported socialism on the Soviet model or its equivalent. Especially in countries of the "francophone family," these illusions partly arose from the ardent optimism of students reacting against neocolonial miseries or subjections, and partly from the prestige, as it then was, of the countries of "actually existing socialism." These, too, poured their "experts" and "advisers" into whatever African states that would accept them and, incidentally, pay for them. These Eastern pundits, like their rivals from the West, were sure that they "knew better" and in any case insisted upon its being agreed that they did in fact know better. One or two examples may be useful.

Among them is the republic of Congo, a little territory that had once been the French Moyen-Congo, lying between Gabon on the Atlantic coast and Zaire in the continental basin of the Congo River. Though potentially a fairly rich and promisingly self-dependent country, this "People's Republic" offers a perhaps extreme example of the "socialist" absurdities that have flowed from colonial partition and from neocolonial nation-statism. By the end of the 1970s its population was approaching 2 million, of whom some 65 percent were to be living in towns by the middle 1980s, with its capital of Brazzaville having 56 percent and constantly growing.[17] This urban population achieved a political leadership that was generally or ostensibly determined to maintain the primacy of the "social" over the "national," but in any case at the cost of the large minority of people living "in the bush." Here we have another "Marxist-Leninist" state in which the peasantry, the domestic food producers, have been treated as politically irrelevant, and have found the state to be their enemy and exploiter.

Though an oil producer on a minor scale, this "Congo-Brazzaville" is therefore heavily dependent on foreign aid, principally from France, whether to subsidize the employment of its urban population, or to provide the urban food that the country's peasants can or will no longer deliver in sufficient quantity. In practice, its oil-exporting capacity, as in other countries so placed, has had seriously negative results, for it has "exacerbated the already dangerous economic and political imbalances" between an urban sector dominated by the political "classes" in the towns and the more or less powerless people of the countryside. It has led—as in Nigeria, as often elsewhere—"to greater neglect of the vital agriculture sector."[18] In spite of a consequently decisive dependence on the West, notably on France, whether for imported food or other means of support, its demagogic leadership nonetheless proceeded, in 1970, to adopt a Soviet-style constitution and a policy devoted to the realization of "scientific socialism."

The reality has proved riotously different from whatever "scientific socialism" was supposed to promote. This "Marxist-

Leninist" state, ostensibly aimed at maintaining the primacy of the "social struggle" and the defense of the mass of its inhabitants, has behaved in fact like an extreme case of a centralized bureaucratic structure with an impoverished rural periphery. Between 1960 (at its independence from France) and 1972 its bureaucracy grew by 636 percent or from 3,000 to 21,000 persons, after which it continued to grow at an even faster rate, totaling by 1987 some 73,000 persons. These included a "national army" of 8,500 effectives, but with no external enemy in sight, and able, in any case, to call on reinforcements from France whenever the neocolonial applecart might seem threatened with upset. By the end of the 1960s this relatively immense and useless civil and military service was eating up around three-fourths of the national budget, and its members enjoyed a far higher standard of living than most Congolese. And it had become, of course, the effective internal political power of this rigidly centralized administration. It remained that to the 1990s, and became probably more authoritarian than before. Not even the "scientific socialism" of Eastern Europe was ever able to achieve quite this degree of practical self-contradiction.

Splendidly rhetorical, the politics of this republic has regularly deployed an Alice-in-Wonderland level of eloquence matched almost nowhere to the realities of foreign dependence and rural decay. Necessarily clientelist because of its dependent system, Congo-Brazzaville's body politic has shaken and re-shaken itself through many coups and countercoups. None of these has done other than confirm this state's inability to embody the interests of its people. The aims may have been admirable, vowed to self-development; the reality has induced an ever-larger bureaucratic parasitism. Congo-Brazzaville's monopolist

235

"Marxist-Leninist" political party might receive the cherished accolade of Soviet recognition for having become the genuine "revolutionary vanguard" of a people bravely enlarging its independence. Meanwhile, the nine-thousand-odd members of this "vanguard" were becoming ever more dependent on government jobs and therefore on Western subsidies; while the model vanguard, back in the Soviet Union, were entering tough and probably terminal trouble. The Leninist future was to have been very different, but never mind: political chatter has its own rules. Remove, in fact, Congo-Brazzaville's oil and foreign cash, and this nation-state must at once seem bound to sink in the swamps of its own verbiage.

The republic of Benin, formerly Dahomey, along the western Guinea Coast, offers a quite different contrast between doctrinal claim and cool reality. Benin was also a "Marxist-Leninist" state until 1989, with a lavish production of rhetoric; and, like Congo-Brazzaville, Benin is a polity composed of a relatively huge bureaucracy and an apparent conflict between town and country, the rural population here being of the order of 60 percent of the whole population. But there the similarities cease. So does any reliability of the official and statistical record. If the latter were anywhere near the truth, this small and rather relaxed republic would have ceased to function as a state; in reality, Benin has functioned rather well. The reality is well-known even while unadmitted and even unadmissible.

From its independence of France in 1960, until 1970, clientelism produced nine different governments and six military coups, all of these being propelled on kinship-corporation lines. But in 1972 Mathieu Kérékou installed a regime capable of building on the only effective stability in Benin, a stability arising from a stabilized compromise between country and town. This compromise may have worked against any hopeful self-development of the Beninese as a people. But it was able to keep the peace. So true is this that its Marxist-Leninist doctrine could be abandoned overnight in 1989 without the least effect one way or the other.

In this Beninese compromise one sees that harassed peoples can be surprisingly capable of imposing their own solutions. The essence here has been that the constitutional and doctrinal rules of the Beninese nation-state are entirely disregarded as being undesirable or unworkable. But the state remains viable because, while accepting this compromise, it has since 1972 proved itself a better defender of the public weal than the "tribalism" of earlier years. On the one side, the interests of a large food-producing peasantry have been to escape the normal exactions of the neocolonial nation-state; on the other side, the interests of the town-dwelling multitude have been sufficiently satisfied day by day. All this has been achieved not by state doctrine but by a simple tolerance of illegality.

Benin's relative stability is explained by its being able to "act as an entrepôt and the base for one of the world's largest smuggling enterprises," the latter being the economic backbone of the compromise. Benin's imports from Europe and other distant lands go largely to its big neighbor Nigeria, and its exports derive in no small degree from Nigeria, flowing in either case through officially illegal channels to the good and satisfactory benefit of a multitude of operators. So large is Benin's "parallel economy" that a politely disgusted U.S. Department of Commerce found it probable for 1982–84, in this respect not exceptional years, that as much as 90 percent of Beninese trade was officially nonexistent. In short, "Benin's apparently appalling trade balance is an artefact" of purely romantic interest.[19]

This appears to have suited everyone. It has suited the urban petty bourgeoisie because it provides ample sources of unofficial payoff. It has suited the peasants because, in return for meeting low taxes, they are left substantially to their own devices. They are left, for example, to grow food not only for the towns of Benin but, even more, for illegal sale across the border in western Nigeria: and both at prices in the fixing of which they have a big and even decisive say. With this "system," in other words, the peasantry does far better than by having to deliver crops to the towns for export at prices imposed by a surplus-raiding device such as a state marketing board. This peasantry, in short, has not felt itself obliged to turn its back on the state.

Nothing that occurs in the official economy can then produce crisis, save in "artifactual" terms. Capital investment in parastatal industries may go to waste. An expensive cement plant built largely to serve the Nigerian market may operate at a quarter of its capacity because Nigeria finds cheaper cement elsewhere. A still more expensive sugar-producing plant, likewise brought into operation early in the 1980s, may operate at a still smaller fraction of capacity for much the same reason. But the money spent has paid wages, and most of it, after all, has come from foreign loans and grants. So planning targets, to quote Chris Allen again, may turn out to be artifactual nonsense, "wholly unrealistic or impractical," but who is going to say so? Visiting experts have their credibility to think of, not to speak of their salaries; and so does Benin's bureaucracy.

Other virtues attend this Beninese "experiment." Here there

is no overwhelming kleptocracy on the Zairean scale; and if there has been rhetoric at the Congo-Brazzaville level, no evidence suggests that anyone has been seriously taken in by it—to the point, as noted, that Kérékou was able to ditch "Marxism-Leninism" in 1989 without a ripple of public concern. More constructively, there has been a continuous decentralization and devolution of decision-making power to local communities and interests, so that "for the first time in recent history, men (and also youth and women) are representing their villages and communities . . . without having to be also rich, notables, educated, or familiar with French culture."[20] That was in 1977; ten years later, records Allen, "local council elections were still keenly contested."

Admirable in these and other ways, the outcome may nonetheless be condemned as essentially nondevelopmental. For there is no transformation of the petty bourgeoisie. The "middle strata" do not emerge. The reintroduction of a multiparty system seems no more likely to produce an effective parliamentary regime than the "tribalism" of old; it may more probably turn out to be the same thing as the "tribalism" of old. But against this there may be a continued spread of local organs of decision-making, and to that extent a continued reinforcement of the existing compromise. One may even argue that the people of Benin, in thus finding their own solutions within their own traditions, may be found to have opened a useful route into the future.

Others, meanwhile, had been searching in desperate circumstances for a route to a hopeful future. To them it had to seem that nothing in the Africa they knew could offer a life worth

239

having, a future worth working for. They defied every council of prudence and resignation, and they wrote into the 1960s and 1970s a record of resistance to persecution and a struggle for survival that was never less than impressive. These resisters were the peoples of the Portuguese colonies, shuttered away behind what their nationalist leaders spoke of, and not wrongly, as "walls of silence." Their project, as we shall see, was essentially the fruit of disbelief in the possibility of any partial or neocolonialist independence. And this belief was reasonable, for it arose from the stiffly racist and authoritarian nature of the Portuguese political system. But they had to launch their bid for freedom in times when a partial or neocolonialist independence was generally accepted, and even applauded, in the rest of Africa. So their project had to seem to other Africans a madness of unrealism, a mere wild adventure bound to fail, while to all the orthodox in the Western world, devoted then to Cold War succor of the dictatorship in Portugal, it had to be denounced as a disgraceful subversion of all that was right and proper.

This "madness" of the project, given the overwhelming odds against success or even physical survival, was apparent to those set to carry it out. Their leaders stood in the midst of nowhere, one could say of them, and yet boldly affirmed that they knew where they were going, and, moreover, that they would surely get there. In 1970 I found myself walking the endless bush of eastern Angola, of the "lands at the end of the earth," as the Portuguese called those regions, with the Angolan rebel leader Agostinho Neto. Before the insurrection in Angola, Neto had been a medical doctor practicing as such. It occurred to me to ask him if he didn't regret leaving his profession. I remember that he stopped walking and looked back at me with some surprise: the question, clearly, could be of no interest because the answer must be obvious. "Oh yes," he said in that midst of nowhere, in that moment when the war of liberation seemed bound to be as endless as the bush itself, "I enjoyed being a doctor. But there is now this business. We have to finish it first." The tail of our little escort of fighting men was closing on our heels. But Agostinho Neto might, I think, have added some words spoken years later by Thomas Sankara when briefly president of the little West African republic of Burkina Faso, formerly the French colony of Upper Volta, shortly before Sankara's supposed companions shot him down. Reviewing the stagnations of neocolonialist independence, Sankara remarked in 1988 that "you cannot carry out fundamental change without a certain amount of madness." This madness had to come from the courage to turn your back on old formulas, it had to come from the courage to invent the future. That being so, "we must dare to invent the future."[21]

Sankara had little chance or time to show what he meant by inventing the future; gunmen of the present got him first. The revolutionaries in the Portuguese colonies were also to be baffled, eventually, in their attempt to "invent the future." They would be reduced to "accepting the present," no matter how wretched that must have to be. Their brave bid to close the gap between People and State would be swept from sight and rapidly dismissed. And this would be done, above all, by most of the "media" in the know-better world, during those very years of the 1970s when "the present," the actually existing condition of the postcolonial nation-state, came ever more dreadfully under siege by the pirates of violence and corruption. The years now ahead, the years of the 1980s, might indeed be called the decade of the handiest automatic weapon then available: the AK-47.

Pirates in Power

On a grim day in October 1990 a journalist in Monrovia, the capital city of the West African republic of Liberia, finds himself invited to watch a video on a TV set whose owner lives on the city's Stockton Creek. With mixed feelings, he accepts. The house at this moment is occupied by a leader of one of the "armies" fighting for power during the overthrow of the supposedly legitimate regime led by a former master sergeant in Liberia's supposedly national army, President Samuel Doe. This Doe, himself a man of violence, has just been done to death.

Proudly shown by the killers, the video is the eyewitness to this death. The journalist and some others are given chairs in the front row for this replay, and beer is brought for them. Behind them men of this particular rebel "army" close in to watch the film. This now begins, and is gruesome. Warlords have often done this kind of thing, but rather seldom cared to boast of it.

"Doe, his face bruised, flabby and naked except for his underpants, his hands tied behind his back," looks up from the camera

243

which is placed, the journalist tells us, in the room next to the room where the killing took place. "Doe watches his death approaching as his captors yell orders at each other, and his underpants soak up more blood from the gunshot wounds received in his legs when he was captured three weeks ago." The film continues to unwind. We hear its soundtrack.

" 'Cut off his ears,' Prince tells his men." Prince is the Liberian warlord in command here. And "the camera swings to the victim. The rebels stand on his body, laying him flat. A knife flashes in the bright lights. The knife saws through the screaming president's ear and the ritual has begun."

"Doe shakes his head to prevent them cutting off the other one. But somebody grabs his head hard. The scream pierces the air. For a second the audience round the camera is silent, then they clap." The journalist hears this applause in counterpoint to the hushed silence of Stockton Creek. Africa hears it too. Doe at last is dying. " 'Doe cried all night. He died at 3:30 A.M.,' says the man in the next seat. 'Now Prince is acting president, and everything is going to be all right.' "[1]

The rivalry for Doe's succession goes on; the killing too.

Poor Liberia: yes, there is no doubt of that. This was the black American republic launched in 1847 for the benefit of former slaves and their dependents in North America, a black republic conceived so as to exercise "the genius of free government" over "this seat of ancient despotism and bloody superstition," as its founders valiantly claimed.

The words are those of one of the founding fathers, the former New Yorker Alexander Crummell (1819–98) who was himself the grandson of an African seized on this West African coast and taken into bondage across the Atlantic. Though not themselves recaptives in the old sense, Crummell and his colleagues and fellow settlers were thus another version of the old Freetown elite, but still more alienated from the cultures and realities of Africa. They saw as their mission the introduction of the elements of civilization, in Liberia, to a "vast population of degraded subjects." They knew, of course, almost nothing about this indigenous African population.

In 1990, here, the outcome of this long experiment in civilizing Africa by denying Africa's own history and achievements was to reach its ultimate degradation. The intentions had been the best. "Africa, to become regenerated, must have a national character"—such had been the central affirmation of the black American emancipationists of the 1850s. But this national character could not be African in its derivation or formation, for Africa's own character was one of misery and violence. It was in Africa, after all, that all the forebears of the Americo-Liberian settlers had been thrust into slavery. The national character must be imposed.

Convinced of this, generations of Americo-Liberians proceeded to rule their "degraded subjects" by a contemptuous tyranny presented to the outside world, whenever that might seem useful, as a right and proper anteroom to manhood suffrage and representative democracy. But the anteroom was found to lead to no such result. Democracy was not encountered.

What finally emerged in 1980, at the culmination of many miseries, was the master sergeant who made himself President Samuel Doe. And in Doe's brief and violent life one may inspect the acutely pathological phenomena that appear in colonial and postcolonial dramas played out by men who have possessed the

245

strength and character to seize power, but not the wisdom to control it. Such men seize power and greed sets in, whether for more power or its fruits. Soon enough, sycophancy walls them round with fearsome mysteries of plot or private hope, and then the praise-singers punctually arrive to chant their anthems of ruin. Now the dictator is lost between greed and fear, and in the stifling grasp of this solipsism he will perish. Many others will have perished in the meantime.

Men like Doe are the children of their own ancestral cultures. But they are also the product of an alienation which rejects those cultures, denies them moral force, and overrides their imperatives of custom and constraint. Such cultural hybrids, to borrow a term of the Gold Coast (Ghana) nationalist Kobina Sekyi, may be said to have become "lost between two worlds"—and this saying has at least the merit of suggesting the mental confusion in which their seizure of power forces them to live. They turn to the AK-47, and use it with the blindness of the damned, at which point their power rebounds upon itself and becomes a route to suicide. It has happened in every culture dispossessed by another, and thereby riven to its roots.

Such persons, and Doe in those years was not the worst among them, are destined to a tragic fate, or would be if the squalors of their degradation deserved to be called tragic. They are destroyed as though they had never been, but in their lifetimes they have been all too dreadfully present: Amin, Bokassa, Macias-Nguema—the names pile up, symptoms of a political self-destruction of which Africa has been all too rich in examples. They have demonstrated, time and again, just why it was that leaders of an entirely different mold and mentality, men strong in their wisdom such as Cabral in Guinea-Bissau, so clearly warned that armed violence was a road to be entered with austere reluctance, and traveled with an ever-present fear of its infections.

The pathology is explicable, but only in terms of alienation. The ancestral cultures of the peoples of Liberia, as with those of neighbors near and far, knew plenty of abusive violence. But they possessed rules and regulations for the containment and repression of abusive violence; and these were the rules and regulations, before the scourge of the slave trade and the colonialism that followed it, that enabled them to evolve their sense and value of community.

To persons outside that background who may think of this sense and value as an arbitrary and vicious free-for-all, there is little to be said. They have yet to understand how communities, anywhere and at any time, are able to emerge and grow strong in their rules and structural restraints but are also able, if these should become lost or cast away, to fall into utter disarray or self-destruction. In Europe, for example, such critics have had to watch the Germany of Goethe and Heine give way to the Germany of Hitler and Himmler, and have tried fumblingly to explain the decay by speculations on the nature of the German character, speculations which are then found to have explained nothing. In Liberia the perversion of community can be rationally explained as arising from the consequences of the slave trade.[2] But alienation from ancestral community was then carried further, and systematized, by imposition of the culture of an imported oligarchy, an oligarchy whose ignorance of local realities was easily encouraged, by the corruptions of power, into a contempt for the peoples who lived in these realities. And Doe, with others, was the eventual product of this systemic alienation. Though a "native from the bush," and not the alumnus of an Americo-Liberian academy of imported manners, Doe was equally the victim of another typical pathology of the times that formed him: the pathology, that is, of a colonial or neocolonial "tribalism" or clientelism which, itself, was a product not of Africa's precolonial development, but a desperate mode of self-defense by citizens whose state could not or would not protect them.

It may be objected that the sheer extremism of the "Doe period" in Liberia was exceptional even on the African scene of the 1980s. And it is true that the toters of the AK-47—excellent as a weapon, but now a mindless symbol of the "man with the gun"—were by no means everywhere present. The thuggish simulacra of Romania's Securitate might have a free run here, but not often and certainly not everywhere. The 1980s also had their peaceful and constructive zones of democratic development. Dictatorship was not everywhere admired, and democracy was often worked for. When the Stalinist dictators of Europe were overthrown in 1989, or reduced to pretending they were democrats, there were strong signs of approval in many parts of Africa, very possibly in all parts of Africa. This was not because that overthrow in Europe "taught useful lessons to Africa," Africa's own traditions and expectations of independence requiring no such lessons, but because it suggested that the years of the AK-47 might after all be drawing to a close.

Yet "the Doe period" was not all that exceptional. Other "Doe periods," even longer and still continuing, were already unrolling their own particular films of stupefying violence—even, indeed, more often than before. To place the 1980s in perspective one may usefully look at the "film" of a little hillside state in East Africa, that of Burundi, having in these years a population of some 4 million, almost double that of Liberia's. Like its neighbor Ruanda, Burundi was the postcolonial descendant of an old kingship in these pleasant uplands along the southern reach of the East African Rift.

The general nineteenth-century move toward more emphatic forms of centralized power had developed the dominance of a minority people, the Tutsi, over a Hutu majority. But the manner of this nineteenth-century dominance was mild, and was regulated by "lord and vassal" relationships which had some resemblance to the simpler forms of European feudalism. "The rich man in his castle, the poor man at his gate" appear to have been the outward and visible forms of a mutually acceptable relationship between Tutsi and Hutu; at least in principle these forms represented an agreed sharing of rights and duties.

Colonial enclosure changed all that. Invading Burundi early in the twentieth century, the Germans found it convenient to exercise their rule through this existing system, the result being, as elsewhere in similar "systems" of what was called indirect rule, that the Tutsi rulers-by-contract became colonial dictators. As the tools of colonial rule, these dictators now took orders and handed them "down"; and the mutually acceptable relationship perished between Tutsi and Hutu. That might still have been restored. But the Belgians who acquired Burundi from the Germans, after the German defeat in 1918, upheld the German method of indirect rule and carried it further. They thoroughly bureaucratized all structures of government, and these, in the nature of the case, had to be authoritarian structures. From the Hutu standpoint these structures were Tutsi-operated tyrannies, made no less intolerable because the Tutsi, for the most part, had assumed the Hutu language and abandoned their own. In these ways the ruling Tutsi group—in Ruanda as in Burundi—became a ruling caste. But independence called for democracy.

Independence came in 1962. It produced in Burundi a modified form of what we shall find to be "the Mobutist paradigm" in the vast land of Zaire (ex–Belgian Congo) next door. Not in Ruanda, however, for there the Hutu majority at once unseated the Tutsi minority and moved toward a form of government, at least by intention, that was reasonably acceptable to most of the population. In Burundi the reverse occurred. The Tutsi ruling group, though an emphatic minority, proved able to sustain its power. Hutu insurrections followed but were crushed. These seemed to reach a climax in 1965, when one more Hutu rebellion provoked a veritable Tutsi massacre of all politically active Hutu who failed to escape it. Implicated in this rebellion, or said to be, many thousands of Hutu peasants were slaughtered out of hand. Yet another Hutu attempt at unseating the Tutsi, this time in 1972, was put down with still larger killings, massacres so furious and immense that there proved to be no telling, in the aftermath, whether the numbers of Hutu slain were around 100,000 or as many as double that total.

Much the same scenario continued to unfold through the 1980s, with still one more outbreak of mass killing in 1988 when some 5,000 Hutu peasants were openly admitted to have been slain by the Tutsi-manned army. It mattered little by this time that these last massacres were triggered by the Hutu killing of one Tutsi shopkeeper-peasant or of two or three. Fear and revenge seemed by now to have finally swept away all capacity to rebuild the precolonial tolerance which historical accounts have described. In those precolonial times, we are told, the king and his princely henchmen, the *mwami* and his *ganwa*, had been able to hold a structural balance of interest and obligation between Tutsi and Hutu. This was the balance which colonial overlordship had destroyed. Even thirty years after Belgian withdrawal, a Tutsi army of mercenaries still held the land in thrall.

It may be that this is where the central count against the colonial process is to be found. The colonizing process was invariably presented by its promoters, and explained by its propagandists, as a "modernizing process." In fact, as we have seen, it induced in practice one after another form of moral and political disintegration. The decolonization process has repeated this downward slide. Once the force of the "social struggle" of the colonized was spent, the drive against social inequalities and perceived injustices was supplanted by a "national struggle" within the institutional "containers" of an imported nation-statism. At this stage there ensued, and evidently could not but ensue, a dogfight scramble for state power by would-be ruling groups acting outside and against the rules and restraints of historical cultures and their compromises. To reach for the AK-47 was then a step both short and easy.

The result, as these years most copiously show, became the reverse of whatever may be meant by "nation building." Rather, it promoted the destructive spread of kinship "tribalism." And from this to "Doe-ism," to a form of "killing on command," has proved to be an even shorter step. After that there can be nothing to be done save "invent the future," as Thomas Sankara put it before they killed him too, however hard this invention may be and however long it may take to realize.

251

*   *   *

By the middle of the 1980s, this generalized collapse of the nation-statist project was widely perceived, whether inside or outside Africa. But what now became scarcely less obvious were the incapacities of the outside world, of the "developed world," to act on any self-critical analysis or even to refrain from purely negative interventions. Of these interventions there were various and many. Some were of an economic nature, designed to protect the industrialized countries' advantageous terms of trade with primary producers. Others were political measures aimed at overtaking governmental blunders or comparable disruptions. Others again were simple acts of militarized violence, adding to the legions of licensed or merely criminal gun toters who were now unleashed upon this hungry continent. More and more of the latter were the puppets, often murderous puppets, of aims and forces they could neither have understood nor even have known a way of understanding. "After the South African police had failed to respond to a series of warnings that an attack was imminent," John Carlin reported from the Transvaal in January 1991, "gunmen opened fire with AK-47 assault rifles, in the early hours of yesterday, on some 300 mourners at a funeral vigil in Sebokeng, massacring 35 and wounding at least 40. The victims were all sympathisers with Nelson Mandela's African National Congress."[3] In the last-ditch writhings of the apartheid nation-state, such scenes became common. Their all-too-likely consequences cast a grim shadow over the years ahead.

Whatever unconfessed motives may have directed the South African police on this and many such occasions—and the subversive involvement of both South African police and government became clear and was admitted in 1991—other hidden

252

hands were easier to see. Among the manifestations of the latter may be paired, for their fruitless sowing of disaster, the Soviet program of arming and rearming the post-1976 military dictatorship in Ethiopia, engaged as this was in internal wars of repression with immensely destructive consequences and, far to the south, the American promotion of violent subversions in Angola, again with ferocious consequences. The old colonial powers had at least taken responsibility for what they did and caused to be done; but the Great Powers in this case seemed neither to care nor even to know what their agents were up to. And what by 1990 could seem still more deplorable was that these Great Power programs of externally directed killing still went on even after the Cold War between them was acknowledged to have come to an end. The U.S. administration went on with its promotion of UNITA banditry, however perversely, at a time when the official justification for doing this—that the established Angolan regime was "pro-Soviet"—was manifestly void of sense. By way of comparison, even in 1990 the Mengistu dictatorship in Ethiopia, then about to topple, still enjoyed formal Soviet support.

It may be argued that these truly desperate situations could promise hope as well as fostering despair, if only because defense against them called out new energies and moral solidarities, notably, in my own experience, among the participants at whatever level in the Eritrean national movement. Yet other situations of violence, although with less foreground loss of life, seemed cast adrift in hopelessness. Nothing within them appeared capable of any self-liberating release. New revolts might be attempted, but these would fail as others had failed before. Reforms might be proposed, but these would come to nothing.

And all the while, as stagnation ruled, the ground for possible recovery grew narrower with the continued transfer of wealth to foreign beneficiaries or to private havens in the banks of Switzerland.

These were the situations of a paradigm now become familiar to those who studied these matters. Quintessentially, this was the Mobutist paradigm constructed in the vast lands of Zaire.

Anyone who has floated for days along the current of Zaire's majestic rivers, grand arteries of never-failing flood that urge their way through the rain forests of the Congo Basin, and who for countless lost hours has watched those anonymous forests slide past in silence and solitude as though rooted in eternity, will know that every pretense of power or politics can seem, in these latitudes, to be a very distant legend. Who cares? Who is there in any case to ask the question, let alone respond to it?

The river steamer checks its dilatory pace once a day or sometimes more, and halts at small log quaysides, each with its handful of humanity. But these are figures in a brooding void. Days ahead there will be a riverside townlet belonging to the "modern world" of futile busywork. But this will be a brief glimpse of urban dust and decay before the bush and the trees close in again, and everything is once again as it was before. Nothing changes; there is only the immemorial merging of one day into the next.[4] What can the nation-state and all its anxieties have to do with this?

And the traveler's impression has this amount of truth in it, that the huge country called Zaire, enclosing enormous zones of middle Africa, regions almost one-third the geographical extent of all the United States, is not so much a mystery as a myth. This state called Zaire may exist in the categories of political convention, but otherwise, as a real phenomenon, it barely exists at all, nor do any of its countries and provinces. History has told us that this was not always so. Kingdoms and republics organized to represent and protect their citizens were born here and survived through centuries of social evolution so vividly successful as to produce fine arts and memorable artifacts. They were invaded and dispossessed in the 1880s by Europeans in the service of a Belgian king called Leopold. The Congo Free State which they formed was a monster but no kind of myth. Its worst miseries were terminated in 1908 when the Congo Free State became the Belgian Congo colony. No fine arts or artifacts could flourish there, but the Belgian Congo was a state meticulously organized and governed with the greatest care for the benefit of Belgium and its overseas partners. However deplorable for Africans in its consequence, that state was no myth.

In 1960 the Belgian state withdrew its administrative and military presence, and the country's name changed several times until it became Zaire. This is when the state became increasingly a myth, a mere verbal usage, an idea without an existential content.

Surprisingly little time was needed for this to happen. Between 1960 and 1965 there was uproar and contention because there were many people in the country who thought that the future ought to be, and could be made to be, altogether better than the present or the colonial past. They failed in their hopes, and in 1965 a "strong man" called Mobutu Sese Seko became the country's dictator by promotion and protection of the West; and the prospect of a different future, whether for better or the same, vanished from the scene. Rivalries for power were now settled in the simplest way. Some contenders were shot to death. Others were consigned to exile. Others again were driven into zones of forest or mountain where, since then, they have been disturbed by little other than a river steamer's chuntering passage now and then. The newly independent nation-state of Zaire—ex–Belgian Congo, ex–Congo-Kinshasa, ex-this and ex-that—was abolished in all save name and category in favor of a kinship or extended-family network relying on police and prisons, sudden death or the absence of "missing persons," and therefore on bribery and corruption in every practicable form. Generally presented by Western propaganda (or, when useful to it, by Eastern propaganda, chiefly, in this case, of Chinese fabrication) as being deplorable but convenient, here was the effective pattern of this postcolonial independence: the pattern of a polity stuck fast in its own stagnation.

Life continued, of course. In company with neighbors not much better placed, this country called Zaire could honestly claim a rapid growth of population. By 1990 it was credibly thought to contain some 35 million people, or more than twice as many as had inhabited it during the closing years of the Belgian Congo. With the countryside largely abandoned to itself, they lived increasingly in towns, maybe a dozen large urban sprawls and more smaller ones. These towns grew frantically in size. They became ten times bigger than any of them had been before.

And this "urban" growth continued, stubbornly affirming life over death, while the country's economy "drifted from one calamity to another" both before and after the export price of copper plunged in 1974, and while the "unparalleled personal power" of the Mobutist paradigm went increasingly together with "crisis and decay." All these descriptions of Zaire in the 1970s and 1980s, I should add, are those of qualified specialists with no axe to grind.[5]

It continued while the capital at Kinshasa, a giant spider at the hub of a subcontinental web, acted as an "overwhelming suction pump" absorbing all attainable rural resources as well as whatever might be milked from foreign donors and investors.[6] To every practical purpose, whether legally or illegally extractive, the state was now reduced to Kinshasa and its satellites, to zones of mining or cash-crop production for export, and to air communications between these, just as the "commanding heights" of its administrative bureaucracy were contained and used by the Mobutist kinship network and its dependents.

The state of Zaire, in other words, had become a myth. Outside its coercions and corruptions the country was left to survive as it might, or else to rot. In 1960 the authoritarian but well-ordered Belgian Congo had possessed 88,000 miles of usable road; by 1985 the total length of usable road was down to 12,000 miles, of which only 1,400 were paved.[7] Vast rural areas from which no wealth could easily or any longer be extracted were abandoned to their own devices; and it was now, early in the 1970s, that hunger appears to have become endemic across wide if otherwise silenced regions.

Official statistics by this time had lost credibility through the distortions and defalcations of illegal or "parallel" trade, as well as through administrative incompetence or simple idleness. But they, too, pointed to deepening impoverishment. Writing of the middle 1970s, René Lemarchand felt able to assert that "about 60 percent of Zaire's high mortality rate" should be attributed to malnutrition.[8] Huge food imports, true enough, were arriving in the urban constellations. They were paid for by the export of mining wealth, and were vital to the regime's "law and order" in those parts of Zaire, prominently "urban," that were necessary to the regime. But the needs of rural producers and their dependents, even now a big majority of the whole population, were decisively ignored.

Between 1969 and 1976, fairly characteristic years in this respect, less than 1 percent of the state's budgetary expenditure went into the improvement or support of farming. And why, after all, spend more? So long as mining wealth could be sold for food imported to feed the Mobutist state—the bureaucracy and its clients, the towns, a few essential services, an army for internal use and a copious force of police—there could be no profit in helping peasants. The forests and savannahs outside that state might fester in their brooding solitudes. They might revert to the control of village governments, or shelter clans of "revolutionary guerrillas" more or less bewildered by the despair of magic and divination, or simply provide a refuge for "masterless men" adapted to one form of piracy or another. But who should care? The aircraft of the state and its beneficiaries flew high above the forests and savannahs; passengers would not even notice that the roads below were drowned in all-engulfing vegetation.

The hunger, it has to be noted, could prove inconvenient. It struck into the towns as well. It sorely disturbed accepted orthodoxies. In 1976—quite early in this spreading hunger—the Archbishop Kavanga of Kinshasa, duly flanked by his suffragan spoke in a pastoral letter of "agonising situations" in which "the thirst for money transforms men into assassins . . . and whoever holds a morsel of authority or means of pressure, profits from it to impose on people and exploit them."

The archbishop's lecture did no good even while it spoke volumes for the nature of this paradigm. "How many children and adults die without medical care," it asked without reply, "because they are unable to bribe the medical personnel who are supposed to care for them? Why are there no medical supplies in the hospital, although these can be found in the marketplace? Why is it that in our courts justice can be got only by fat bribes to the judge? Why are prisoners forgotten in jail?" adding the reason: because "they have no one to pay off the judge who sits on the dossier."[9]

There could no longer be any point in asking such questions of the rural areas, for no such services functioned there or were claimed to function. The rural areas of the Congo Basin had suffered badly during colonial times, whether from the exactions of the Congo Free State or those of later concession companies; but it seems that they suffered as badly now, or even worse. "Rural poverty is not a new phenomenon in Zaire," comments Lemarchand of these ferocious 1970s, but "what is new is the unprecedented scale of pauperization, the depth of the social dislocations it has engendered, and the mechanisms and attitudes that lie in the background of this massive affliction."

What these mechanisms and attitudes could mean in a wide and "normative" sense was illustrated, as Lemarchand shows, in a booklet by a certain Tshitenyi-Nzambale entitled *Devenez Riche Rapidement.*[10] It seems to have had an approved circulation. Its key advice aims at "liberating the mind of all doubts as to the legitimacy of material wealth," for "the world," says this booklet, "belongs to the rich. A man is more than a man

259

when he has more wealth. Become rich; and the rest will follow of itself," to which is added, and I give it in its French for the full savor of it: *"Vous devez aimer l'argent et le poursuivre inlassablement. Aimez l'argent à la folie. Adorez-le en pensée et en acte."* The distinguished Zairean writer, a diplomat *de son état*, would be able to point, if he thought it worthwhile, to even more distinguished exponents of the "wealth at all costs" philosophy in the Europe of the 1980s. Like them, one should love money to the point of madness, inexhaustibly pursue it and adore it; as for the price for doing that, let others pay. What M. G. Schatzberg, also writing of Zaire, has called the "state as bandit"[11] now proved as savage a master as the absolutist regime of the Leopoldian Congo, of which, explains Crawford Young, it was now a "modernized version."[12]

Within this paradigm, by the 1980s empowered in one degree or another in many African states besides that of Zaire, even if Zaire may have realized it in the most flagrant shape and form, the question must still arise as to whether such polities are to be regarded as having become truly stuck fast in their own stagnation? The facts of impoverishment and stasis have appeared beyond any serious questioning, and are unrelievedly negative—but were the conclusions so generally drawn from these facts unhelpfully rhetorical? Have they not indulged in a sentimentalist despair? The case could be argued, and the reason why it could be argued was already becoming apparent by the late 1980s. This was that the state's banditry could also be used against the state.

The Mobutist paradigm, in other words, may at least to some extent be made to yield its own antidote. This has become obvious in rural areas of production: as in many African states during the 1970s, farmers increasingly withdrew from the state economy that abused or oppressed them and found ways of producing and trading outside the reach of the state. Now in the 1980s the same process of disengagement from the state began to flourish in towns as well: a "disengagement from the state in order to escape the excessive appropriations of the ruling class," in Janet MacGaffey's finding.[13] One may read this, if one prefers, as organized theft by those without bureaucratic or other executive power. But this would be to miss a good deal of MacGaffey's point. For the disengagement in question was not simply by persons outside the executive network. Increasingly, as poverty struck inward, it was disengagement by that same network as well.

This process of disengagement had gone so far by late in the 1980s, on MacGaffey's persuasive evidence, as to have become "significant for class formation, because some of its activities allow considerable accumulation."[14] A most pointful question of "development" is thereby raised. If the central or at least the formal aim of policy is to promote a capital-owning bourgeoisie as the decisive factor in establishing a capitalist *system*, where none otherwise exists or has ever existed, cannot this be done by unorthodox means? If foreign-aid injections, bankers' prescriptions, and all the tutelary lessons of existing and successful capitalism have failed to produce a true and necessary bourgeoisie, may this not still be achieved against the rules by "methods of banditry"? Indeed, has the the thing ever been achieved except by "methods of banditry"?

Looking at Zaire in the 1990s, such questions may not be merely rhetorical. Of Kisangani in 1988, Zaire's second or third city, MacGaffey reports the emergence of "a new middle class" that is the product of illegal trade: in other words, of "disengagement" from the state economy. "Its members," she tells us, "make up 22 percent of substantial business owners in the city. They enjoy a middle-class life-style and constitute a nascent true bourgeoisie since, in contrast to the political aristocracy [she is referring to the executive kinship network], they invest their profits in expanding their enterprises and managing them effectively."[15]

I am bound to say that for me this projection of a future capitalist system *in posse* fails to convince, not least as the comparable paradigms in much of Latin America have continued to unfold their miseries after much more than a century of trying. But human initiative is happily persistent. This new illegal middle class in Zaire's handful of cities may be able to make its way. Whatever else has appeared in Zaire seems little more than stagnation gone beyond recall.

A time for climbing out of this abyss of muddle and misfortune would surely come; but this time would evidently not be yet. Meanwhile, the problem of the 1990s, as thoughtful men and women in a good many African countries had begun to see and even to say, was the absence of a clear political catalyst that could break into the stagnation so as to set new ideas moving and new hopes stirring. Just as evidently, this catalyst, whatever it might turn out to be, was not going to take the form of some grand ideological "breakthrough." The ideas for that were not at hand, or were not sufficiently mature; or else, in the measure that these ideas emerged in the participatory schemes and policies of the anti-Portuguese liberation movements of the 1960s and 1970s, they were ideas that seemed defeated by the middle

of the 1980s. All that was otherwise available, in terms of teleo-
logical salvation, was one or another manifestation of a religious
fundamentalism, chiefly Islamic, from which nothing fruitful of
peace and progress could be expected.

Social revolution, meanwhile, had vanished into a verbiage
become absurd by empty repetition, even though, in practice, a
revolution of existing structures of stagnation remained ever
more urgently desirable. If "inventing the future" had so far
failed, this was certainly not from any lack of the need for it.
There were, in practice, trends of political renewal flowing now
from many sources, mostly obscure, and I will come back to
these. But the foreground seemed only to show a debilitating
sense of waiting for transport to the future which simply refused
to come, of waiting in a byroad of history, as it were, through
which no traffic flowed. Or of standing still while, at the same
time, slipping irreversibly back.

And even when transport now and then arrived, transport at
least going somewhere or claiming it, there was the strange
spectacle of drivers, conductors, and self-appointed guides who
seemed to have no interest in the passengers. For what may
after all be most deplorable about these fruitless years was not
the hunger and frustration on every side, bitterly painful though
all that might be, but the absolute hostility between rulers and
ruled.

Notwithstanding all the manifold linkages of kinship, the gap
between "have and have not," even between "have-something
and have-nothing," appeared to become uncrossable once the
power lines were set. It was as though these nation-statist structures had functioned and must function so as to rob the best-
intended wielders of power—and these, here and there, were

far from lacking—of any real capacity to share their power with those it was supposed to benefit. The continent whose past development had rested on a real participation in the use of power was now in this dead-end where power and participation had become sore enemies of one another.

And this was the point, climactic in 1989, at which certain parallels with Europe, above all with Central and Eastern Europe, became instructive. There in Europe, too, liberation from the crassly colonial subjections of Hitlerite invasion and enclosure had briefly signaled, in 1945, the chance of a new beginning. But there had followed, very rapidly, enclosure within a Stalinist system that was even more markedly "neocolonial" in its demands and impositions than were the far less direct demands and impositions of postcolonial structures in Africa. And there, too, in Central and Eastern Europe, if of course in differing degrees of severity and modes of practice, this Stalinist "neocolonialism" had induced a moral and institutional stagnation. There, too, if in varying forms and features, the "Mobutist paradigm" had grasped society in its killing hand of bureaucratic repression and corruption, and sometimes, as so clearly in the Romania of Ceauşescu and his kinship networks, whether personal or political, with a painfully close family relationship. There, once again, power and participation in power had reached a state of apparently irreducible conflict with each other. But then quite suddenly the political landscape was utterly changed. Pent-up social forces, tremendous powers at least in their potential, broke upon the scene. Yesterday's dour silence was swallowed in a fury of passionate debate. Padlocked frontiers creaked and bent and burst wide open. Prisoners walked free. A new age seemed to have begun.

But where was it going, what did it intend? Whether this massive escape from empire could find its way to a political culture of tolerance, and whether that culture, when found, could hold its own against new extremes of destructive nationalism—most obvious among the Serbs and Croats, but everywhere present—these were matters that remained to be seen. Meanwhile, for Africa, all this being so, the parallel in Europe acquired a close and fascinating interest.

The European Parallel

In the Europe between Germany and Russia—broadly, Eastern Europe—the question acutely raised in 1989, when Soviet imperial hegemony disintegrated, was not so much the prospect of a democracy of rights and responsibilities. That would be desirable, of course. But the immediately feasible prospect was one of an autonomous future freed from Great Power interventions. If that kind of future could be got, these many and diverse peoples might then at last, having for so long seen their fields trampled by foreign armies and their governments bullied by foreign interests, embark upon a self-development denied to them for centuries. With exceptions in mountainous strongholds, Eastern Europe had known no such self-development since modern times began; and whenever in later times freedom has managed to find a voice, its songs of peace have come usually from emigrant voices whose owners were on their way to the Americas, not planning to return.

Some forty years before the formal end of empire in Africa, the formal end of empire in Eastern Europe had been likewise celebrated by the emergence of nations and nationalities. Quite a few of these, thanks to a benevolent Wilsonian dispensation, would form themselves into nation-states. The wisdom of doing this was no more discussed here than it was later on in Africa; meanwhile, the great thing was that they were free at last to do as they wished, or at least much more free to do it than before.

About a dozen new nation-states thus took shape in Europe out of the collapse of the old internal empires. Many more were going to emerge in Africa from the collapse of the external empires: some fifty new nation-states in all. The circumstances of emergence varied. But the process of emergence was much the same.

As later in Africa, the doctrine of the sovereign nation-state in Europe was accepted as the supreme problem-solving formula for peoples emerging from foreign rule. It was accepted more easily than in Africa, if only because the cutoff from the precolonial past in Europe was less drastic and complete. This was because the new frontiers in Central and Eastern Europe corresponded, often enough, with major ethnic groupings or historical memories. Constitutions could be devised for peoples who had possessed independent states, or something like them, in a more or less recent past—most obviously, perhaps, in the case of the Poles and Hungarians and Serbs—and for all these constitutions (again, as it was going to be in Africa) the sovereign models were taken from the history of England and France. Parliamentary freedoms, thus installed, were supposed to be placed on the firm foundations of capital-owning "middle strata," and these freedoms were to be guaranteed, it was said, by the steady progress of bourgeois democracy. None of this seemed open to serious question save by those who, briefly in the afterglow of the Bolshevik revolution, mistook the history they were living through, and thought that some kind of socialist equality was to be the wind of the future.

That was not going to be its fate. But with a few exceptions, most obviously in the Czech lands of Bohemia and Moravia, nor was the development of bourgeois democracy. One by one, these new nation-states pledged to the unfolding of their peoples' sovereignties collapsed more or less painfully into the clutch of militarized dictatorships, even in Serbia, where ancient traditions of egalitarian self-determination had been unusually strong.

Whether this collapse of postcolonial European nation-statism could have been averted has been a matter much discussed; in any case, it was not averted. What is relevant here is that the reasons for this collapse into new forms of subjection all refer, in substance, to governing conditions that were to become present in Africa as well. One of these conditions was the political weakness signaled by the incapacity of "middle strata" to impose their domination—or, if you prefer, their leadership— upon these new states. Another was the economic weakness that reduced all of the new states into a more or less complete submission to external controls; to forms of "neocolonial" control, even if this term was never used. Most of them were what would later on, in reference to Africa, become known as "less developed countries"; only in small enclaves here and there, and even then partially, could this fate of indirect but close external control be eluded. This "neocolonialism" was at first exercised mostly by Britain and France; after German expansion began again in the 1930s, it became all-pervasive.

And the banal consequences duly followed. While the Soviet

Union, if also at the cost of fearful self-inflicted wounds, was able to isolate itself from the economic depressions of capitalism, the rest of Europe was caught by the same scissors that were cutting into the whole of the continent, though worst of all in the old imperialist lands. Writing of the plight of those lands in this interwar period, the British economist Michael Barratt-Brown has shown that "primary-product prices were halved in the 1930s compared with the levels of the 1920s," and harsh recession struck at every source of income.[1] The European part of the colonial or ex-colonial "Third World" was hit with much the same severity as African "Third World" countries later on. And the result was dismally parallel. By early in the 1930s the average East European regime was an open or barely disguised militarist bureaucracy capable of little more than "holding the ring" on behalf of foreign patrons or paymasters. Appropriately enough, with Hitlerite expansion in the 1930s, it was Germany's most powerful bank that made itself the arbiter of policy.

It would be easy to enlarge this brief economic sketch with the tale of social and political degradations and turmoils that rapidly advanced across the scene. If parliaments continued here and there to exist in name, they seldom had more than decorative value. Wherever old aristocracy managed to survive, as for example in Hungary, an impoverished and resentful "ruling elite" played out the game of government and opposition while real power remained with police and army. And wherever the ending of the old empires had allowed forbidden nationalities to escape from their obscurity, notably in the South Slav lands, deepening social frustrations tore into interethnic peace and laid the ground for coming massacres. Everywhere, in short, the "national question" of state power had overridden the "social question" of moral and material improvement. Everywhere in line with this, save in the Czech lands of relative economic development, there was the widening spectacle of bureaucratic corruption and idleness. Here, as in Africa, the great ideal was not to do a job but to occupy a salaried post. Here, as in Africa, urban poverty was subsidized by rural immiseration; and one regime of gross incompetence followed upon another.

Police and army power went down the same road of degradation. Generals were ousted by colonels and colonels by majors, majors by captains and captains by sergeants; while, increasingly through the 1930s as Hitlerite pressures grew stronger and more violent, these otherwise insignificant "changes of the guard" acquired the accents of Fascism or its agents. "Inventing the future" became one means or another of inventing death. All this was in the history of Central and Eastern Europe between the two world wars, just as it was going to be in the history of Africa a few decades later.

Surely there was no lack of rebels and revolutionaries, protesters or reformers, appealing to the liberal visions of half a century earlier or else, if they had managed to stay alive, to the apocalyptic promises of Russia's revolution. No year passed without some desperate initiative on behalf of useful change or even of reconciliation. None prevailed; instead, prisons were crammed with dissenters and graveyards with insurgents. The militarist animal inside the nation-statist shell proved too strong for any such persons, realist or utopian, to make headway against it. And once Hitlerite expansion finally assailed the last feeble bastions of sovereignty in these lands, nothing remained but surrender or war; and most surrendered.

A new German empire was prevented only at unspeakable

human cost, and the peace of 1945 brought another dawn that promised, once again, to promote freedom from the subjections of the past. But the victory of 1945 brought its own cost, and the price was paid in unforeseen ways. Central and Eastern Europe was soon trenched within the western bulwarks of a Soviet sphere of command which then became the extensions of a new Russian empire, while the anxious fears and ambitions of the Western Powers ensured that this severing of Europe into two hostile "blocs" should stand firm for another forty years. Who was chiefly to blame for this disaster, and in what degree or with what malice or stupidity, are questions that history has yet to answer; and perhaps history's eventual answer will say that the disaster was not in any case avoidable. What is meanwhile certain is that the consequences for the peoples living between Germany and Russia were increasingly painful.

During these forty years, if with varying impact, these consequences were in forms of Soviet control of a "neocolonial" nature. This control was exercised, by preference, from behind the scenes, and therefore had its parallels, at the same time, in much of Africa.

Often this Soviet "neocolonial" control was extremely close, closer even than anything of its kind that appeared in Africa. There was even an oil refinery in Bulgaria, it appears, which was incapable of refining any oil except Soviet-produced oil. One may compare this with the American-financed bauxite smelter built in Ghana that was unable, in practice, to smelt Ghanaian-produced bauxite. The bauxite for the smelter was brought from Jamaica, but at least the dam that powered the Ghanaian smelter produced electricity that stayed in Ghana.

Generally, the "neocolonial" consequences worsened as the

years went by. This was not so much because the controlling Soviet hand grew heavier and more oppressive, although it could be both and usually was whenever its dominance was threatened (as, for one example, against Hungarian rebels in 1956), as because its local agents or beneficiaries grew more isolated and therefore more fearful.

Socialist policies and programs might retain their solid attachment to the general good. Contrary to the received Western wisdom of 1989–90, it seems that those policies and programs often did do this in terms of social responsibilities for welfare and public education; but they were increasingly hobbled, or even wiped out altogether (as most obviously in Romania), by the deepening demoralization that ensued from stagnation and political repression. For nothing in the rigidly commandist structures of the Stalinist or para-Stalinist structure was allowed to change. Wherever industrial expansion really took place, as it did in several of these countries, it was at the cost of ferocious pollutions of the environment—pollutions taken to a point at which wide plains and ancient forests ceased any longer to be fit for life by any reasonable estimate of survival value.

Wherever literary and artistic culture had responded to the liberating call of social revolution—and this it had certainly done to notable effect after the miseries of the 1930s and the Hitlerite war—it had now to face the censors' wrath, or worse. Above all, perhaps, there was continuing decay in the quality of the rulers. Earlier years had produced self-sacrifice and high ideals. But the Stalinist degeneration ruined them, too, or else slaughtered them in judicial "trials" that would have been atrociously absurd if their outcome had not been tragic. Now there were no revolutionaries or ardent reformers in power, but only gray figures of a drear but dangerous Soviet obedience. The names and deeds of leading men and women in these countries had once been names and deeds to conjure with. Now the names and deeds of such persons, after the 1940s, seemed barely worth remembering.

In all these ways the "neocolonial" condition, just as in Africa, induced the denial of its own legitimacy. Now the state was one thing, but the people quite another. Quantities of words might be expended to demonstrate the contrary; they made no difference. In all these countries the ruling party—or rather the ruling bureaucracy, for the concept of political party in every legitimate sense had ceased to apply—was itself the state; and this state, effectively, had ceased to have any citizens. Its condition of "having no citizens" was every bit as complete, if sometimes less blatantly obvious, as, for example, in the Mobutist paradigm of Zaire in the 1980s. Citizens might remain present as existential phenomena; they were absent as participating actors. As early as 1953 the German revolutionary poet Brecht, no doubt Europe's most poignant voice in this desperate epoch, satirized a final reversal of revolutionary aspirations in scathing lines written of East Germany, where he lived. After the Berlin rising of that year, official leaflets of the government informed "the people" that they had "forfeited the confidence of the government"—in which case, asked Brecht, would it not be simpler "for the government to dissolve the people and elect another?"[2] When destiny overtook this bureaucratic nightmare in 1989, the state collapsed like a house of cards. One day the "German Democratic Republic" was there, solid and immovable; the next day it had vanished from the scene of practical affairs: leaving, of course, its problems unresolved.

Needless to say, there remains more to be said. Exceptions have to be taken into account, and some of them, as in Africa, have been important and remain important. In Eastern Europe, including Greece, the principal exception has been Yugoslavia. Here, too, the year of 1989 signaled a virtual collapse of the established constitutional order, and yet this order had emerged from an undoubtedly successful and enlightened federalism, itself the product of Yugoslavia's victorious war of self-liberation from 1941 to 1945. One might have expected protest against inefficient government, poor standards of living, incompetent bureaucracy, and various forms of human failure. The culprit that emerged, however, was something different. All the evils of federal Yugoslavia, it was discovered in 1989, were the fault of its federalism. A truly frenzied outbreak of nationalism, of extremist nation-statism, erupted on every side.

There was imminent civil war, separatism, an utter rejection of wartime gains. Given that this Yugoslavia had broken from the Stalinist empire in 1948, and had traced since about 1955 a path of its own, how and why should this destructive fragmentation of internal loyalties and purposes have come about? Just when Western Europe was turning away from traditional nation-statism, why should this Yugoslavia, precisely, turn toward traditional nation-statism?

The case of Yugoslavia, as would rapidly become clear after 1990, in no way undermines the case against nation-statism in the world of today. It merely shows that one can try one's hand, and even possibly succeed, at putting the clock back.

The "first Yugoslavia" was the "Triune Kingdom" of the Serbs, Croats, and Slovenes, born in 1919 and enduring until 1941;

and while its ending was unforeseeably disastrous, one is still bound to say, and not only with hindsight, that here was a kingdom certain to fail. This was for the simple reason, apparent even at the time, that all the non-Serbian peoples of the country felt themselves to be, and in practice often were, subject to constrictive Serbian domination. This was why the kingdom could never achieve the democratic aspirations of its birth or even of Serbian history itself. For an African parallel one may even suggest, without any great distortion of the evidence, that the condition of seething discontent present in that first Yugo-slavia, within some years of its birth, was much like the condition that could have been expected in postcolonial Ghana if, at independence in the 1950s, the whole of the country had been placed under the command of the king of Asante. The king would no doubt have felt that history warranted the domination of all Ghana by the Asante kingship and its people; large numbers of other Ghanaians would surely have made violent objection.

For this and other reasons the Yugoslav state formed in 1919 became rapidly a bureaucratized and militarized shell, and when the invading armies of Germany, Italy, Hungary, and Bulgaria fell upon it in April 1941, it collapsed within days. The invaders carved it into pieces. Slovenia fell under military occupation. Croatia became a puppet state under a Fascist-type regime pro-tected by Germany and Italy. Most of Serbia was left to Serbian puppets under strong German or Italian control. Other regions were variously occupied or divided. Much of Macedonia was handed to neighboring Bulgaria, with the rest remaining under Italian military occupation. The Vojvodina, whose fortunes we have followed earlier, was dismembered into three pieces. One

275

of these, the Banat, remained under direct German military control. Another, the Bačka, also north of the Danube, was annexed to Hungary although three-fourths of its population was not Hungarian. And a third fragment, Srem, south of the Danube, was incorporated in the puppet state of Croatia even though most of its people were Serbs.

That was in 1941, and it invited trouble. But the Germans and Italians, or those who ruled them then, were confident that they could deal with any amount of rebellion. They were to learn better as the war proceeded, but in Yugoslavia they began to learn better almost at once. Armed resistance to enemy occupation began and persisted on a rising scale, and could not be mastered. In 1944 and 1945 the partisan armies of Yugoslavia's self-liberation drove their enemies to final defeat, needing for this little more than peripheral Soviet assistance on their frontiers with Romania and Bulgaria, and some Western aid in arms, ammunition, and medical facilities.

Now this was truly a people's victory in the full sense of the term "people." No matter how dogmatic the Communist partisan leadership may have been—and it was at that time sharply dogmatic in its Stalinist loyalties—the partisan armies were drawn from all parts of Yugoslavia and from all sectors of society, while behind them stood the overwhelming support of a probably clear majority of Yugoslavs. The internal opponents of the partisans were in comparison small men more or less fatally stained by service with a ruthless enemy, or else by outright betrayal of every democratic principle. These internal opponents, mostly old-style nationalists when they were not blatant sellouts to the enemy, had nothing new to offer but a dismal repetition of past conflicts. The partisans, by contrast, had much to offer that was new. These sentiments may sound pro-partisan, but were they not to be confirmed by the revived aggression of those same old-style nationalists after federal collapse in the 1980s?

Against old-style nationalism, drenched as it was with the blood of countless nationalistic massacres perpetrated between 1941 and 1944, the partisan leadership in 1945 offered an enlightened and innovating federalism. The men and women in their fighting brigades had marched to no tunes and slogans of nationalism, but for the ideals of *bratsvo i jedinstvo*, of brotherhood and unity, such as could and did rise above old conflicts, and promise to establish a real ground for postwar reconciliation among all these harried peoples.

Launched in 1942 in the midst of many battles and appalling enemy reprisals, above all in this period in Croatia and Bosnia, this federalizing program was refined and improved until, at war's end, a new Yugoslavia could take shape. A modernizing society arose from the ruins of the old. It now consisted of six federated republics and two self-governing regions, each with far-reaching powers of internal self-government and an undoubted scope for the promotion of these various national cultures. This decentralizing and participatory achievement was and has remained, all recent events notwithstanding, innovative and impressive; but its virtues have been little appreciated in the outside world. The Soviets rather understandably feared that a federalized Yugoslavia, following lines of democratic participation (however reduced by one-party rule), would develop outside the centralized rigidities of Moscow's control, while the

Western powers, enwrapped in their Cold War worries and myopia, thought that it must in any case be hostile if only because it took place in a Communist-ruled country.

Yet this federalism, judged also in hindsight, may far better be reckoned as one of the truly developmental initiatives to have derived from the upheavals of the Second World War. Except in the case of Kosovo-Metohija, where the claims of a local Albanian population struck hard against Serbian traditionalism, the new dispensation proved to be shrewd and successful. Old sources of dissidence and rebellion were impressively relieved. The Macedonians, for example, achieved a national autonomy for the first time in modern history, at least so far as their people inside Yugoslavia were concerned. While Macedonians in neighboring Bulgaria continued to be treated as Bulgarians, and those in neighboring Greece as Hellenized Slavs, the majority of Macedonians acquired a republic of their own as part of federal Yugoslavia. The same was true of Bosnian Muslims after suffering, during the war, from ferocious massacres at the hands of Croat Fascists.

This strong program of reconciliation, forged though it had to be in the midst of harsh warfare against enemy powers, drew its strength from various traditions. One of them was an old conviction that there could be no peace in the Balkans as long as Balkan states and governments were powerless to resist external influence or control. The need, therefore, was to overleap a nation-statism which was bound to play into the hands of stronger powers.[3] This need would be met only if nationalist enmities and rivalries could be made to give way to intra-Balkan forms of federalizing unity. What united this mosaic of peoples, in short, could then become stronger than what divided them, provided that an equality of rights and interests could be made to prevail. In other words, so long as "the national question" had priority over "the social question," there would be no peace; any such peace that might be patched up would always fall victim to rivalries couched in nationalist terms. That is what had happened in the first Yugoslavia between 1919 and 1941. But the partisan resistance had introduced the factor of social revolution, and a different outcome could be possible.

One may remark in passing that this introduction of the factor of social revolution was essential to the possibility of widespread partisan insurrection and its eventual success. This was not because the partisan brigades and their civilian support organizations were filled with men and women fighting for Communism or socialism or any such doctrine. The slogans might say that. But the reality was different. What they were undoubtedly fighting for was to end a hated and feared enemy occupation, yet to end it in such a way that some wide if often vaguely understood social renewal might become possible. They wanted a modernization of these peasant societies that could thrust old hatreds and disabilities behind them. They wanted a clear and positive break with the past.

This was what their internal opponents, whether old-style Serbian nationalists (known as Chetniks) or new-style Croat Fascists (ustaša and the like), could not offer. All they could offer was a return to the past under narrowly nationalist dogmas. Here in the partisan movement, in other words, the "social" had overtaken the "national," even while it remained no less true that the partisans were also fighting for a nationwide liberation from enemy control. These peoples went to war in excruciating conditions of loss and danger not for "the ideas in anyone's head"—as Amílcar Cabral was to say of the insurrectionary peasants whom he led in West Africa in the 1960s—but "in order to see their lives go forward, and be able to live in peace." This being so, the concepts of a practical and self-regulating democracy could become real and appealing for the first time in every Yugoslav region.

The acid test of this truth could perhaps best be seen at work and evolution in the plains of the Vojvodina. There the peasants rose and fought in multitudes—no matter that they had no mountains or deep forests in which to shelter—so as to end a hated foreign tyranny and then "to see their lives go forward." Often they were relatively privileged peasants in fertile lands where there was normally plenty to eat and drink or trade with; a Marxist would have described them as kulaks, peasants who in the usual run of things might be counted as prudently conservative. But they still responded far more eagerly to the partisan call for social change and progress than to any appeal based on the ideas of Serbian nationalism: here in these sundered fragments of northern Serbia, there was no nostalgia for the Great Serbianism of royal Yugoslavia.[4]

Why, then, was the collapse of the whole Stalinist project in Eastern Europe accompanied also by Yugoslav disintegration? Why should the vividly imaginative federalism of the liberation movement yield so readily, and tumultuously, to the old slogans of separatist nationalism, bidding Serbia "to arise," or Croatia "to arise," or some other variant on bankrupt ideas and doctrines? Such questions seemed all the more pressing because the Yugoslav Communists, unlike their neighbors, had cut loose from Soviet control in 1948 and, having done that, began soon after to cut loose from internal Stalinist programs and oppressions as well. They held to their federalism but went further. They persisted in policies and efforts designed to reduce the heavy-handed centralism of their Stalinist state system. They introduced complex and ambitious forms of economic self-management. They went far to hand over power to local bodies and initiatives. They tried to achieve a system of mass participation that should be able to defend itself from bureaucratic rigidities and corruptions.[5]

But in this they had, and perhaps could only have had, a mixed success and eventual failure. The reasons lay both in structural breakdowns and the frailties of human nature, for the project was splendidly innovative and difficult. But it seems likely that history's judgment, if one may imagine it, will say that the principal reason for failure lay in the persistence of a single-party authoritarianism unable or unwilling to reform itself. For it appears to have remained largely true, as journalist Misha Glenny has observed, that "the structure of the Yugoslav League of Communists, as the party was renamed in the mid-50s, remained Stalinist in essence . . . and those who disagreed were either isolated or imprisoned," while "Yugoslavia's internal security machine," at any rate up to the end of the 1970s, "was one of the most powerful in the whole of Eastern Europe."[6]

Thus it came about that federalist decentralism, in practice, was not what it claimed: to a more or less large degree, the single all-Yugoslav oligarchy was displaced (at any rate for nonmilitary affairs) not by decentralized organs of democracy, but by six or seven regional (republican) oligarchies which behaved as outright rulers. These oligarchies were at first in loose alliance with each other but soon in fractious and eventually destructive conflict. There developed an increasingly abrasive free-for-all between and among these oligarchies for possession of scarce resources. The ideal of brotherhood and unity became more and more a camouflage, as more and more citizens came to see it, for unfair discriminations and nest featherings, or worse.

There was thus induced the kind of atmosphere, and sometimes of hard reality, of political disintegration that had led to the collapse of Triune Yugoslavia in 1941. Ambitious demagogues, beating the chauvinist-separatist drum, began to flourish. Slovenia and Croatia drew ever more sharply away from a Serbia now gripped by nationalist dementia; and the malady unavoidably spread. Anxious eyes in Western Europe, having welcomed the demise of Tito's Yugoslavia, were now dismayed by a prospect of the "gates of the West" being besieged by a mob of mutinous Balkan states which had not been viable in the past, or in some cases had not even existed in the past. While Western Europe was turning toward federalist structures of one kind or another (however labeled), it appeared that Eastern Europe had fallen back on the nation-statism of the 1920s, yet with no better hope of making this work.[7]

In the ideological and cultural void induced by Stalinism, it was no doubt entirely natural to "turn to the West," and to look for solutions in a more or less blind aping of Western ideas and structures. But to find escape in that direction was to suppose that the scope and time and resources to bring into existence a groundwork for Western structures in Eastern Europe were present, or could rapidly be summoned. They were not so present, and summoning proved more than difficult. The 1990s opened on a scene of nation-statist uproar and confusion.

*   *   *

Elsewhere it was much the same. The sclerosis of single-party statism on the Soviet pattern, made almost everywhere more acute by political illusions or sheer political ignorance long fostered by an absence of public debate and information, seemed to leave no alternative but to return to multiparty structures which had briefly existed before the Second World War. Yet this "parliamentary solution" on bourgeois-capitalist lines had invariably failed in the prewar years, save in the Czech lands, because it lacked its necessary social basis. Capitalists without strength and cohesion had all in various ways found themselves sucked into the whirlpools of militarized dictatorship. "Middle strata" parties had all gone down in defeat for want of any sufficiently nourished middle strata. It had been argued—as it would be argued in Africa—that development and the passage of time would make good this want of capitalist middle strata. But war and disaster had arrived instead.

And now the position was worse than before, even much worse. What could be said about Romania at the end of 1989 was widely and even generally true: that the Stalinist monocratic system had not only dominated political life, but actually destroyed every alternative social structure, erecting instead a gigantic bureaucratic apparatus of repression. That apparatus had made itself hatefully odious and despised, but how was Romania to be governed without it? New parties were formed, many parties modeled on the conservative parliamentary parties of the West. Their leaders were available but not, it seemed, their troops.

A reversion to crude nationalism was perhaps unavoidable. Yet this was clearly no solution to the ideological void. This was rapidly proved by the example of Romania's Hungarian minority in the great upland province of Transylvania. That minority's complaints of Romanian oppression were now heard to repeat the very same words used before the Second World War, and with much the same justification. All good sense indicated that the interests of Romanians and Hungarians in Transylvania could best be satisfied by a mutual sinking of nation-state sovereignties between Romania and Hungary, and that nothing could be gained on either side by purely nationalist policies. But the lessons of all the years since 1919 seemed to have gone for nothing. In early 1991 it was even reported that the Hungarian government was seeking to buy the national armory of a defunct East Germany, so as to rearm Hungary in case of new aggressions—which, all too clearly, could only come from nationalist disputes. The "new Romania" seemed bent on the same kind of folly.

Meanwhile, another act in this ludicrous tragedy assailed in-terethnic peace in the Vojvodina. In 1989 a renewed Great Serbian nationalism had destroyed the autonomous stature of the Vojvodina, adding it simply to Serbia. By July 1991 the Serbian parliament in Belgrade declared that Serbian was to be the only official language of the Serbian republic. What this did, among other deplorable things, was to outlaw the public use of the Hungarian language by Hungarians whose forefathers had lived in the Vojvodina since at least the eighteenth century; and this minority now was no smaller than some 400,000 persons. This backward step was taken for absolutely no good reason of sense or value, but of course was bound to strike hard at the cultural peace that the federalism of 1945 had promoted and maintained. No wonder that it now seemed that the anti-Stalinist "revolutions" of 1989 had turned back on themselves, with Serbs today doing to Hungarians what Hungarians in Kossuth's time had done to Serbs.[8]

To all this sowing of confusion, the last years of a dying century added major breakdowns within the Soviet Union itself. Here, too, while fears of repression were lessened and forbidden thoughts began to be uttered again, large minorities and whole constituent peoples across a vast Euro-Asian continent began to call for separatist sovereignties, and were not in the least held back by consideration of the conflicts between them that might ensue. This was easily understandable; but it was not therefore promising of peace or progress. The real interdependence imposed by profound technological and economic changes in the world were thrust aside, however blindly, by the clamors of this insurgent nationalism. And yet there also appeared, everywhere in the wake of Stalinism or its equivalents, something like a collective collapse of political and social self-confidence, rather as though nothing could be done but await salvation by an immediate installation of "Western prosperity." It seemed, quite often, as though these peoples had lost all belief in their capacity to think and act for themselves except, fatally, by repeating the blunders of the past.

Perhaps more time had to elapse before the nation-statist mirage could be seen for what it was; all the old songs of nationalism still had emotive force. Yet all the lessons of the twentieth century were there to drive home the unavoidable conclusion that if these peoples were not to die together they would have to find out how to live together. What grew ever more visible, as the uproar continued, was the uselessness, or rather the helplessness, of the nation-statist project. This perception in no way denied the value of nationalism, of national pride or feeling, as a vehicle of culture. Just as in ex-colonial Africa, these ex-colonized European peoples had everything to gain from the flowering of their cultures. Their languages and their arts, their customs and pleasures of community and all their beauties of singularity, were such that any worthwhile European civilization would be impossible without their concourse. These cultures had every good reason to insist on their survival. But to cramp and confine their strivings into the nation-statism of exclusive and abrasive sovereignties would now be the obvious action of a blind despair.

Here, as in Africa of the 1990s, it appeared that new containers for national cultures were required; otherwise, the miseries of the past would have to be repeated. And if this was true, wisdom would have to look in the direction of some rational federalism. A hopeful future—a postimperialist future, a postneocolonialist future—would have to be a federalizing future: a future of organic unities of sensible association across wide regions within which national cultures, far from seeking to destroy or maim each other, could evolve their diversities and find in them a mutual blessing.

The Wilsonian containers of 1919 had been well intended; but these nation-states had not worked. It began to be seen that something different and much more flexible was now required; and something different seemed to be in the cards. No one said this better, as our blood-encrusted century closed, than a West German—but one can now simply say German—political thinker. This was the stalwart Erhard Eppler; and he offered a mighty contrast to the German political thinkers of earlier times whose frantic nationalism did so much to foster a Europe of nation-states. "What is new," Eppler told the West German parliament in 1989, even before the great upheavals of that year had reached their climax, "and what I find encouraging, is that national identity today is no longer tied to nation-states, or even aims at creating nation-states, but is often rooted in older kinds of community."[9]

It might well be, Eppler went on to say, that the nation-states of Europe were now being eroded in their sovereignties from two sides at once: "by the European Community, and, from below, by regional traditions, languages, dialects, and cultures." This could mean, as it proceeded, that a future European Community could progressively find room for the self-affirmation of all those identities and cultures—Scots, Welsh, Basque, Catalan, many more—that nation-statist frameworks had oppressed or stifled. Then indeed, this wise German might have added, a federalizing European Community could find out how to accommodate all those minorities divided from their mother cultures by the accidents of history—such, for example, as Hungarians in Romania—who were grossly disadvantaged, or felt themselves to be, by the nation-statist sovereignties in which they were enclosed.

The application of these thoughts to Africa is clear enough. And with all this the idea began to gain ground, if not easily or smoothly, that nationalism need not imply nation-statism: that there could be life after nation-statism, and a better life than before. For was it after all so sure that newly clamorous nationalities in, for example, Soviet Asia were shouting for nation-statism; or were they not in revolt, rather, against being governed from afar, governed by a rigidly centralized system they could seldom influence, and therefore governed badly? Could a proliferation of new nation-states promise any good outcome to the end of the Soviet empire? Or would a new mob of mutinous nation-states provide a happy sequel to the collapse of federal Yugoslavia? To think so would be to forget the last hundred years or so of internecine strife.

The circumstances of Africa, it may be objected, differ in many ways from those of Eastern Europe. I am far from sure of this, but in any case the circumstances here relate to speeds of change, notably of ideological change. Europe has needed more than two centuries to go through its experience of nation-statism from its formative beginnings—in most explanations, those of the French Revolution—to the unfolding thought that nation-statism has come near the end of its useful life. But it seems that Africa has covered this ground in just half a century.

While the bureaucratic nation-state may still claim to exist in Africa, at least on paper, the thought that it may be near the end of its useful life is more advanced. The African snail, it would appear, has in this respect outpaced the European hare. The African warlords of the bureaucratic nation-state may still rage and strut, but pretty well everyone save themselves has begun to see their fruitlessness; which is not in the least to impugn those honest generals and soldiers—for example, in Nigeria—who have not governed and do not govern as warlords but who have striven and do strive to advance the public good. It is a fruitlessness proclaimed even from the housetops. As experienced an observer as Edem Kodjo, former secretary-general of the Organization of African Unity, went out of his way in 1987, when writing for a wide audience, to deplore the African nation-state as "a shackle on progress." What weighty opinion has disagreed?

Unavoidably, the question arose—and arises—of how this

black man's burden can be shifted. This is no doubt one of those questions that historians are not supposed to answer. But I have noticed that historians always do answer. What I can do is to conclude this book with a kind of survey that may also be a kind of answer. Even, if cautiously, a hopeful answer.

Conclusion

IF THE postcolonial nation-state had become a shackle on progress, as more and more critics in Africa seemed to agree by the
end of the 1980s, the prime reason could appear in little doubt.
The state was not liberating and protective of its citizens, no
matter what its propaganda claimed: on the contrary, its gross
effect was constricting and exploitative, or else it simply failed
to operate in any social sense at all. Its overall consequences
were in any case disastrous. And the prime reason for these
consequences was something else that was widely agreed upon.
It was powerfully stated by the hero of the Nigerian novelist
Chinua Achebe's memorable *Anthills of the Savannah*, published in 1987 but reflecting that writer's mature conviction.
The prime reason, Ikem reflects before he, too, has to meet
disaster, "can't be the massive corruption though its scale and
pervasiveness are truly intolerable; it isn't the subservience to
foreign manipulation, degrading as it is; it isn't even this sec-
ond-class, hand-me-down capitalism, ludicrous and doomed."

All such miseries of malice and incompetence or greed could

be blamed for "the prime failure of this government." But they were not the cause; they were the effects. The cause was to be found elsewhere. It lay in "the failure of our rulers to re-establish vital inner links with the poor and dispossessed of this country."[1] It was the failure of postcolonial communities to find and insist upon means of living together by strategies less primitive and destructive than rival kinship networks, whether of "ethnic" clientelism or its camouflage in no less clientelist "multiparty systems."

Anxious visitors picking over the ruins of neocolonial experi-ence had therefore good reason for pessimism,[2] just as, some years later, other visitors would return from Eastern Europe with similar forebodings. All the copious plans and projects for postcolonial progress and "development" had supposed the more or less rapid and even automatic arrival of "middle strata" capable of building systems of capitalism on the best-advocated models, whether those of Western Europe or of North America, after which, as all the models were held to prove—vast interne-cine wars and other disasters being somehow held to be momen-tary pileups on the mighty highways of free enterprise—there would be steady advance to "high mass consumption." So it was prophesied. But no such middle strata had arrived, much less "high mass consumption." Or else, it was contrarily argued, still more desirable routes and objectives would be found under the magic guidance of Marxism-Leninism. This Marxist-Lenin-ist vision vanished utterly in 1989. But maybe the free-enter-prise vision could still be made true?

The pessimists of the 1980s generally thought not. In their view the ex-colonial countries, now fashionably categorized as the countries of the "Third World" or simply as LDCs (less developed countries) had missed the bus. For them it was too late. They would not now be able to escape from the constrictions of a "world order" designed most clearly to put them in their place and keep them there. Japan, of course, had escaped; but Japan had never been invaded and dispossessed. One or two large Latin American countries—perhaps Brazil, conceivably Argentina—might still be able to escape, and build a capitalist system of their own, a self-orientated and sufficiently stable system; but the results of their trying to do this over the previous hundred years were more than discouraging. In recent times the "four little dragons" of Asia—Hong Kong, South Korea, Singapore, and Taiwan—might be on their way to being capitalist "blue chips" in terms of system as well as production. But their circumstances were nothing if not specific to themselves: the "little dragons" were islands unlikely to be joined to "the main." Otherwise the future for the "Third World" appeared bound to be a restatement of stagnation and decay.

To this the optimists of the 1980s—surprisingly, there were still some to be heard—have replied that pessimism of this built-in type is equally bound to be defective history. It empties the whole grand panorama of social being, they have argued, into a sack of negative conclusions. It writes off the story of Africa, but not only of Africa, as though it can never, in a postcolonial sense, begin again. Whereas very much, in truth, has already begun again. In all those arts and initiatives that derive from the dynamics and development of peoples, as distinct from the mere trajectory of things such as "gross national product," the anticolonial liberations have not failed.

All its defects and diseases notwithstanding, the Africa of the 1990s is immeasurably different from the Africa of the 1930s, and in all those ways that signal renewal and creativity, this Africa is also immeasurably more alive. Achebe's Ikem had powerful reasons for pessimism in 1987; but this was an Ikem that an Africa of half a century earlier could never have possessed. And since I have ventured on parallels with Eastern Europe, I would suggest that the same may be true of Eastern Europe between 1930 and 1980, no matter how sorely the Stalinist systems have cut down the liberating consequences of the anti-Nazi war. Here, too, the pessimists of the 1980s may have all too easily forgotten the miseries of the decades before the anti-Nazi war.

The pessimists, on this general view of matters, may be said to have overstated their pessimism and to have forgotten that peoples can never for long be confined to the cages of any neat scenario. But however this can be, what has remained common cause to pessimists and optimists alike is that the systems in place have all failed, whether neocolonial capitalist in Africa or Stalinist in Europe, and that the prime badge of their failure, as Ikem said, has lain in the brutal divorce between rulers and ruled. The African texts to this effect were many and forceful by the end of the 1980s, and no serious person had yet been heard to deny their truth.

"Development strategies in Africa, with minor exceptions, have tended to be strategies by which the few use the many for their purposes. They are uncompromisingly top-down. There is not, and never has been, popular participation in political and economic decision-making." Everything, on the contrary, is done "to prevent the expression of popular interest, and to ensure acquiescence in policies which are hostile to the public interest."[3] And this had become true, added this Nigerian wit-

point that "development has turned into concerted
against the common people, producing a theatre of
alienation."[4]

The writer was not, as it happened, a disgruntled academic sniping at his masters, but Claude Ake, a highly competent analyst speaking from close experience; and the same view has come from spokesmen of the established order. Criticizing the command economies of Eastern Europe, the top-down economies of the Stalinist dispensation, Chief Emeka Anyaoku, the British Commonwealth secretary-general, has argued that such economies could never in any case realize "national potential for development";[5] and the application to Africa was directly clear. Only "popular participation in development," he affirmed, could realize this potential. The whole option of and for representative democracy—and the words here are those of Nigerian President Ibrahim Babangida speaking in October 1989—has to be "hinged on mass participation; and this is the cardinal principle which will sustain it."[6]

Was this, then, the route of escape from the fearsome dilemma of the 1980s: the dilemma which taught that a strong state had to mean dictatorship but a weak state must collapse into clientelism? If so, the key to progress, even to survival, was not to be found merely in the multiplying of party rivalries at the centers of executive power, however much a structured rivalry might be desirable. It would be found, rather, in devolving executive power to a multiplicity of locally representative bodies. It would be found in reestablishing "vital inner links" within the fabric of society. Democratic participation would have to be "mass participation." And "mass participation," patiently evolved and applied, would be able to produce its own version of a strong state: the kind of state, in other words, that would be able to promote and protect civil society.

Now ideas such as these, as it happens, have a history of their own. Whether they can be made to work in the modern world is another question; and I will confront that question a little further on. But there can be little doubt that they could be made to work in the precolonial past. For "mass participation," however variously mediated by this or that structure of representation and control, was at the heart of all those African societies which had proved stable and progressive before the destructive impact of the overseas slave trade and colonial dispossession had made itself felt. And an historian may note that these ideas on mass participation, on practical democracy, can also be seen as a revised completion of those developmental projects launched more than a century earlier by the prophets of a regenerated Africa in the British West African settlements, some of whom framed the Fanti constitution of the 1860s. The essential argument of those early prophets was that a progressive Africa, one that would be capable of facing the outside world, must depend on the development of progressive institutions. They turned to Europe for those institutions, and we have seen what has come of that. The prophets of mass participation in the 1980s, on the contrary, were meditating concepts more or less related, in one reformulation or another, to those whereby their ancestors had held society together and, when necessary, put down the mighty from their seats.

How far such concepts have a real affiliation with those of the precolonial past may be argued elsewhere. My own view is that the years ahead will increasingly show this affiliation, and will give the struggle to escape from stagnation or regression a new base in African historical experience. However one views this, these same ideas also have a modern history of their own, even if obscure and brief. Before looking further into the capacity of mass participation to provide "the route of escape," this is a history that deserves to be recalled.

The first modern attempt at the practical application of the ideas of mass participation appeared with some of the anticolonial movements of armed struggle, notably those in the Portuguese African colonies. These movements and their insurrections have been copiously described but rather little studied, not least in their moral and psychological aspects. One may hope they will be better studied in the future; meanwhile, I want to draw attention to their moral aspects.

These could be seen, as I wrote some years ago, in "the demand that men and women should rise above themselves, take inspiration from their cause, grow larger in companionship" while, on the side of negation, "there were the miseries of hardship, danger and solitude, the temptations to withdraw into neutrality, the longing for food and sleep and safety when no such safety, let alone for food or even sleep, was anywhere to be looked for or even to be hoped for." Beyond that, in these African guerrilla movements, there were "other demons that assail, the demons of the forest or the wilderness that are not the demons of the ancestors but the demons of doubt, distrust of absent comrades, nagging fears of intrigue, surges of despair, the ever-repeated question of knowing what best to do and how to do it."[7]

Large numbers of young men and women lived and fought under these conditions, seldom better and often worse, for long successive years; and one is bound to ask what ideology or belief could have sustained them. Much was said at the time, principally by their enemies, of the influence of Marxism and its revolutionary teachings; and for a handful of educated persons in guerrilla ranks this influence was real and inspiring. Much was said about the huge provocations of a Portuguese colonialism that would yield no concessions, and give no ground for peaceful change; this particular influence, generally, was far more important in these movements, and would probably have sustained them without any other influence.

These were wars against a colonialism of Fascist type, reflecting the dictatorship which reigned in Portugal: a colonialism of a most brutal nature. But while its provocations were unyielding and severe, and revolutionary hopes and thoughts became powerful in the leadership of these movements, mature reflection suggests that another factor was also at work. This factor is hard to pin down without inviting misinterpretation, for these are matters both subtle and little understood. These ragged peasants—almost all were peasants, save for a few "second-generation" peasants from colonial towns—could well seem merely primitive in their motivations, primitive insurrectionaries obeying "primitive customs," "atavistic" customs as was charged, for example, against the Mau Mau insurrectionaries in the Kenya of the 1950s; but there is more to be said. Along with such loyalties to insurrection—actually underlying them—one can perceive something else. This has been the missing factor in all Europe-centered histories of Africa: the deep and lasting sense of injury, above all of moral injury, that colonial dispossession was felt to have done to the way that people had lived and should live. It is the factor of moral legitimacy.[8]

Understood in this light, as I believe they have to be, the "primitive customs" of national-liberation warfare join others in the precolonial pantheon—I am drawing here on the work of social anthropologist Meyer Fortes, writing in the 1950s of various situations—as media "for giving tangible substance to moral obligations." These loyalties and the duties they imposed on the volunteers of these wars (for there were none but volunteers on the African side) reflect "a conviction that there is a moral order in the universe, and that man's well-being depends upon obedience to that order as men see it."[9] The colonial intrusion and its monstrous coercions had wrecked that moral order. To restore it would be enormously difficult. But without restoring it—without, that is, restoring its legitimate successor—there could be no peace or self-respect: just as, in fighting to restore it, men and women could win back self-respect and possess at least the prospect of an eventual peace.

All this may be hard to accept in a world that has generally seen the colonial dispossessions as an acceptable price of progress or, at least, as a generally benign process of "development." Obviously, too, men and women joined these anticolonial wars with every sort of motivation and often remained in them, as soldiers will, because there was no sufficient case for leaving them. Yet the strategies with which the wars had to be fought, if they were going to be won—and each of the insurrections in these Portuguese colonies was clearly successful—had their own momentum and compulsion. These strategies came together in what their memorable political philosopher Amílcar Cabral, who was no less a memorable man of action, called "a determinant of culture": of sociopolitical culture, of moral culture. In this lay their great originality.

Irrespective of whatever alliances or semialliances of theory or of convenience that these movements may have had abroad, they had to follow the bidding of their own conditions; and these conditions demanded absolutely that the peasants, with the few townsmen who joined them, participate out of their own will and understanding. The alternative was defeat. A few stalwart revolutionaries would decide to take up their rifles and "begin." They would be overcome and eliminated by a massively stronger enemy unless they could rapidly fulfill two conditions for survival. The first and preliminary condition was that they should gain local peasant sympathy and support. The second, much harder, was that they should then transform this support into active participation. That they were able to do this—not always, but surprisingly often—is what has given these movements in the Portuguese colonies their true place in history. This *participação popular*, as it came to be called, responded of course to practical needs—for the risking of life, for the porterage of ammunition, for the building and running of bush schools and clinics, for the meeting of local forms of self-government wherever the colonial dictatorship could be lifted away; beyond these, however, *participação popular* responded to the needs of moral restoration.

Its central process aimed at giving rural multitudes a real measure of practical self-government. This would have been hard in any case; in the case of the Portuguese colonies it was extremely difficult. Still more than other colonial powers, the Portuguese had governed solely by the imposed hierarchies of administrative decree, whereas *participação popular* meant self-administration by local assemblies and their elected executives. It was a process that had time and opportunity to succeed very well in a few regions, and to reach an early stage in some other regions; but, as was expected, it barely appeared at all in provinces not yet heavily influenced by armed insurrection. But where it did succeed, its workings could be remarkable.

"Consider," wrote Cabral of this process, "the features of an armed liberation struggle" necessary to its success. These are "the practice of democracy, of criticism and self-criticism; the increasing responsibility of populations for the governance of their own lives; the creation of schools and health services; the training of cadres from peasant and worker backgrounds. All these features, and others, enable us to see that the armed liberation struggle is not only a product of culture. It is also a *determinant* of culture." From it a double effect would follow. The thought and behavior of "those who began," of leaders, would converge upon and meld with the thought and behavior of those who followed, who joined in participation: and each would change.

The leaders, he continued, would lose their petty-bourgeois opportunism and "sense of superiority." They would "learn a new respect for the multitude and strengthen their grip on reality." At the same time, "the mass of workers and in particular the peasants, who are generally illiterate and have never moved beyond the confines of the village universe, would understand their situation as decisive in the struggle. They would break the fetters of that village universe and integrate gradually with the country and the world."[10]

There were risks apart from the perils of warfare in which many perished. These perils were unavoidable. "We were, therefore, left," reflected the Mozambican leader Eduardo Mondlane, writing later of the decision to fight, "with these alternatives: to continue indefinitely living under a repressive imperial rule, or to find a means of using force against Portugal which would be effective enough to hurt Portugal without resulting in our own ruin."[11] Yet these leaders went to war reluctantly, knowing that violence could always be a two-edged weapon. "We had to follow this route of armed struggle," in the words of the Cape Verdean leader Aristides Pereira, referring here to the insurrection in neighboring Guinea-Bissau on the mainland, "because there was no other way. And yet it was an act of violence on our peasants too: a violent changing of village mentality, a dangerous route!"[12] Hence their wartime slogan, repeated so often by Cabral: "We are armed militants, we are not militarists."

This distrust of violence, including their own violence, is really what marked them off more clearly than any aspect of their programs from the generalized mayhem into which so much of Africa was falling. They saw that the necessary acceptance of violence might well destroy the very objectives they sought to achieve; and I think it is true—at least on the basis of having watched in the field all three of the principal fighting movements in the Portuguese territories—that they used violence under the best disciplines they could manage to evoke.[13] This distrust of violence undoubtedly became a factor in the political successes they were to score. Knowing the unbridled violence of the colonial dictatorship and its armies, they held that if this morbid violence were to be allowed to govern their own projects, they would end in a misery no better than the one they were pledged to defeat. And just how right they were in thinking this was to be displayed, later on, by the murderous violence of the externally created and directed "opposition movements" raised against them: by the UNITA (National Union for the Total Independence of Angola) "movement" in Angola and the analogous RENAMO (Mozambican National Resistance) banditries in Mozambique.

Meanwhile, pursuing their *participação popular* in its civilian as well as its military aspects, the genuine anticolonial movements in the lusophone colonies—PAIGC (African Party for the Independence of Guinea and Cape Verde) in Guinea-Bissau, FRELIMO (Mozambique Liberation Front) in Mozambique, the MPLA (Popular Liberation Movement of Angola) in Angola— were able to achieve impressive gains. By 1968 the little "army of armed militants" of Cabral's PAIGC in the tropical forests and savannahs of Guinea-Bissau had won control of half the territory, and was able to secure the rest by early in 1974.[14] In Angola the insurrection of 1961 had been drowned in blood, but a remnant of Angolan nationalists had managed to survive and was able to achieve leadership by 1975. In Mozambique, meanwhile, the nationalist "front" called FRELIMO was similarly able to overcome initial confusions and defeats, and, again in 1975, concluded its war with striking success.[15] These successes changed the whole balance of power in southern Africa in favor of democratic progress not only against colonialism but also, and now more importantly, against the racist system in South Africa.

It remains that the record after independence became, in all three cases, a story of defeat and even of disaster. Much has been written on the subject, and more will come to hand as distancing years bring firmer analysis.[16] At this stage two principal reasons for this failure seem evident. One of these was internally produced, the other externally created. Both in various ways relate to the whole nation-statist project.

The internally produced reason, or group of reasons, lay partly in the sheer difficulty of proceeding with the project of mass participation once the driving disciplines of the war were no longer present. Angola and Mozambique were vast in size, enormous in their plains and forests, scarcely tied together by all-weather roads or railways; and of many of their remote peoples little was understood by the nationalist policy-makers. Here there were communities which had lived for decades under the heel of an alien authority that they had feared or hated and in any case had done their best to evade. The nationalists were welcomed as liberators but still had to remain, to some extent, an authority hard to accept.

Meanwhile, no matter how hopefully the policies of *participação* had made their mark, the end of the wars brought social and economic emergencies that were extremely hard to handle. Literates were few, politically competent literates fewer still, reliable policy-makers fewest of all; some of the best of them, including Cabral, had given their lives during the struggle, and could in no case be rapidly replaced. Courage and enthusiasm might still be present, but so was the mental and bureaucratic legacy of colonial rule. This legacy weighed heavily on the necessary initial balance between statist centralism and the demands of democratic participation: heavily and negatively. The effective arena of "people's power," of *poder popular*, became ever smaller and beset with troubles.

Soviet bloc advice in planning and application—the more readily accepted because of the continued hostility of the United

States and other Western countries—was soon added to the negative side of the balance. This advice was of course the product of socioeconomic systems of an extreme centralism and commandism, systems that were at the opposite pole from the devolutions of participation. Crudely put, one may say that the Soviet bloc saw salvation for Angola and Mozambique in the rapid development of urban-based industry financed by "peasant surplus"—in its essence, the same policy that Stalinism had carried to ruinous extremes in the Soviet Union. This proved fatal. Clearly, a policy of gradual industrialization was desirable, supposing always that its extraction of peasant surplus was never carried to the point of provoking peasant rejection. Unhappily, it was carried well beyond that point. The externally created banditries that followed would feed on consequent peasant rejection.

The destructive outcome was perhaps especially clear in Guinea-Bissau. Here the level of peasant participation had by 1974 reached a notable effectiveness, and the independence movement, led by Cabral until his murder in 1973 by agents of the Portuguese dictatorship, still pinned its faith to a policy of maintaining the primacy of peasant interests, there being in any case only one town of any size in the whole country, the city of Bissau. But with or without Soviet bloc advice, the policy was soon thrust aside, and wartime perspectives were abandoned. By 1983, in the words of a well-informed observer, "the country's internal and external resources were concentrated in the city [of Bissau], but without any significant increase of production: either in the countryside, which had no access to adequate resources, or in the city itself, where application of those resources was not productive. And so it evolved that external finance, instead of constituting the initial means of development, became ever more the crucial axis of the economy; and this dragged the country into a difficult posture of dependence."[17] This dependence—mainly in this case on Western, not East bloc, partners—became ever more pronounced after the Cabral-inspired regime which had won sovereignty from Portugal was overthrown in 1980 by a semimilitary succession.[18]

Worse followed in Angola and Mozambique. There the same centralizing trend was overtaken and engulfed by ferocious factions launched by and from South Africa and variously encouraged by some of the Western friends of South Africa's racist system. These groups—UNITA in Angola, RENAMO in Mozambique—were in no sense aimed at political programs more democratic or effective than those of the MPLA in Angola or FRELIMO in Mozambique, for they possessed and put forward no such programs. They were aimed simply at dragging down the independence regimes into a mire of violence and confusion. As it was, they infiltrated from South Africa into rural zones where centralizing policies had produced a certain dissidence: the product, as has been said, of a "basic contradiction," inherently a nation-statist contradiction, "between an economic strategy of modernisation and industrialisation, and a political stragety of popular mobilisation and democracy."[19] They failed in their objective of unseating the independence regimes, but they left in their wake a trail of death and impoverishment which had something of the same effect.

The banditries increasingly realized the violent degradation foreseen by leaders like Cabral and Pereira: for many of these bandits, bereft as they were of any sociopolitical restraints and divorced as they had become from ancestral moralities, blind destruction seems to have become the staple of their existence. "Although it is true," one careful observer of Mozambique was writing in 1991 of the RENAMO activities, which still continued, "that most of RENAMO's combatants were forced to join the rebels [against the FRELIMO regime], evidence has shown that many are deeply traumatised by their experiences, and have accepted terrorism and banditry as a way of life. Many of these indoctrinated fighters who have not been tempted to respond in some part to the government's amnesty may feel that continuing fighting is their only option."[20] And of course the infections of this violence could also spread to demoralized fighters in the army of FRELIMO itself.

The result was the wild and indiscriminate wrecking of every social achievement of the liberation won against colonial rule in 1975. In Mozambique, between 1981 and 1988, "291 health units were destroyed" by RENAMO violence, "and another 687 looted and at least temporarily closed. By the end of 1989, 3,096 primary schools had been forced to close, more than half of the primary schools in Mozambique. More than 200 teachers and health workers have been killed." The consequences were especially destructive for infants and young children bereft of parents, shelter, or any succor that could be effective. U.N. estimates in 1989 concluded, for the years 1980 to 1988, that there had been 494,000 Mozambican deaths of children under five for reasons deriving from what was called "destabilization": banditries and other such activities, that is, aimed at undermining the legitimate regime. All in all, this "destabilization" had driven about 1 million Mozambicans into exile as refugees while, inside the country, perhaps as many as another million had lost their lives.[21]

Direct South African military invasion of Angola, over many years since independence was won in 1975, went similarly hand in hand with an externally created "destabilization"; and again the outcome was appalling in loss of life and social destruction. Even when the agents of "destabilization" were disarmed, and the interventions ended, it would be many years before Angola, like Mozambique, could hope for any solid measure of peaceful or progressive development. In spite of every achievement, whether individual or collective, these movements had met with adverse forces too strong for them. Their bid to "invent the future" had ended in defeat.

But the vision of a different future embodied in their ideas and practice of participation in self-government and self-liberation was not therefore proved false. On the contrary, wherever it was able to evolve and spread its influence, this vision was shown neither to be wishful thinking nor impractical romanticism. For this there was the evidence of what had been attempted and achieved in colonial regions from which the colonial power had been sufficiently evicted—in "liberated zones," as they were usually called. Here it was sometimes possible, even while the wars continued, to watch the revival and practical operation of forms of local self-administration.

Nor was the influence of this same order of ideas confined only to the movements in the Portuguese colonies. Embryonically, at least, it had been present in other anticolonial movements of armed struggle. And these had not been few. If one counts only the big insurrections against one or another imperialist enclosure in Africa after the Second World War, they begin with the massive Malagasy rebellion against French control of Madagascar in 1946 and they continue, in one territory or an-

307

other, up to the success in 1990 of anticolonial insurrection in Namibia, passing along the way through huge and most painful upheavals in Algeria and other parts of the French North African empire.[22] In all these various movements, in one degree of success or another, the leaders' need to win a large and active participation of rural and even urban peoples had promoted the concepts of devolved powers resting on local initiative and control. "Mass participation" had become a vigorous aspect of all that scene which lay unfolding, from the colonialist standpoint, on "the other side of the lines." The colonialist authorities might refuse to believe it, but mass participation had become a mode of popular culture reaching deeply into the idioms of daily life.

Just as surely, it failed in these cases to survive the wars of liberation so as to open, after independence had been won, a route of escape from the nation-statist dilemma: the dilemma between a strong state which threatens or becomes dictatorship, and a weak state which collapses into clientelism. There have of course been exceptions or partial exceptions to this failure. One of these, at least for the first fifteen years after independence between 1975 and 1990, unfolded to widespread admiration all over the world in the little archipelago of Cape Verde off the West African coast; and this has been an exception which seems likely to be remembered.[23] Another took shape in circumstances still more remote from worldwide notice. This was the success of an Eritrean liberation movement fighting against Ethiopian imperialism, not only in the military field but also in building an Eritrean "grass roots" politics of self-government in their country along the Red Sea coast.[24]

Even so, the route of escape still had to show a general validity.

Other dramas of the 1980s could be called into evidence on the now decisive issue of whether or not the ideas and practice of decentralization and mass participation could offer escape from the pirates and their crisis. The underlying economic scene and prospect were bleakly discouraging. Could these ideas be more than a slender hope, a poor grasping at straws in a time of continental misery?

Even a selectively optimistic look at the evidence—and any such look, to be comprehensive, would have to mean several books as long as this one—will show that these ideas concerned with mass participation had failed more often than they had succeeded. In 1974 a great upheaval in the ancient state of Ethiopia, amounting as many said to a social revolution, promised far-reaching devolutions of power to regional and ethnically diverse claimants. But the promise was not made good; instead, after 1976, a still more centralist and authoritarian dictatorship emerged. This dictatorship was overthrown in 1990 by undoubtedly popular rebellions imbued with policies of mass participation. It still remained to be shown that these ideas could now prevail.

In neighboring Somalia, also in the period from 1974 to 1976, a reforming regime had likewise attempted an experiment in the devolution of power to local assemblies and their elective executives. This was done as a means of promoting a democratic alternative to military dictatorship, under which Somalia was then governed, as well as to the chaotic "multipartyism" that had preceded that dictatorship, a multipartyism of more than sixty supposed parliamentary parties which in practice were no more than personal or clan pressure groups.

Against this background—of a strong state requiring dictatorship or a weak state riven by clientelism—Somalia's experiment in mass participation had promising aspects. It went together with the writing of the Somali language in an effective script for the first time in history, and this in turn was made to serve the cause of widespread adult literacy campaigns, the opening of primary schools where none had previously existed, and, at an administrative level, the promotion of local self-government in democratic forms never achieved before. All this, however potentially fruitful, was swept into oblivion by hurricanes of interstate warfare after 1976. Somalia by 1990 had ceased even to be a nation-state; nothing seemed to remain save clan warfare and destruction. Yet it could not be said that Somalia's brief attempt to follow "the route of escape" had failed for reasons inherent to itself: in this sense, rather, the attempt had succeeded. But the circumstances in which it could persist and mature were simply not present.

What was generally present, instead, was a collapse of belief in the possibility of any collective escape from crisis. The sensible man would build a retreat for his family and himself, and barricade the doors. Moderate policies of reform had produced pitifully little. The remedies of "actually existing socialism" had reached worse confusion. All the solutions of "actually existing capitalism" had led to deeper poverty and hunger so far as the majority of people were concerned. A widening sense of helplessness could not be wondered at. Since the 1950s there had been no lack of self-denial and even of self-sacrifice by innovators striving for the public good. Yet everything they had striven for, as it seemed, was after all reduced to muddle and corruption. Trained and educated men and women slipped away to distant countries, filling whatever safe niche they could find, or else took refuge on family farms until the storms should blow wildly past them. The plague of AIDS meanwhile began to threaten a further catastrophe.

Yet it was in this dire situation, however paradoxically, that some of the worst sufferers from misrule and militarized mayhem had begun to present evidence of social renewal. A regime of reconstruction in Uganda headed by Yoweri Museveni after years of strong-arm misery under Idi Amin or Milton Obote was a case in point, rare but by no means unique. This regime of Museveni's National Resistance Movement reached power late in the 1980s when the whole of Uganda was in the last extremes of disintegration, and the odds against its survival, let alone recovery, had to remain heavy. Yet its early years into the 1990s produced the makings of peace and reconciliation where no hope of either had existed before. Fear retreated. The possibility of civil government instead of executive abuse began to emerge. Genuine moves toward the democratization of executive power thrust up their challenge to despair. It was even as though Uganda's long years of clientelist tyranny had cleared the way for grass-roots political life to push a harvest of renewal up through soil that had seemed irretrievably ruined.

"Resistance committees at village, parish and district level have been encouraged by the National Resistance Movement to elect local leaders," Victoria Brittain reported in 1987. These began to form themselves into nine-person local executives which "take care of community security and the distribution of basic commodities such as sugar, salt or soap, which had simply vanished with the collapse of [Uganda's] economic and social infrastructure." And as may really happen in times of renewal "at the base of society," all this began to create "new local initiatives, which range from brick-making, maize processing, brewing, to co-operative shops, football pitches and chess clubs for youths" who "used to roam about with the soldiers, fighting, thieving, raping, outside any family or village life."[25] Yet all this was then found to be more than a flash in the pan of optimism. Three years later Britain would report that "the old strongmen" of Uganda's statist structures had been successfully "challenged by the resistance committees, many of them made up of peasants," to a point at which "local decision-making, including the settlement of land disputes, has given the committees control over the lives of their communities."[26]

Could this democratic process endure and grow into a state power accountable to the people whom it claimed to serve and protect? The evidence remained contradictory. But what now began to be noticed was that the process, or efforts toward launching it, seemed to be spreading. In Ghana, however unexpectedly for a country that appeared entirely to have lost its way since its pioneering lead of the 1950s, a reforming regime under an air force officer, Jerry Rawlings, took power in 1981, and soon developed a strong critique of top-down forms of bureaucratic government. Turning to the grass roots in order to put executive power at local levels into "the hands of the people" and create "an opportunity for a genuine participation in the government of the country," this regime set itself to promote self-government by a democratic elective process. By March 1988 no fewer than 7,269 men and women had been elected to district assemblies by Ghana's 110 electoral districts. This was at least a start toward displacing an authoritarian bureaucracy by persons "at the bottom of the heap." It had to be a lot better on paper than in practice, if only because habits of bureaucratic command were deep-rooted. But indications of helpful change still seemed to be present.

A similar struggle between theory and practice evolved in the twenty-one-state federation of Nigeria. Here, too, the sharp conflict between a strong state under direct military rule and a weak state under multiparty clientelism (invariably, in Nigeria, known as "tribalism") had gone through many painful phases by the end of the 1980s. But miseries of one kind or another had tended to mask what was in fact a notable national success. Since breaking itself apart in a civil war from 1967 to 1970, this amazing country of some 100 million people, speaking a multitude of languages and with dozens of different ethnic loyalties, had somehow managed to arrive at a basic stability, even while the political air continued to be rent with tumults of dispute. If little recognized, this relative stability was seen to rest on a persistent trend underlying the public uproar. This trend has consisted in a real decentralization of administrative power, and at least an initial attempt to promote real forms of local government.

In 1960 the British had left Nigeria with three large regions, to which a fourth was soon added. But rather than splitting into as many or more separate nation-states—each of which would have been much larger than most of the ministates of French-speaking West Africa—Nigeria has evolved into a federation of twenty-one autonomous but interlinked and interdependent states. Each of these, in turn, proceeded to construct its own network of local assemblies and executives. These structures of self-government were to have three levels or "tiers": federal government at the "center," autonomous government in the federated states, and, underpinning all this, networks of purely local or municipal government.

All this went together with healthy argument which had produced, by 1990, a solid doctrine concerned with various aspects of "mass participation." It responded to the view, robustly put, that "top-down" government was the source of much evil. "The bane of local government in the Third World," said one Nigerian critic in a fairly typical statement, "has been the over-kill of central supervision, rather than the chaos or corruption of independent existence." Central government, he urged, must have the nerve and vision truly to accept the three-level autonomies of central, state, and local organs: for "what will get Africa out of her present food and fiscal crises is not the clamping down of more governmental controls, but the release of the people's organisational genius at solving their community problems."[27]

How far such doctrine was a modernized reflection of Nigeria's own historical structures of participation and accountability remained far from sure; the necessary research, so far as I know, was lacking at this stage. Peoples like the Yoruba and their neighbors had certainly developed complex and successful systems of constitutional checks and balances in relation to the use of executive power, and these were engrained in popular memory as well as folklore. Yet the compensatory power balancing of ancient institutions such as the *oyo mesi* and *bashorun*, or corresponding matchings of power elsewhere, belong to a time that is gone. No one was seriously supposing that the structures of the past could be revived; history doesn't, after all, retrace

its steps even when we should like it to. What the processes of
Nigerian history nonetheless confirmed is that the modern state
can become stable and progressive only in the measure that it
wins back for itself the popular legitimacy it has lost or never
sufficiently possessed, and that it can do this only by processes of
participatory democracy, no matter what the actual mechanisms
may be found to be.

In favor of this venture there is undoubtedly a long history
of relative success in the precolonial past. But the precolonial
past is not recoverable, while most political development since
then has backed away from democratic participation or has flatly
destroyed it. Decades of bureaucratic dictatorship have bitten
deep into capacities for self-government. And they have done
this to a point at which, by the 1980s, it could appear that
most Nigerians had ceased to be able to take part in governing
themselves. As Dele Olowu has put it: "Institutions that were
established to promote participation, such as parliaments, political parties, local governments and independent print media,
have either been legislated out of existence, or transformed into
institutions which are clearly dominated by their executives."[28]
No matter what Nigeria's reforming constitution of 1979 might
affirm on paper, the state governments, according to Olowu,
"were able to circumvent many of the provisions aimed at reducing their overbearing nature." Years of civilian rule then slipped
by, it appears, without serious attempt to strengthen and enlarge
the local elective process which, naturally, withered on the vine
wherever it had been briefly able to grow. No elections to local
governments, it seems, were held. In place of these absent
elected bodies, governors of states "have packed the local-
government committees with their favourites and nominees,"

315

writes Olowu. Such assemblies, on this credible account, were persistently deprived of financial resources and, politically, "run not by the people's representatives, but by party stalwarts nominated by state government, some of whom had little or no political base in the local-government areas" which they were supposed to represent.

This route of escape into participation, in short, has been barricaded with snags and pitfalls, and travel along it made much less than safe. But, then, nothing else could be expected, given that human nature is frail of purpose and prone to falling by the wayside. Besides, it was never said that this was a route that had to reach, or indeed ever could reach, its destination: what is sought along it is not Utopia but a decent society to live in. To that end, this is a route that can offer a crucial means of moral and political restoration. It is the making of the journey that will count, not the arrival.

Already by 1991, as it now transpired, this "making of the journey" was beginning to count for a lot. One obscure little republic after another, chiefly at this stage in French-speaking regions of extreme neocolonialism, began to shake and tremble with popular outbursts of one kind or another, sometimes violent but more often usefully disputatious. So-called national conferences of any number of political participants and protestants surfaced with demands for "sovereignty of political decision"; and such was the atmosphere of democratic expectation—perhaps a little by osmosis from Eastern Europe but much more from indigenous good sense—that even the worst pirates in power began to rock in their seats and yet refrain, as never before, from ordering in their gunmen. Even in tightly shuttered Zaire there was open talk of Mobutu's "rapidly faltering regime," along with claims that he be jailed as soon as anyone could manage to overthrow him.

As all this unfolded during weeks and months, gruesome secrets were seen creeping from the skirts of official silence. While, for example, the Republic of Togo's "national confer- ence" rolled on, "more and more revelations came tumbling out" to the angry satisfaction of the delegates. Ex-Sergeant- Major Étienne Eyadema, gun-installed president of Togo since 1967, "was accused of setting up a 'death camp' at Kassaboah, where people were tortured and killed." The same accusation, stoutly made without denial that I have heard, "indicated that there had been 'public murders' in the President's home village. The bodies of victims were hung from helicopters and thrown to wild animals."[29] And so it continued, on and on, in this republic or in that; and all of it, in substance and at times appalling detail, gave forth the stench of shameful truth. Harsh setbacks followed, but at least the truth was being told.

At this point the daily chronicle takes over and the historian retires. But out of the bubbling tumult there began to come the suggestion of some longer-term conclusion. Overtones of anger were easy to hear, and might or might not indicate a refusal to suffer as before. Certain of the pirates remained firmly seated, and political life would continue to be dangerous to lives as well as to careers. Yet events had begun at least to suggest undertones of another kind: of relief at the fall of monsters but also, beyond the relief, of hope in the feasibility of a new politics of minds and capacities, a politics that might at last be able to confront the real problems of the continent and begin to solve them. This hope could only be the fruit of a stubborn optimism. And yet there were signs that it was not without some ground to stand on. These signs were such that Roland Oliver, the doyen of Britain's academic historians of Africa, now felt able to conclude a finely measured survey of the continent's history by affirming of the 1990s that "the era of mass participation in the political process was about to begin."[30]

The old miseries of apartheid South Africa were still strongly present, while the removal of that particular black man's burden, another legacy of colonial dictatorship, was at once threatened by plots, corruptions, and killings by various official hands, some hidden and others not. And yet the most cautious critics could scarcely deny that the end of the worst, built-in evils of apartheid was now much closer than could have seemed possible a few years earlier. So true was this that democratic planning for a postapartheid, integrated southern African region—a region that could reach from Zambia to the Cape of Good Hope—was already beginning to be discussed and to take shape in political designs. If that could be realized, then almost two centuries of foreign imperialism and dispossession in this southern "half" of Africa might be within sight of its end.[31]

Contradictions obviously persisted. They were observable elsewhere: in West Africa, now with its clamor for democratic liberties and its spreading demand for a politics of democratic participation, and, if more tentatively, along the Mediterranean seaboard of North Africa. The same contradiction between despair and hope was present overwhelmingly in East Africa. There, by 1991, the warring clans of Somalia, Hawiya against Darod above all, were literally shooting each other to pieces. They had fought often before: "but in this century nothing like the present slaughter has ever occurred"; and any sanity of

318

political behavior among these vengeful or frightened rivals, now wrecking their country with a suicidal ruthlessness, seemed far to seek.[32] Much the same was true in the republic of Sudan, after 1956 another would-be nation-state, where old regional differences between Muslims and Christians, "northerners" and "southerners," were exasperated beyond all good sense by "fundamentalist" extremism of one sort or another. On the other hand, in absolute contrast, the prospect in Eritrea and Ethiopia was now turned sharply away from strife toward tolerant reconciliation.

Here in these long-bedeviled countries a politics of decentralization and grass-roots participation in self-government had taken the upper hand and now promised to retain it. In Eritrea, after some twenty-five years of insurrectionary warfare against an Amharic imperial rule directed from Addis Ababa, a national transitional government—transitional to constitutional status—was preparing the way for a multiparty system based, too, on its wartime program of forming and operating local assemblies and elective executives. Next door, in Ethiopia, another transitional government issued from successful insurrectionary warfare was likewise preparing a constitution designed to make good the promise of the aborted "revolution" of 1974, the promise that equal rights in self-government should be assured to all of Ethiopia's many nationalities. There must be a long way to go. Yet these were beginnings that were full of a reasoned hope.[33]

No doubt, generally, there were and will remain plenty of well-nourished reasons for despair. All objectively expert judgments—whether on Africa or on Eastern Europe, the two great zones I have compared in this book—shared in subscribing to these reasons. It appeared as good as certain that no kind of easy and prosperous future could now be achieved anywhere in the poor man's world, the ex-colonial world: existing systems of wealth exploitation, with their ever-continuing transfer of resources from the impoverished to the privileged, stand too solidly in the way. But while despair is all very well for those who can afford it, despair comes too dear for those who can't. For those who can't, a ground for hope is a necessity.

I find it obvious that this necessity is far from assured. No matter what strivings for democracy there may be in the upheavals of the 1990s, there is no guarantee that a culture of tolerant consensus, a culture able to promote a politics of self-development, is going to be possible. In Eastern Europe a philosopher-poet may become president of Czechoslovakia, but is Václav Havel more than a lucky chance? If a democratic Serbia could be engulfed by militarist dictatorship in the 1920s, could it not happen in the 1990s? If one or other pirate falls in Africa, what promises that another will not take his place? And so on down the line, always looking over our shoulders at the old devils of nation-statist violence.

In this book I have aimed to provide a guide through puzzles and complexities bearing on old devils and new devils, chiefly African but also European, for the parallels are instructive; and in doing this to point the way to understanding a central riddle of times present and times past: the riddle posed by nationalism and by the embodiment of nationalism in the armored shell of the nation-state. From this analysis it emerges that the ground for hope for those people who can't afford despair, meaning most people as things now stand, lies in one or another mode of the politics of participation. This politics claims to raise a means of defending all those people who live now on the losing side of the existing world system, the poor and the very poor, and offer them a means of survival.

On past showing, this may seem to be claiming more than any such politics can deliver. And yet times have changed. No matter how old devils may posture and threaten, the two great contests of our epoch have gone against them: the crushing of Nazi-Fascist imperialism and the subsequent curtailment of other imperialisms; and then, against old devils become younger devils, the peaceful winding down of the East-West Cold War and its drive to terminal disaster. These tremendous facts build no new world, but they give sure scope for building one. And the core of this scope, it seems, lies in this building of a new politics, a postimperialist politics such as has not been possible before. If this has to mean new developments in democracy, as the evidence suggests, then the democracy of the early twenty-first century will be the politics of participatory self-commitment—or else it will be empty rhetoric, mere soapbox verbalism with different words.

What the analysis then goes on to demand, all this being so, is the invention of a state appropriate to a postimperialist future. To those who prudently reply that it can't be done, the answer will be that it can certainly be thought of. Cases spring to mind. It was already beginning to be thought of, even during the dreadful 1980s, in the projects of the sixteen-country Economic Community of West African States, and, potentially again, in those of the nine-country Southern African Development Coordination Conference launched a little later. Each set of projects has supposed a gradual dismantlement of the nation-statist legacy derived from imperialism, and the introduction of participatory structures within a wide regionalist framework. And if it is objected (as it often has been) that these are aims beyond realistic reach, because these are nation-states which will never accept a lessening of their sovereign powers and privileges, another confident answer is that such aims were already in process of being reached in that most unlikely of regions, Western Europe, the very seat and cradle of nation-statism. As things were moving in the 1990s, even those most nationalist of peoples, the English and the French, might before long find themselves without sacred and sovereign frontiers between them. It could sound improbable; to many it must sound impossible. And yet as Galileo said in another dawn of dizzying change, *Eppur si muove*. And the earth, it has turned out, really does move around the sun.

Notes

INTRODUCTION

1. See a copious bibliography by the World Bank, the U.N.
   Economic Commission for Africa, and many specialists.
   Generally, I am assuming that the politics of modern nation-statism are inseparable from the economics of mature
   capitalism in its transnational or "multinational" forms of
   development and rivalry, and that the reader will take this
   for granted.
2. Crawford Young, "The Colonial State and Post-Colonial
   Crisis," in Prosser Gifford and Wm. Roger Louis, eds.,
   Decolonization and African Independence (New Haven:
   Yale University Press, 1988); and ibid., "The African Colonial State and Its Political Legacy," in Donald Rothchild
   and Naomi Chazan, eds., *The Precarious Balance: State
   and Society in Africa* (Boulder, Colo.: Westview Press,
   1988), passim.
3. *West Africa* (London; weekly), 11 September 1989.

4. Edem Kodjo, *L'Occident du Déclin au Défi* (Paris: Stock, 1988), p. 230.

5. Basil Davidson, *African Nationalism and the Problems of Nation-Building* (Lagos: Nigerian Institute of International Affairs, 1987), p. 19.

1: AFRICA WITHOUT HISTORY

1. Lieutenant (Patrick E.) Forbes, *Six Months' Service in the African Blockade* (London, 1849; reprint, London: Dawsons, 1969), passim. The *Bonetta* barely survived the infamous trade she was fitted out to suppress, being broken up at Deptford in 1861, only twenty-five years after she had been launched. I am grateful to Mr. D. J. Lyon at the British National Maritime Museum for valuable information on Forbes and his command.

2. The classic and compendious source on recaptive history in Sierra Leone is Christopher Fyfe, *A History of Sierra Leone* (Oxford: Oxford University Press, 1962).

3. Christopher Fyfe, "Africanus Horton as a Constitution-Maker," *Journal of Commonwealth and Comparative Politics*, vol. XXVI, no. 2, July 1988, p. 247.

4. E. A. Ayandele, *The Educated Elite in the Nigerian Society* (Ibadan, 1974), p. 42 and passim.

5. J. Ayodele Langley, *Pan-Africanism and Nationalism in West Africa* (Oxford: Oxford University Press, 1972), p. 133 and passim.

6. David Kimble, *A Political History of Ghana: The Rise of Gold Coast Nationalism, 1850–1928* (Oxford: Oxford University Press, 1963), pp. 207–8.

7. Fyfe, "Africanus Horton as a Constitution-Maker," p. 174.

8. James Africanus Horton, *West African Countries and Peoples* (London, 1868; reprint, Edinburgh: Edinburgh University Press, 1969).

9. Attoh Ahuma, *Gold Coast Nation and National Consciousness* (Liverpool, 1911; reprint, London: Frank Cass, 1971), p. 11.

10. John Mensah Sarbah, *Fanti National Constitution* (1906), here quoted from M. J. Sampson, *Gold Coast Men of Affairs* (London, 1937; reprint, London: Dawsons, 1969), p. 221. I am grateful to Dr. Ray Jenkins for generous help with ideas and references on early African nationalist interest in Japan.

11. Fyfe, "Africanus Horton as a Constitution-Maker," p. 174.

12. Quoted in Hollis R. Lynch, ed., *Selected Letters of Edward W. Blyden* (Millwood, N.Y.: Kraus-Thomson Organization, 1978), pp. 460–61.

13. M. R. Delany, *The Condition of the Colored People of the United States* (Philadelphia, 1859), p. 210.

14. Alexander Crummell, *Africa and America* (1891), in this citation from an address of 1870, quoted here from H. S. Wilson, *Origins of West African Nationalism* (London: Macmillan, 1969).

15. A governor-general of Angola to Lisbon, 14 October 1885, Archivo Historico Ultramarina, quoted here from D. L. Wheeler, *Angola* (London, 1971), p. 102.

16. Quoted in Christopher Fyfe, *Sierra Leone Inheritance* (Oxford: Oxford University Press, 1964), p. 216.

17. Ibid., p. 300.

18. K. W. Deutsch and W. J. Foltz, eds., *Nation-Building* (New York: Atherton, 1963), p. 117.

2: THE ROAD NOT TAKEN

1. K. Onwuka Dike, *Trade and Politics in the Niger Delta* (Oxford: Oxford University Press, 1956).
2. R. S. Rattray, *Ashanti* (Oxford: Oxford University Press, 1923), p. 287.
3. Ibid., p. 289.
4. Naomi Chazan, "The Asante Case," in S. N. Eisenstadt et al., *The Early State in African Perspective* (Leiden: Brill, 1988), p. 60.
5. Ivor Wilks in J. Friedman and M. U. Rowlands, eds., *The Evolution of Social Systems* (London: Duckworth, 1977), p. 487. My debt of learning to Professor Wilks is large, and will be obvious.
6. Deutsch and Foltz, eds., *Nation-Building*, p. 117.
7. Ivor Wilks, *Asante in the Nineteenth Century* (Cambridge: Cambridge University Press, 1975), see esp. under "Asante National Assembly" and "*odwira*."
8. T. B. Freeman in *The Western Echo*, no. 1 (March 1886), p.8. And see Wilks, *Asante in the Nineteenth Century*, pp. 388–89.
9. R. S. Rattray, *Ashanti Law and Constitution* (Oxford: Oxford University Press, 1929), p. 82.
10. Discussed in T. G. McCaskie, "R.S. Rattray and the Construction of Asante History," in *History in Africa*, vol. 10, 1983.
11. H. E. Egerton, *British Colonial Policy in the XXth Century* (Oxford: Oxford University Press, 1922). In 1922 Egerton was professor of colonial history at Oxford University.

12. W. E. F. Ward, *A History of Ghana* (London: Allen & Unwin, 1958), 2nd ed., p. 280.
13. Wilks, *Asante in the Nineteenth Century*, p. 705.
14. For example, A. F. C. Ryder, *Benin and the Europeans, 1485–1897* (London: Longmans, 1969), chap. 1, passim.
15. Wilks, *Asante in the Nineteenth Century*, p. 652.

3: SHADOWS OF NEGLECTED ANCESTORS

1. *African Historical Demography*, seminar proceedings, Centre of African Studies, University of Edinburgh, April 1977, pp. 2–6.
2. Ibid.
3. Basil Davidson, *The African Genius* (Boston: Atlantic Monthly Press/Little, Brown, 1969), p. 120.
4. Gwyn Prins, *The Hidden Hippopotamus* (Cambridge: Cambridge University Press, 1980), p. 102.
5. Max Gluckman, *The Ideas in Barotse Jurisprudence* (New Haven: Yale University Press, 1965), passim.
6. Chazan in Eisenstadt, *Early State in African Perspective*, p. 40.
7. Ibid.
8. Roy Willis, *A State in the Making* (Bloomington: University of Indiana Press, 1981), passim, for the precolonial history of Ufipa.
9. J. R. Strayer, "The Historical Experience of Nation-Building in Europe," in Deutsch and Foltz, *Nation-Building*, p. 24.

10. H. R. Trevor-Roper (Lord Dacre), in a BBC lecture, *The Listener*, London, 1963.
11. Quoted in Davidson, *The African Genius*, p. 181.
12. Claude Meillassoux, "The Role of Slavery in the Economic and Social History of Sahelo-Sudanic Africa," in J. E. Inikori, ed., *Forced Migration* (London: Hutchinson, 1982), p. 82.
13. Ibid.

4: TRIBALISM AND THE NEW NATIONALISM

1. John Iliffe, *A Modern History of Tanganyika* (Cambridge: Cambridge University Press, 1979), esp. chap. 10 for an excellent explanation of this process.
2. Ibid., p. 324 and passim.
3. David Kimble, *A Political History of Ghana: The Rise of Gold Coast Nationalism, 1850–1928* (Oxford: Oxford University Press, 1972), p. 196.
4. Lord Hailey, *An African Survey* (Oxford: Oxford University Press, 1938; 2nd ed., 1945); and Hailey, *Native Administration in the British African Territories*, 5 vols. (London: H.M. Stationery Office, 1950–53).
5. Obafemi Awolowo, *Path to Nigerian Freedom* (London: Faber, 1947), p. 63.
6. Thomas Hodgkin, *African Political Parties* (London: Penguin, 1961), p. 139.
7. E. W. Blyden, *Liberia's Offering* (New York: Gray, 1862), p. v.

5: THE RISE OF THE NATION-STATE

1. In G. M. Trevelyan, *Garibaldi and the Making of Italy* (London: Longmans, Green, 1914), where the story is told in graphic detail, p. 105.
2. As quoted in G. M. Trevelyan, *Garibaldi and the Thousand* (London: Longmans, Green, 1909), p. 53.
3. Trevelyan, *Garibaldi and the Making of Italy*, p. 290.
4. Elie Kedourie, *Nationalism* (London: Hutchinson, 1960), p. 9.
5. As quoted in Eric Hobsbawm, *The Age of Revolution* (London: Weidenfeld, 1962; Sphere ed., London, 1973), p. 164.
6. Kedourie, *Nationalism*, p. 73.
7. Hans Kohn, *The Idea of Nationalism* (New York: Collier, 1944), p. 10.
8. Eric Hobsbawm, *The Age of Capital* (London: Weidenfeld, 1975), p. 15.
9. Trevelyan, *Garibaldi and the Thousand*, p. 219.
10. Hobsbawm, *The Age of Capital*, p. 15.
11. As quoted in R. W. Seton-Watson, *A History of the Roumanians* (Cambridge: Cambridge University Press, 1934), p. 199.
12. See, for example, the *Memoirs of Moses Gaster*, edited and collated by Bertha Gaster, printed privately (London, 1990).
13. R. W. Seton-Watson, *History of the Roumanians*, p. 214.
14. Ibid., p. 222.
15. Ibid., p. 225.
16. Alexander Herzen, *My Past and Thoughts*, translated by Constance Garnett (London: Chatto & Windus, 1924–27), vols. 1–6.

17. Ibid., vol. 3, p. 130.
18. As quoted in R. W. Seton-Watson, *History of the Rouma-nians*, p. 397.
19. Hugh Seton-Watson, *Nations and States* (London: Meth-uen, 1977), p. 162.
20. Mila Čobanski et al., *Novi Sad u Ratu i Revoluciji, 1941–45* (Novi Sad: Institut za Izučavanje Istorije Vojvodine, 1976), vol. 1, introduction.
21. Sava Petrić, "Tri Palanke u Bačkoj," in *Zbornik: Radova o Nastanku* . . . , Kniževni Klub "Dis," Bačka Palanka, no. 1 (1988), p. 31.
22. Kohn, *The Idea of Nationalism*, pp. 550–51.

6: THE CHALLENGE OF NATIONALISM

1. As quoted in Basil Davidson, *Black Star: A View of the Life and Times of Kwame Nkrumah* (New York: Praeger, 1964; reprint, Boulder, Colo.: Westview Press, 1989), p. 86.
2. Jacques Rabemananjara, *Nationalisme et Problèmes Mal-gaches* (Paris: Présence Africaine, 1958), p. 122.
3. As quoted in Kedourie, *Nationalism*, p. 89.
4. In *The Crisis in Africa*, conference proceedings, Union of Democratic Control, London, October 1950, p. 17.
5. A. H. M. Kirk-Greene, ed., *Africa in the Colonial Period*, vol. III, *The Transfer of Power*, contribution by Sir Hilton Poynton, "The View from the Colonial Office," symposium proceedings, Inter-Faculty Committee for African Studies, Oxford University, 1979, p. 15.
6. Minutes by Gambia Colonial Secretary, 1937, in J. Ayodele

Langley, *Pan-Africanism and Nationalism in West Africa* (Oxford: Oxford University Press, 1972), p. 137.

7. Chef de la Colonie of Senegal: note to Paris. In archives of Service de Liaison avec les Originaux des Territoires de la France d'Outre-Mer (SLOTFOM), rue Oudinot, Paris, undated roundup of revolutionary propaganda, evidently in 1929.

8. Kirk-Greene, *Africa in the Colonial Period*, p. 12.

9. Ibid., pp. 43–50. And see p. 50, comment by Sir John Fletcher-Cooke, sometime deputy governor of Tanganyika: "So far as I am aware Africans, whether in Tanganyika or elsewhere, were never asked for their ideas as to whether the Westminster Model [for postcolonial sovereignty] would be suitable, whether any modification should be made, or whether any African practices or institutions could be associated with it."

10. Ibid., p. 107, comment by G. L. Aitchison, sometime deputy permanent secretary, Northern Nigeria; and comparable comment on other pages of this memorable symposium.

11. J. D. Hargreaves, "Toward the Transfer of Power in British West Africa," in Prosser Gifford and Wm. Roger Louis, eds., *The Transfer of Power in Africa: Decolonization, 1940–1960* (New Haven: Yale University Press, 1982), p. 125, quoting the Elliot Commission on Higher Education in West Africa.

12. Ronald Robinson in Kirk-Greene, *Africa in the Colonial Period*, p. 181.

13. In Gifford and Louis, *Transfer of Power*, p. 231.

14. Parliamentary Debates, 11 April 1959.

15. Cranford Pratt, "Colonial Governments and the Transfer of Power in East Africa," in Gifford and Louis, *Transfer of Power*, p. 260.
16. Ibid.
17. G. E. von Grunebaum, "Problems of Muslim Nationalism," in R. N. Frye, ed., *Islam and the West* (The Hague: Mouton, 1953), p. 659.
18. J. E. Ade Ajayi and A. E. Ikoko, "Transfer of Power in Nigeria," in Prosser Gifford and Wm. Roger Louis, eds., *Decolonization and African Independence* (New Haven: Yale University Press, 1988), p. 246.
19. Henry Collins, "Economic Problems in British West Africa," in Basil Davidson and Adenekan Ademola, eds., *The New West Africa* (London: Allen & Unwin, 1953), p. 102.
20. James Coleman, "Tradition and Nationalism in Tropical Africa," in Martin Kilson, ed., *New States in the Modern World* (Cambridge: Harvard University Press, 1975), p. 14.
21. As discussed in J. M. Blaut, *The National Question* (London: Zed Books, 1987).
22. David Fieldhouse, *Black Africa, 1945–1980: Economic Decolonization and Arrested Development* (London: Allen & Unwin, 1986), p. 15.
23. J. van Wing, S.J., *Bulletin* of the Institut Royal Colonial Belge, no. 2 (1951).
24. Basil Davidson, *The African Awakening* (London: Jonathan Cape, 1955), p. 95.
25. Fieldhouse, *Black Africa*, p. 36.
26. Ibid., quoting the British diplomat Sir Roger Stevens, p. 8.

7: THE BLACK MAN'S BURDEN

1. K. A. Busia, *Report on a Social Survey of Sekondi-Takoradi* (Accra: Crown Agents, 1950), a pioneering study in African urban degradation.
2. Jean Suret-Canale, *La République de Guinée* (Paris: Éditions Sociales, 1970), p. 13.
3. Ibid., p. 191.
4. Chris Allen et al., *Benin, The Congo, Burkina Faso* (London and New York: Pinter, 1989), p. 24.
5. Ibid., pp. 145–236.
6. See detailed record and analysis in J. M. Allman, *The Quills of the Porcupine: The National Liberation Movement and Asante's Struggle for Self-Determination, 1954–57*, forthcoming.
7. Boubacar Barry, "Neocolonialism and Dependence in Senegal," in Gifford and Louis, *Decolonization and African Independence*, p. 289.
8. Discussion in Fieldhouse, *Black Africa*, p. 227.
9. Allen et al., *Benin, The Congo, Burkina Faso*, p. 134. These estimates were made by the U.S. Department of Commerce.
10. Olaniyi Ola, "Smuggler's Paradise," *West Africa*, 27 March 1989.
11. A large bibliography. The quote here is from Jean Suret-Canale, *French Colonialism in Tropical Africa* (London: Hurst, 1971), p. 279.
12. Paul Richards, *Indigenous Agricultural Revolution* (London: Hutchinson, 1985), p. 43.
13. Fieldhouse, *Black Africa*, p. 6.

14. Ibid., p. 44.
15. Peter P. Ekeh, "Social Anthropology and Two Contrasting Uses of Tribalism in Africa," *Comparative Studies in Society and History*, vol. 32, no. 4 (October 1990), p. 660. I should like to recommend this brilliant paper from Nigeria to all interested readers. Ekeh writes with a cool and long perspective from inside his subject.
16. *West Africa*, 5 October 1990.
17. Allen et al., *Benin, The Congo, Burkina Faso*, p. 256 and note on p. 231.
18. Ibid., p. 214.
19. Ibid., pp. 134 and passim.
20. Philippe Leymarie as quoted in ibid., p. 62.
21. *Thomas Sankara Speaks* (New York: Pathfinder Press, 1988).

8: PIRATES IN POWER

1. Mark Huband, *The Guardian*, 3 October 1990.
2. Walter Rodney, *A History of the Upper Guinea Coast* (Oxford: Clarendon Press, 1970), and bibliography.
3. *The Independent on Sunday*, 13 January 1991.
4. Of this scene, see my own impressions in *The African Awakening*, pp. 13–22.
5. Most of them have been American scholars, notably Professors Crawford Young and René Lemarchand.
6. Crawford Young and Thomas Turner, *The Rise and Decline of the Zairean State* (Madison: University of Wisconsin Press, 1985), p. 81.
7. John A. A. Ayode, "States Without Citizens," in Donald

Rothchild and Naomi Chazan, eds., *The Precarious Balance: State and Society in Africa* (Boulder, Colo.: Westview Press, 1988), p. 196.

8. René Lemarchand in Guy Grau, ed., *Zaire: The Political Economy of Underdevelopment* (New York: Praeger, 1979), p. 238.

9. Young and Turner, *The Rise and Decline of the Zairean State*, p. 72.

10. Lemarchand in Grau, *Zaire*, p. 248.

11. M. G. Schatzberg, *The Dialectics of Oppression in Zaire* (Bloomington: University of Indiana Press, 1988), p. 53.

12. Young and Turner, *The Rise and Decline of the Zairean State*, p. 43.

13. Janet MacGaffey, "Economic Disengagement and Class Formation in Zaire," in Rothchild and Chazan, *The Precarious Balance*, p. 183.

14. Ibid.

15. Ibid., p. 184.

9: THE EUROPEAN PARALLEL

1. Michael Barratt-Brown, "The Capitalist Revolution," *Endpapers* (Nottingham: Spokesman, 1989), p. 33. Barratt-Brown has set out this thesis at detailed length in his *After Imperialism* (London: Merlin, 1963; rev. ed., 1970), see esp. pt. 2, p. 216.

2. Translation of "The Solution" by John Willett, in *Bertolt Brecht: Poems 1913–1956* (London: Methuen, 1976), p. 440. Original, "Die Lösung," in *Brecht: Gedichte* (Frankfurt am Main:. Suhrkamp, 1964), vol. 7, p. 9.

Wäre es da
Nicht doch einfacher, die Regierung
Löste das Volk auf und
Wählte ein anderes?

3. See esp. Svetozar Vukmanović-Tempo, *Borba za Balkan* (Zagreb: Globus, 1980); in English, *Struggle for the Balkans*, translated by Charles Bartlett (London: Merlin, 1990). Vukmanović was Tito's plenipotentiary in Macedonia during the liberation war; his testimony remains indispensable.

4. I draw on personal war experiences in the Vojvodina, as well as a large local bibliography: esp. Jovan Beljansky, *Sećanja* (Novi Sad: Inst. za Istoriju, 1982); Jovan Veselinov, *Iz Naše Revolucije* (Novi Sad: Inst. za Istoriju Sociajilistička Misao u Vojvodinu, 1974); Djorge Vasić, *Hronika o Oslobodilačkom Ratu u Južnoj Bačkoj* (Chronicle of the Struggle in Southern Backa) (Novi Sad: Vojvodina u Borbi, 1969).

Though passionately Serbian, the Serbs of the Vojvodina showed no wish to become part of a "Great Serbia" such as the Chetnik programs demanded during the war (and, of course, again after 1989). Among their countless peasant songs, as I recall, the Vojvodina partisans sang one with a chorus which ran: *"Vojvodina naša dika, bićes Republika"* (Vojvodina our treasure, a republic you shall be). As it turned out, they managed to make the Vojvodina into an autonomous region of the Serbian republic until 1989, when a renewed "Great Serbianism" undermined that autonomy. Cold War polemics have sunk the memory of realities like this.

5. Some time will pass before a final analysis of the collapse of Yugoslav federalism is feasible. For a general overview, see esp. Duncan Wilson, *Tito's Yugoslavia* (Cambridge: Cambridge University Press, 1979). For Yugoslav self-management in its various and original aspects, see esp. Edvard Kardelj, *Slobodni Udruženi Rad* (Belgrade: Radnička Stampa, 1978); Milojko Drulović, *Self-Management on Trial* (Nottingham: Spokesman, 1978); Ljubo Sirc, *The Yugoslav Economy Under Self-Management* (London: Macmillan, 1979); and much else on several sides of the argument.
6. Misha Glenny, *The Rebirth of History* (London: Penguin, 1990), p. 120.
7. In tortuous negotiations and various standoffs, there was also talk of "confederalism," but ambitions were now running too high for compromise. See the discussion in the contemporary press, esp. issues for this period of the partisan veterans' weekly, *4 Jul*, and especially Sladjan Ajvaz, "Konfederacija—iluzorno rešenje," 20 November 1990. In the situation which had now developed, he was undoubtedly right.
8. The ban on the public use of the Hungarian language in Serbia was reported in *The Independent*, London, 5 August 1991.
9. Erhard Eppler to Bundestag, Bonn, 17 June 1989, my translation.

CONCLUSION

1. Chinua Achebe, *Anthills of the Savannah* (New York: Anchor Books/Doubleday, 1988), pp. 130–31.

2. My own thoughts at a slightly earlier stage of Africa's crisis are set forth in *Can Africa Survive?* (Boston: Little, Brown, 1974).

3. Claude Ake, *Newsletter* of the African Association of Political Science, Lagos, December 1989, p. 8.

4. Claude Ake, in *West Africa*, 26 March 1990.

5. In *West Africa*, 8 August 1990.

6. Ibid., 16 October 1990.

7. Basil Davidson, *The People's Cause: A History of Guerrillas in Africa* (London: Longman, 1981), p. 7.

8. There is a large bibliography relating to the sense of moral legitimacy in precolonial societies, mostly from the researches of social anthropology. For an introductory overview, see my *African Genius* (Boston: Atlantic Monthly Press/Little, Brown, 1969), esp. pts. 2 and 3. British ed., *The Africans* (London: Longman, 1969).

9. "Tangible substance . . ." Meyer Fortes in Max Gluckman, ed., *Essays on the Ritual of Social Relations, Custom and Conflict in Tribal Africa* (Manchester: Manchester University Press, 1962). "Conviction [of] moral order" discussed in E. W. Smith, ed., *African Ideas of God* (Edinburgh: Edinburgh University Press, 1950).

10. Amílcar Cabral, *Unity and Struggle* (New York: Monthly Review Press, 1979), passim; collected writings of prime importance in this whole context. See also contributions to a symposium, *Continuar Cabral*, Praia, Cape Verde, January 1983; among these latter, Basil Davidson, "On Revolutionary Nationalism: The Legacy of Cabral," reprinted in *Race and Class* (London), vol. 27, no. 3 (1986), also in *Latin American Perpectives*, vol. 11, no.2 (1984), together with

contributions by R. H. Chilcote, Nzongala-Ntalaja, Dulce Duarte, Sylvia Hill, and Yves Benot.

11. Eduardo Mondlane, *The Struggle for Mozambique* (London and Baltimore: Penguin, 1969), p. 125.

12. In Basil Davidson, *The Fortunate Isles: A Study in African Transformation* (Trenton, N.J.: Africa World Press; London: Century-Radius, 1989), pp. 82–83.

13. There is a copious literature from many angles on the anticolonial struggles in the Portuguese African colonies. For recent work, and bibliographies of earlier work, see for example on Angola: Bettina Decke, *A Terra é Nossa* (text in German) (Bonn: Informationsstelle Südliches Afrika, 1981); A. and B. Isaacman, *Mozambique: From Colonialism to Revolution* (Boulder, Colo.: Westview Press, 1983); Giuseppe Morosini, *Il Mozambico Indipendente* (Milan: Franco Angeli, 1984); Barry Munslow, *Mozambique: The Revolution and its Origins* (London: Longman, 1983), and other books in these notes. A comprehensive history of the anticolonial war in Guinea-Bissau, and of its personalities and policies is Basil Davidson, *No Fist Is Big Enough to Hide the Sky* (London: Zed Books, 1984). I myself made five journeys to and through guerrilla-held territory, chiefly in "liberated zones" in Guinea-Bissau (1967, 1972, 1974), Mozambique (1968), and Angola (1970).

14. Detailed account in Davidson, *No Fist Is Big Enough to Hide the Sky*, p. 121.

15. See Munslow, *Mozambique*, and bibliographies listed in his book; and A. and B. Isaacman, *Mozambique*, also with valuable bibliographical notes.

16. See esp. Joseph Hanlon, *Mozambique: The Revolution Un-*

339

der Fire (London: Zed Books, 1984; U.S. distributor, Biblio
Distribution Center, 81 Adams Drive, Totowa, N.J. 07512);
and Bertil Egerö, *Mozambique: A Dream Undone* (Uppsala: Scandinavian Institute of African Studies, 1987; in
English).

17. Ladislau Dowbor, *Guiné-Bissau: A Busca da Independência
Económica* (São Paulo: Ed. Brasiliense, 1983), p. 40.

18. Peasant participation in social and political self-government
was well developed in liberated areas of Guinea-Bissau by
the early 1970s (see Davidson, *No Fist*, and references) but
was little attempted or failed in the economic sphere. On
this, see esp. Lars Rudebeck, "On the Class Basis of the
National Liberation Struggle of Guinea-Bissau," AKUT
(Uppsala University), May 1983; and Kenneth Hermle and
Lars Rudebeck, "Political Alliances and Structural Adjustment," AKUT, May 1989, the latter being an analysis of
participatory decay and its collapse after the military takeover in November 1980.

19. Egerö, *Mozambique*, p. 14.

20. Alex Vines, *RENAMO: Terrorism in Mozambique*
(Bloomington: Indiana University Press; London: James
Currey, 1991), p. 132 and passim.

21. Joseph Hanlon, *Mozambique: Who Calls the Shots?*
(Bloomington: Indiana University Press; London: James Currey, 1991), p. 41 and passim. Hanlon's book is indispensable
to any understanding of Mozambique since about 1985. His
findings on "destabilisation" should shake the most callous
reader. Of Mozambicans who were children during the 1980s,
he concludes that "this is the generation which should have
led Mozambique to victory over development. Instead, it will

be a crippled generation that will have to be supported for life by its parents and children, extending the impact of destabilisation well into the next century" (p. 42).

22. A review of these insurrections is in Davidson, *The People's Cause*. The bibliography, again, is vast in several languages, some of these unusual in the Africanist field: for example, by far the most informative book on the Algerian insurrection (1954–62) when seen from the Algerian, rather than the French, side is in Serbo-Croatian, Zdravko Pečar, *Alžir do Nezavisnosti* (Algeria up to Independence) (Belgrade: Prosveta, 1967). Dr. Pečar was Yugoslav envoy to the Algerian independence front (FLN) during the Algerian war, having previously fought as a partisan in the Yugoslav war of liberation. So far as I know, unhappily no translation so far exists.

23. For Cape Verde in this context, see Davidson, *Fortunate Isles*, passim, and *O PAICV e o Exercicio do Poder Político*, programmatic document of PAICV Third Congress, Praia, June 1988.

24. For Eritrea, background and development, see John Markakis, *National and Class Conflict in the Horn of Africa* (Cambridge: Cambridge University Press, 1987); Stefano Poscia, *Eritrea: Colonia Tradita* (Rome: Edizioni Associate, 1989); Lionel Cliffe and Basil Davidson, eds., *The Long Struggle of Eritrea*, (Trenton, N.J.: Africa World Press, 1988); and bibliographies.

25. Victoria Brittain, *The Guardian*, 24 April 1987.

26. Victoria Brittain, *The Guardian*, 24 February 1990.

27. Dele Olowu, *Newsletter* of the African Association of Political Science (Lagos), April 1989, p. 13.

NOTES

28. Ibid.

29. Quotes in these paragraphs from "Waves of Independence," a report by staff and correspondents of *West Africa*, 12 August 1991.

30. Roland Oliver, *The African Experience* (London: Weidenfeld and Nicolson, 1991), p. 264.

31. See esp. Bertíl Odén and Haroub Othman, eds., *Regional Cooperation in Southern Africa* (Uppsala: Scandinavian Institute of African Studies, seminar proceedings no. 22, 1989); and various publications on behalf of the Southern African Development Coordination Conference (SADCC), notably Phil O'Keefe and Barry Munslow, eds., *Energy and Development in Southern Africa* (Uppsala: Scandinavian Institute of African Studies, 1985), being pts. 3 and 4 of successive volumes devoted to technical and structural issues of nine-country integration.

32. Pietro Petrucci in *Il Mattino*, Rome, 4 August 1991.

33. See the Transitional Period Charter of Ethiopia adopted by a multiethnic conference of Ethiopians, representative of the postdictatorship regime, in July 1991. Article 1 of this charter pledged the right of all Ethiopians "to engage in unrestricted political activity." Article 2 pledged "the right of nations, nationalities and peoples to self-determination" within a democratized Ethiopia. Each should "administer its own affairs within its own defined territory, and participate effectively in the central government on the basis of freedom and of fair and proper representation." Ethiopian Peoples' Revolutionary Democratic Front (*News Bulletin*, vol. 1, no. 11 [Addis Ababa, 7 August 1991].)

Index

Macaulay, Herbert, 111
Macedonians, 278
MacGaffey, Janet, 261–62
Madagascar, Malagasy rebellion in,
    307–8
Maghrib, *regna* of, 93
Mali, *regnum* of, 93–94
Mandela, Nelson, 252
Marx, Karl, 134
Meillassoux, Claude, 94
Mengistu Haile Mariam, 253
Miletić, Svetozar, 157–58
Mitchell, Sir Philip, 179–80
Mobutu Sese Seko:
    dictatorship of, 255–56
    open criticism of, 316–17
Moldavia, 140–41
Mondlane, Eduardo, 300–301
Mossi, 63, 102
Mozambique:
    destabilization of, 305–7
    mass participation in, 302–6
    socialist system of, 222
Muhamed, Murtala, 229
Museveni, Yoweri, 311
Mussolini, Benito, 4

Naples, Kingdom of, overthrow of
    Bourbon rule in, 122–26, 147
Napoleon, Louis, Emperor of France,
    121, 123
nationalism and nationalists, 74,
    164–67, 169–71
    aims of, 49
    ambitions of, 166
    analytical impoverishment of, 183
    anti-racist, 52
    brutalities of, 16–18
    chauvinistic, 161, 283–85
    costs of, 147–48
    crimes and horrors committed in
        name of, 115–16, 165–66, 169
    crisis of social disintegration
        inherited by, 191
    definitions of, 11, 164

divisions of Africa crystallized by,
    13
doubt about other people's, 147
egotism associated with, 147
embodied in nation-statism,
    118–29, 132–33, 138, 320
in Germany, 130–33, 135
in Hungary, 15–18, 151–52, 154
ignorant masses and, 108–9
inspiration of, 149
in Italy vs. Africa, 128
Janus-like nature of, 18, 52
naïveté and fervor of, 131
nation-statism embraced by, 99,
    106, 113–114
new, *see* new nationalism
in nineteenth-century Europe,
    119–60
on obstructive nature of colonial
    legacy, 181–84
opposed by core peoples of *regna*,
    95–96
as oppressing force, 14
as ordinance of nature, 116
populism of, 134
as reaction against consequences
    of imperialist rule, 158
riddle posed by, 320
in Romania, 140–47
as route to progress, 162
as state of mind, 132
as thing of extremes, 149
and tribalism, 11, 75–76, 101
virtues of, 49
as way to rescue people from
    disunity and despair, 147
nation-statism and nation states:
    absence of serious quarrels
        among, 202
    class stratification associated with
        rise of, 133–34
    definitions of, 91–92
    dismantling imperialist legacy of,
        321–22
    dividing line between nations and,
        91

economic weakness of, 268–69
as escape from colonial condition,
  99, 113–16, 164, 267
federalism as alternative to, 106,
  113–14, 183–84, 192, 274,
  277–82, 286–88, 313–16
fruitlessness of, 288
generalized collapse of, 252
as harbinger of democratic
  benefits, 168
helplessness of, 285–86
as inheritors of dictatorships, 208,
  223
legitimizing of, 159
manifest destiny practiced by, 138
national vs. social objectives of,
  138
neocolonial, 12–13, 106
obscuring implications of legacy
  of, 166
optimism over, 195–98, 201
policies of oppression launched by,
  132
potentials of, 168–69, 171–72,
  175
as product of national
  consciousness, 138
as reductive, 98
as shackle on good sense and
  policy, 115–16, 288, 290
as successors and inheritors of
  colonial states, 169
supposed eternality of, 133, 138
untouchable sanctity of rights and
  conduct arrogated to, 133
weight and influence of, 183
Neto, Agostinho, 240–41
new nationalism, 99–117
  alleged radicalism of, 109
  and Britain's residuary legatees,
    102–6, 109–113
  demands of, 107
  ignorant masses needed by,
    107–11
  old vs., 73
  self-assurance of, 116–17

and social vs. national conflicts,
  112, 114
tribalism and, 99–105, 111–113
Nicholls, C. C. and Laura, 46
Niger, attempt to grow cotton in
  middle delta of, 216
Nigeria:
  agents of Christianity and
    Constitution in, 27–28
  anticolonial nationalism in, 164,
    167
  author's first visit to, 5–8
  Benin's trade with, 237–38
  civil war of, 197, 229
  decolonization of, 181
  federalism of, 313–14
  mass participation in, 313–16
  under military rule, 229
  new nationalism and, 108–10
  parliamentary constitution of, 207
  peasants of, 145
  political incompetence of British
    administrators in, 176
  positive role of tribalism in, 111,
    113
  smuggling wheat in, 213–14
  social vs. national conflict in, 112
Nile Valley, Iron Age in, 77, 79
Nkrumah, Kwame, 103–4
  Britain's agreement with, 162–63
  overthrow of, 197, 231–32
Nyerere, Julius, 175, 222
  East African federation
    recommended by, 183–84

Obasanjo, Olusegun, 229
Obote, Milton, 311
Obradović, Dositej, 156, 158, 161
Oduduwa, Egbe Omo, 111–12
Oliver, Roland, 318
Olowu, Dele, 315–16
Organization of African Unity,
  12–13, 186, 202, 288

Passfield, Lord, 170
Pereira, Aristides, 301, 305

slave trade, 19–26
British blockade of, 22–25, 30
death and devastation resulting
from, 80
end of, 67, 80
and failure of Africa to meet
challenge of imperialism, 65
mortality rate in, 22
perversion of communities as
result of, 247
privations of, 21–23
profitability of, 24
ships used in, 22–23
tribalism and, 226–27
Slovaks, 151–52, 157–58, 188
Slovenes, 274–75, 282
Small, E. F., 170
Somalia:
Hawiya vs. Darod in, 318–19
mass participation experiment in,
309–11
Songhay, *regnum* of, 93–94
Soninke, 97–98
South Africa, 102, 302, 318
anticolonial struggle in, 198
in destabilizing Angola, 195, 305,
307
Iron Age in, 77
violence in, 252–53
Soviet Union, 193–95, 268–69
African influence of, 194–95
in Angolan politics, 195, 303–4
breakdowns within, 285, 287–88
88
and British withdrawal from West
Africa, 32
Eastern and Central European
hegemony of, 15–16, 248, 264,
266, 271–74, 280–83
in Ethiopian politics, 222, 253
in Guinean politics, 304
Hungarian rebellion against,
15–16
and militarized violence in Africa,
253
in Mozambican politics, 303–4

new nationalism associated with,
109
and radical innovation in Africa,
194
socialism on model of, 233–34,
236
U.S. rivalry with, 193
Yugoslavia and, 276–78
see also Russia
Spain, 111, 186–87
Strayer, J. R., 91–92
Sukuma, 100–101
Suret-Canale, Jean, 203–4

Tanganyika:
independence declared by, 180
political incompetence of British
administrators in, 175–76
social vs. national conflict in, 112
tribalism in, 101
Thiongo, Ngugi wa, 150
Tito (Josip Broz), 282
Tolstoy, Leo, 148
Touré, Sékou, 105
Trade and Politics in Niger Delta
(Dike), 52–53
Trevelyan, G. M., 128
tribal unions, 101–2, 291
as agents of destruction, 228
disguised as political parties, 227
as enemies of state, 227–28
in formation of parties of nation-
statist independence, 111–12
politicians in manipulating of, 228
and reassertion of Fipa, 90
Serbian ethnic movements
compared to, 154
status of, 227
tribes and tribalism, 11–13, 99–
104, 224–30
in Benin, 239
and Britain's residuary legatees,
102–3, 113
civil society undermined by, 11
and clientelism, 12, 206–7,
224–25, 248

tribes and tribalism (*cont.*)
    comparison between rise of
        feudalism in Europe and rise of,
        225–26
    creation of, 11–12, 100–101, 225
    definitions of, 11, 99–100
    democracy vs., 75
    and ethnic diversity, 99–101
    history of precolonial, 75–76
    and military rulers, 228–29
    and modes of loyalty and self-
        defense, 224–26, 230
    and nationalism, 11, 75–76, 101
    and new nationalism, 99–105,
        111–113
    positive value of, 111, 113
    regional and territorial interests
        misinterpreted as, 206
    in rivalry between progress and
        tradition, 103–5
    and slave trade, 226–27
    and socialist states, 236–37
    and social vs. national aspects of
        anticolonial struggle, 185–86
    subversions of, 229–30
    in Uganda, 197
    and violence, 251
Turkey, 140, 152–53
Tutu, Osei, King of the Asante,
    54–57
Twining, Sir Edward, 175–76

Ufipa, 88–91
Uganda:
    independence declared by, 180
    mass participation in, 311–12
    spread of tribalism in, 197
United States:
    on absence of precolonial self-
        government experience, 74–75
    African Iron Age and, 80
    Garibaldi's fame on, 122, 126
    in identifying and promoting
        candidates for nation-statist
        leadership, 172

and militarized violence in Africa,
    253
neocolonial control exercised by,
    271
new nationalism and, 107, 110
in opposition to radical innovation
    in Africa, 192–93
transfers of African wealth to, 9,
    220

Victor Emmanuel II, King of Savoy,
    121, 123, 127
Victoria, Queen of England, 70
Vojvodina, 152–56, 284
    aspects of social struggle in,
        154–55
    attempt to Magyarize culture of,
        154
    under Austrian rule, 153–54
    dismemberment of, 275–76
    Hungarian oppression in, 152
    peasants of, 152–54, 280
    under Turkish rule, 152–53
    see also Serbs

Wallachia, 140–41
War and Peace (Tolstoy), 148
Ward, W. E. F., 67
West Africa, 13, 295
    Christianizing of, 42–43
    cleavage between own history and
        borrowed nation-statism in,
        104–5
    colonial racist rule over, 41–48
    cultural diversities in, 102–3
    decolonization of, 29–36, 177
    disputes over residuary legatees
        in, 32–38, 102–5, 109–13
    in failing to meet challenge of
        imperialism, 65
    Horton on, 37–38, 41–42
    impact of slave trade on, 80
    new nationalism in, 105–6
    white establishment on literate of,
        45–46

ABOUT THE AUTHOR

BASIL DAVIDSON is a writer and historian of Africa whose books and writings have appeared in many languages. As a major and then lieutenant colonel in the British army, he spent some twenty-one months from 1943 to 1945 on active service with armed resistance forces in Yugoslavia and northern Italy. He first took up the study of Africa in 1950, visiting the continent numerous times since then. He has made the study of historical conditions and the rise of African emancipation movements a central preoccupation of his work.

Roland Oliver, writing in the *New York Review of Books*, has called Davidson "the most effective popularizer of African history and archaeology outside Africa, and certainly the one best trusted in Black Africa itself." Many of his books on Africa are required reading in courses in Britain, Africa, and the United States. He has lectured on African history at American universities from coast to coast, as well as at British and African universities. Basil Davidson lives in Somerset, England.